ORIGINS of a
CATASTROPHE

WARREN ZIMMERMANN

ORIGINS of a CATASTROPHE

YUGOSLAVIA AND ITS DESTROYERS

TIMES BOOKS

RANDOM HOUSE

To Teeny,
who helped so many to survive

This work was originally published in hardcover
and in slightly different form by Times Books, a division of
Random House, Inc., in 1996.

Portions of this work were originally published in *Foreign Affairs* magazine
and *The New York Review of Books*.
Library of Congress Cataloguing-in-Publication data is available.

ISBN 0-8129-3303-6

Random House website address: www.atrandom.com
Printed in the United States of America on acid-free paper
2   4   6   8   9   7   5   3
First Paperback Edition

As you can see, bad leadership has caused
The present state of evil in the world,
Not Nature that has grown corrupt in you.

>—Dante Alighieri, *Purgatory* (trans.: Musa)

The old question "Who shall be the rulers?" must be
superseded by the more real one "How can we tame
them?"

>—K. R. Popper, *The Open Society and Its Enemies*

A gulf profound as that Serbonian Bog
Betwixt Damatia and mount Casius old,
Where Armies whole have sunk: the parching Air
Burns frore, and cold performs th'effect of Fire.

>—John Milton, *Paradise Lost*

PREFACE

This is a story with villains—villains guilty of destroying the multiethnic state of Yugoslavia, of provoking four wars, and of throwing some twenty million people into a distress unknown since the Second World War. How could this tragedy have happened to a country that by most standards was more prosperous and more open than any other in Eastern Europe? My thesis is that the Yugoslav catastrophe was not mainly the result of ancient ethnic or religious hostilities, nor of the collapse of communism at the end of the cold war, nor even of the failures of the Western countries. Those factors undeniably made things worse. But Yugoslavia's death and the violence that followed resulted from the conscious actions of nationalist leaders who coopted, intimidated, circumvented, or eliminated all opposition to their demagogic designs. Yugoslavia was destroyed from the top down.

This book is primarily about those destroyers. As American ambassador between 1989 and 1992, I saw them frequently and came to know them well. Speaking with me before their faces had become familiar to Western television viewers, they hadn't yet learned the full panoply of defenses against questions from foreigners. They described their plans, sometimes honestly, sometimes deceitfully, but always passionately and with a cynical disregard for playing by any set of rules. This record of their words and actions provides evidence for a coroner's report on the death of Yugoslavia.

The book also recounts the changes in American policy toward Yugoslavia in its death agony. None of these policy decisions were either easy or self-evident. Choices rarely present themselves as clearly when they need to be made as they do later, after their consequences are known. Both the Bush and Clinton administrations made damaging mistakes in the Yugoslav crisis, as I did also. While mistakes never seem like mistakes when we make them, I have tried to be candid about what was right and what was wrong in American policy.

Yugoslavia was the first European country to perish since World War II. The Soviet Union followed soon after. The two cases were different. The Soviet Union was a dictatorship from the center, an ideological tyranny, a despotism exercised by a single ethnic group, and a colonial empire. Yugoslavia was none of those. Thus, while the Soviet Union deserved to die, the fate Yugoslavia merited was less morally ordained.

The Yugoslav experiment in liberal communism from 1945 to 1991 was based on the twin assumptions that diverse peoples who had fought in the past could learn to live together and that communism based on local factors rather than the Soviet model could help them do so. In both conception and implementation, the experiment was flawed. But it offered far more to the twenty-four million Yugoslavs than the sea of misery into which most of them have now been cast adrift. The destruction of Yugoslavia led directly to wars in Slovenia, Croatia, Bosnia, and Kosovo—each war more savage than the one before.

The prime agent of Yugoslavia's destruction was Slobodan Milošević, president of Serbia. Milošević claimed to defend Yugoslavia even as he spun plans to turn it into a Serb-dominated dictatorship. His initial objective was to establish Serbian rule over the whole country. When Slovenia and Croatia blocked this aim by deciding to secede, the Serbian leader fell back on an alternative strategy. He would bring all of Yugoslavia's Serbs, who lived in five of its six republics, under the authority of Serbia, that is, of himself.

Milošević initiated this strategy in Croatia, using the Yugoslav army to seal off Serbian areas from the reach of Croatian authority. His plan in Bosnia was even bolder—to establish by force a Serbian state on two-thirds of the territory of a republic in which Serbs weren't even a plurality, much less a majority. In league with Radovan Karadžić, the Bosnian Serb leader with whom he later broke, Milošević was responsible for the deaths of tens of thousands of Bosnians and for the creation of the largest refugee population in Europe since the Second World War. Then, in 1999, he turned on Kosovo, a province under Serbian sovereignty and with important Serbian memories and monuments, but with a large Albanian majority. In a scheme so ruthless that even NATO military planners were caught by surprise, he set out to denude the province of all of its two million Albanian inhabitants—a people whose roots in the Balkans were planted over two thousand years ago.

Franjo Tudjman, elected president of Croatia in 1990, also played a leading role in the destruction of Yugoslavia. A fanatic Croatian nationalist, Tudjman hated Yugoslavia and its multiethnic values. He wanted a Croatian state for Croatians, and he was unwilling to guarantee equal rights to the 12 percent of Croatia's citizens who were Serbs. Tudjman's arrogance in declaring independence without adequate provisions for minority rights gave Milošević and the Yugoslav army a pretext for their war of aggression in Croatia in 1991. And Tudjman's greed in seeking to annex Croatian areas of Bosnia prolonged the war and increased the casualties in that ill-starred republic.

Slovenian nationalism was different from the Serbian or Croatian sort. With a nearly homogeneous population and a location in the westernmost part of Yugoslavia, Slovenia was more democratically inclined and more economically developed than any other republic in Yugoslavia. The Slovenes wanted to be free of the poverty and intrigue of the rest of Yugoslavia. They particularly detested Milošević, charging him with making Yugoslavia uninhabitable for non-Serbs. Under the presidency of Milan Kučan—a conflicted figure buffeted toward secession by the winds of Slovenian politics—Slovenia unilaterally declared its independence on June 25, 1991. The predictable result, irresponsibly disregarded by Kučan and the other Slovene leaders, was to bring war closer to Croatia and Bosnia.

An ironic feature of Yugoslavia's destruction was the descent into barbarism of the Yugoslav People's Army. The army, heir to the partisan force that Josip Broz Tito had led to victory in World War II, was a genuine Yugoslav institution. Though with a predominantly Serbian officer corps, it drew soldiers from all parts of the country. Its mission was to protect Yugoslavia's integrity and borders. As the country became increasingly divided by competing nationalisms, the army became the tool of Milošević's imperial designs. It tried unsuccessfully to destroy the Slovenian and Croatian leaderships; it helped the Serbs in Croatia seize more than a quarter of that republic; it colluded with the schemes of Milošević and Karadžić to tear away two-thirds of Bosnia; and it committed massive atrocities in Kosovo. The army's shame was symbolized by the rise of General Ratko Mladić, commander of the Bosnian Serb army—a career officer in the Yugoslav army and a war criminal of Nazi proportions.

Because of the intensity of the nationalisms in Yugoslavia, it proved impossible to preserve the country in a way that would have moved it toward democracy. There were many Yugoslavs who tried, and this book also tells their story. The leading figure was Ante Marković, a businessman and economic reformer from Croatia who was prime minister from early 1989 until the Yugoslav flame finally guttered out toward the end of 1991. Had Marković come to office a decade earlier, at the time of Tito's death and before the rise of nationalism, he might have led the country to economic and democratic reform. Instead he was the coda of a tragic symphony. History takes little account of lost causes. This book is in part an attempt to vindicate the valiant efforts of an able man overwhelmed by forces beyond his control.

My most difficult task has been to convey the conviction that all Yugoslavs weren't the bloodthirsty extremists so ubiquitously visible in Western news accounts. Most of the people my wife and I met in six years of living in Yugoslavia were peaceful and decent, without a trace of the hostility on which nationalism feeds. It's true that nationalist leaders have been able to turn many normal people toward extremism by playing on their historic fears through the baleful medium of television, a matchless technological tool in the hands of dictators. What amazed me was how many Yugoslavs resisted, and continue to resist, the incessant racist propaganda. I have tried to describe some of them, because they or their political heirs will one day help to build societies not driven by rabid nationalism.

The death of Yugoslavia and its bloody aftermath proved a debacle for the United States and Europe. The Bush administration believed that it was important to hold the country together as long as that could be done democratically. I shared that belief and the view—which proved tragically accurate—that Yugoslavia's death could come only with extreme violence. This book explores alternatives to President George Bush's "unity and democracy" policy and identifies mistakes in our approach. Still, I believe that no imaginable political or even military intervention from outside could have arrested the nationalist-inspired drive to Yugoslavia's destruction.

When war broke out in Bosnia, however, the United States was not so impotent. The Bosnian war confronted two successive American administrations with the first test of their leadership in Europe since the end of the cold war—a test that, until much too late, they failed to pass. The aggression in Bosnia by Milošević,

Karadžić, and the Yugoslav army went far beyond the bounds of any Serbian grievances, real or imagined, against the Muslim president, Alija Izetbegović.

Had the North Atlantic Treaty Organization (NATO) met that aggression with air strikes in the summer of 1992, I believe that a negotiated result would soon have followed. From July 1992 I urged that course, without success. The war dragged on into the Clinton administration, whose vacillations deferred decisive Western action to the summer of 1995. Then Tudjman's recapture of the Serbian-held areas of Croatia, the pressure on Milošević of international economic sanctions, a decisive two-week NATO air campaign, and an ingenious and determined American negotiating effort achieved an agreement in Dayton, Ohio, at the end of the year. It came three years and more than a hundred thousand deaths after America's first real opportunity to help end the war.

The Dayton result mirrored all the complexities and contradictions that I have sought to describe in this book. It was an uneasy compromise between the multiethnic values of the old Yugoslavia and the nationalistic assertiveness of Milošević and Tudjman and their compatriots in Bosnia. The Dayton formula will succeed only if radical nationalism and its champions are discredited in Bosnia, if Serbia and Croatia stop meddling there, and if the Bosnian people themselves decide that they've had enough of war.

The Bosnian war had frozen the even older and less tractable crisis in Kosovo. After Dayton, Kosovo returned predictably to a dangerous state. In 1998, an Albanian guerrilla group—the Kosovo Liberation Army (KLA)—emerged as the product of Milošević's habitual intransigence and the failure of the moderate Albanian leadership to win any concessions from him. The KLA demanded an independent Kosovo and began to kill Serbian officials. Milošević's reaction was to use paramilitary troops to kill KLA members and supporters and to prepare the expulsion of Kosovo's entire Albanian population. The NATO countries, led by the United States, demanded that Serbia concede autonomy to Kosovo and accept a NATO peacekeeping force to ensure it. When Milošević refused, NATO launched, on March 24, 1999, a campaign of air strikes against Serbia. This NATO intervention, though not as shamefully dilatory as in Bosnia, may still have come too late. Milošević took advantage of the months of negotiation to organize his cleansing operation. When the bombing began, he was able to accelerate the expulsions, driving nearly half the population of Kosovo outside its borders in the first days of the war.

The aggressive nationalism that destroyed Yugoslavia and turned Bosnia and Kosovo into killing grounds can be overcome only by a recommitment to the proposition that different ethnic groups must learn to live together. As of this writing—May 1999—this is still possible in Bosnia. The cynical ruthlessness of the Serb attack against the Kosovo Albanians makes Kosovo a more doubtful case. Even Yugoslavia, imperfect and doomed, had something to teach us about tolerance. The lesson isn't confined to the Balkans. All but a small percentage of the world's peoples live in states containing more than one ethnic group. From India to Israel, Sudan to South Africa, Quebec to Chiapas, the principles of the single nation-state and the multiethnic state are in conflict. The issues fought out with such savagery in Yugoslavia—how to curb a tyrannical majority, how to preserve minority rights, when to recognize claims to self-determination, how to apply international preventive strategies, when and how to use force, how to reshape international institutions to meet ethnic challenges—are being contested around the globe.

This book is also an attempt to deal with these larger questions. I have written it in the form of a memoir, because I was fated by diplomatic assignment to be on the scene for the final three years of Yugoslavia's turbulent history. The role that the United States and other Western countries played in the country's terminal disease and my own role are a part of this memoir. But the story is mainly about the individual people who strode the stage of the last tragic act of this Balkan drama, the people who tried to save Yugoslavia and the people who destroyed it.

NOTE ON
PRONUNCIATION

The pronunciation of Serbo-Croatian names is not as daunting as it seems. Most names end in -ić, pronounced "itch." For reference:

c is pronounced like "ts," as in cats

ć is pronounced like the "t" in future

č is pronounced like "ch," as in chop

dj is pronounced like the "j" in just

j is pronounced like the "y" in young

š is pronounced like "sh," as in hush

u is pronounced like the "oo" in boot

ž is pronounced like the "s" in treasure.

CONTENTS

Yugoslavia Before the Breakup

SOURCE: U.S. Department of State

Bosnia and Herzegovina: The Dayton Agreement

SOURCE: U.S. Department of State

ORIGINS of a CATASTROPHE

DECLINE

*Milošević One and Milošević Two had several
traits in common.*

They say that every diplomat has a special posting, a place that
shines brightest in imagination and memory. For me Yugoslavia
was such a place. The postcard images lost none of their luster in
the reality of the country. Cliffs plunged down to beaches of pink
rock. Mountains were bright with snow or wildflowers. Bronze
Age ruins and Roman amphitheaters made the countryside seem
timeless. Tiny medieval churches perched in valleys of plum
trees. Yugoslavia's Balkan allure featured animated political chat-
ter, grilled lamb, horse-drawn carts, circle dances, and curiosity
about strangers. The richness of its history inspired one of the
great travel books of this century—Rebecca West's 1,181-page
classic *Black Lamb and Grey Falcon.* And the hospitality of its
people was so unaffected that most Western visitors made a point
of remarking on it.

Political Yugoslavia was no less enticing. Even as a communist
country, it was so pleasant that British Labour Party politicians,
looking for political correctness, vacationed there. Its form of
government was non-Stalinist enough to inspire emulation among

left-wing democratic thinkers in Western Europe. It was a founder and leader of a formidable bloc of nearly a hundred so-called nonaligned nations, enjoying a global influence far beyond its modest size and population. Its economy was consistently ahead of its communist neighbors, even Czechoslovakia and Hungary with their Western economic traditions. At its best it stood for civility and tolerance among peoples with different ethnic backgrounds and different historical experiences.

I first went to Yugoslavia as a young foreign service officer with my wife Teeny and three small children; we stayed three years and traveled all over. When I returned as American ambassador in 1989, it still seemed an enchanting country. Now, as I write, Yugoslavia has vanished, the first European country since World War II to be destroyed. Its six republics have been catapulted into the perilous future reserved for unstable ministates. Beginning in 1991 its people suffered four progressively long and bloody ethnic wars. Five million became refugees in their own countries or outside them—the largest refugee population in Europe since the Second World War and a human displacement comparable to that of the Palestinian refugees living in the Middle East diaspora. Its economy was shattered, plunging its inhabitants, bandits and black marketeers excepted, into the worst penury in half a century. Its very name was appropriated—some would say desecrated—by the Serbian regime most responsible for its terrible end.

What happened to this country, which had steered so confidently between two worlds, the communist and the capitalist? Why couldn't it exploit the breakup of the Soviet empire in Eastern Europe just as it had exploited the U.S.-Soviet rivalry during the forty-year cold war? Why were the partisans of peace and economic reform so weak and the advocates of violence and ethnic supremacy so strong? The answers to those questions explain the tragedy of Yugoslavia's death.

In early 1989, shortly after I was confirmed as the new—and, as it turned out, the last—U.S. ambassador to Yugoslavia, I sought out Lawrence Eagleburger, who had just been appointed deputy secretary of state in the incoming Bush administration. Eagleburger's career had been in the foreign service, but there was nothing of the diplomatic stereotype about him. He is a man of Brandoesque bulk with a gruff voice abraded by years of chain-smoking. He has a wicked sense of humor, which he uses to tease rather than skewer. I found him sitting in the small back room adjoining the opulent deputy secretary's office, furtively drawing on a cigarette, which, as an asthma sufferer, he wasn't supposed to have.

Larry Eagleburger was and is one of the foremost American experts on the Balkans. He and I had shared the experience of serving twice in Yugoslavia. Both of us loved the country and the variety of its people of all ethnic stripes. As we talked, we soon agreed that the traditional American approach to Yugoslavia, born in the cold war years, no longer made sense amid the revolutionary changes sweeping Europe.

Yugoslavia was created in 1918 out of the destruction of the Austro-Hungarian and Turkish empires in World War I. It was an offspring of a commitment by Woodrow Wilson to the principle of national self-determination in Eastern Europe. The United States was not only present at its creation; along with France, we were its godfather. The new country was named the Kingdom of the Serbs, Croats, and Slovenes, for the three nations that had joined together to form it. For Serbia, which had been an independent country since 1878, the creation of Yugoslavia provided an opportunity to unite Serbs scattered for centuries throughout the two empires. In recognition of Serbia's heroic role on the winning side in World War I and of the numerical plurality of Serbs—about 40 percent throughout the life of Yugoslavia—the Serbian royal house of Karadjordjević was given hereditary rule over the new monarchy.

Croatia, which had been part of the defeated Austro-Hungarian monarchy, joined the new state in order to be among the winners of the war and to counter Italian ambitions along the Dalmatian coast. Nineteenth-century Croatians had also been the source of the initiative for a South ("Yugo-") Slav state. For the Slovenes, the smallest and westernmost of the three groups, Yugoslavia could provide security against the territorial pretensions of Italy and Austria. There was nothing "artificial" about the creation of Yugoslavia. It was the voluntary union of its three major nations—the same three that seventy years later were to tear it apart.

Invaded and partitioned by the Germans and Italians and their allies during World War II, Yugoslavia was re-created as a communist state after the war by Josip Broz Tito, the former Stalin apparatchik transformed into a redoubtable resistance leader. The Croat Tito—actually he was half-Croat, half-Slovene—fought the Germans more convincingly than his anticommunist rival, the Serbian general Draža Mihailović, who concluded in 1943 that communism was the greater threat. Tito's partisans won the support of the British and the Americans because of their success in tying down some ten German divisions in the mountains of Bosnia and Montenegro, thus making them unavailable for the Western front. Tito expelled the Germans and won the civil war within Yugoslavia against Mihailović's forces and Hitler's puppet state of Croatia. He emerged the unchallenged leader, and communism emerged the unchallenged ideology. When Stalin broke with Tito in 1948, the United States, swallowing ideological scruples, backed the intrepid Yugoslav in an extraordinary act of enlightened statesmanship.

America's support for Tito was geopolitical. The Truman and Eisenhower administrations wanted to show that countries could break out of the Soviet orbit and survive. Yugoslavia's independence deprived the Soviet Union of a potential foothold in the Mediterranean, from which it could have threatened Italy, Greece, and France. Through good luck, Albania's quarrel with Moscow years later also froze the Soviets out of the only other communist country on the Mediterranean. Tito's shutdown of Yugoslavia's massive assistance, including an arms supply line, to the communist forces in Greece helped prevent their victory in the civil war there.

Successive U.S. governments believed that Yugoslavia could become a model for independence as well as for an Eastern European political system that, though regrettably communist, could be more open politically and more decentralized economically than the Soviet satellites. Yugoslavia's position between hostile Eastern and Western camps made its unity a major Western concern. As long as the cold war continued, Yugoslavia was a protected and sometimes pampered child of American and Western diplomacy. Tito and his successors, after his death in 1980, grew accustomed to this special treatment.

By 1989, however, the world had changed dramatically. The cold war was over and the Soviet empire, even the Soviet Union itself, was breaking up. With Soviet leader Mikhail Gorbachev's acquiescence, the Eastern European countries were beginning to slip Moscow's leash. Poland and Hungary had achieved quasi-Western political systems, with Czechoslovakia soon to follow. In view of these circumstances Eagleburger and I agreed that in my introductory calls in Belgrade and in the republican capitals I would deliver a new message.

I would say that Yugoslavia and the Balkans remained important to U.S. interests, but that Yugoslavia no longer enjoyed its former geopolitical significance as a balance between the North Atlantic Treaty Organization and the Warsaw Pact. It was no longer unique, since both Poland and Hungary now had more open political and economic systems. Its failures in the human rights area, which the United States had tended to downplay because of America's security interests, now loomed larger, especially in the province of Kosovo, where an authoritarian Serbian regime was systematically depriving the Albanian majority of its basic civil liberties.

Not least, I would reassert to the Yugoslav authorities the traditional mantra of U.S. policy toward Yugoslavia—our support for its unity, independence, and territorial integrity. But I would add that we could only support the country's unity in the context of progress toward democracy; we would be strongly opposed to unity imposed or maintained by force.

As I was leaving Eagleburger's office that day, just before my departure for Belgrade, he said with a grin, which—for anyone of less than his girth—could be taken as impish: "By the way, I'm going to get you in trouble during your first few weeks in Yugoslavia." He explained that he would soon be called to testify on his nomination for deputy secretary before the Senate Foreign Relations Committee. He would be asked about his relationship with Slobodan Milošević, who had been a prominent banker during Eagleburger's ambassadorship in the late 1970s and was now the communist president of Serbia. Milošević had been in the news for his ruthless suppression of Albanian rights in Kosovo.

Eagleburger told me that he intended to criticize Milošević sharply in his public testimony. I said I was glad he would do this. His public criticism would be consistent with what we had both agreed I would say privately to Yugoslav officials. It would add credibility to my private remarks, showing that they came from the U.S. government and not just from an ambassador with a personal commitment to human rights.

Eagleburger was as good as his word. On March 15, a week after my arrival in Belgrade, he told the Senate that Milošević was playing on Serbian nationalism: "What he has done is create a situation which I think is very dangerous. I don't yet say it's come to the point of a real likelihood of shooting. But it is far the worst situation with regard to the nationality question we've seen since the close of the war." A well-known and popular figure in Serbia, Eagleburger had begun to sketch for the Serbs and the other Yugoslavs the outlines of an American policy that preserved a familiar framework but was adjusting to the times. It was a course correction, not a turnabout, but the fine points were not lost in the republican capitals of Belgrade, Zagreb, and Ljubljana where, for good or ill, policy was being made in post-Tito Yugoslavia.

Teeny and I arrived in Belgrade on March 9, 1989, after an absence of twenty-one years. The city hadn't changed much from the mostly Slav, partly Turkish town we remembered. Perched strategically on a bluff over the confluence of the Danube and Sava rivers, Belgrade had been built by the Celts and fortified by the Romans, but its character was pure Balkan—a combination of dynamism, decay, and seedy charm. The leafy beauty of its wonderful chestnut trees was only partly diminished by the gigantesque architecture so beloved of communist potentates. Between our two diplomatic tours in Belgrade, horses and carts had been banned from its streets, but less than a mile from the city limits antique peasant life resumed its familiar rhythms.

As the capital of Yugoslavia, Belgrade was the center of the eight-man Yugoslav presidency (composed of one representative from each republic and autonomous province), of the federal government, of the federal ministries (defense, foreign affairs, interior, etc.), and of the federal parliament. The city housed officials and journalists from all six of Yugoslavia's republics, most of whom, with the exception of the Serbs, would rather have been elsewhere. With the approach of each weekend, these uneasy visitors took advantage of the subsidized rates on the Yugoslav airline's fleet of Boeings to flee to their republican capitals— Ljubljana (Slovenia), Zagreb (Croatia), Sarajevo (Bosnia-Herzegovina), Skopje (Macedonia), and Titograd, now Podgorica (Montenegro).

On weekends Belgrade was a genuine Serbian city, not just the capital of Yugoslavia. It was fun to poke around the winding streets of the old part of town, where you could get an iron screen cast and beautifully filigreed for a modest price or a book bound for a couple of dollars. The peasant markets sold not only vegetables but old oriental carpets that had been woven in eastern Serbia or Bulgaria. In the evenings the new private restaurants produced decent if pricy meals, but the best place to go was the Serbian Writers' Club, where you could get a good Balkan dinner—grilled lamb, spiced tomatoes, and the ubiquitous cabbage, washed down by Slovenian or Croatian Riesling, Bosnia's green *žilavka,* or the strong black wine of Montenegro. There was also the homemade, clear, and potent *loza* (from grapes) or *šlivovica* (from plums), drunk by real Serbs for breakfast, lunch, and dinner.

The Writers' Club displayed one of the fascinating contradictions of Belgrade's small-town atmosphere. Political liberals and human rights crusaders rubbed elbows there with the most extreme nationalist writers and politicians. I often saw Vojislav Šešelj, the psychopathic bully who was later to revel in the slaughter of Croats and Muslims, at a small table dining quietly with his wife. Except in the summer, when the tables were moved to a leafy outdoor garden, we learned to arrive at the Writers' Club well before eight, by which time the cigarette smoke that had been collecting in a cloud on the ceiling began to descend to the level of the food.

I have spent over a tenth of my life in Belgrade and haven't begrudged a minute of it. The main reason, of course, was the friendships Teeny and I made there. A book like this must inevitably concentrate on extremists rather than normal people, because in crises it's usually extremists who call the shots. Someday the normal people will supplant the extremists in control of many of the broken pieces of Yugoslavia. For now, all I can do is try to dispel the impression that all Serbs are like Milošević or Šešelj. Nothing in their genes makes Serbs irrational or inhuman or "Balkan." They're a product of their history, as we all are. That history explains in large part why Serbia was the key to the destruction of Yugoslavia and to the three wars that followed in Slovenia, Croatia, and Bosnia, and why it will be the key to any resolution, if there is ever to be one.

All Serbs know that they are the heirs to a great medieval civilization that spread throughout the southern Balkan peninsula and left numerous frescoed churches of miniature beauty. Serbia produced a race of warrior kings, as well as ascetics of renown. Serbs are proud of their military tradition; their main archeological and historical collection is housed appropriately in a fort called the Military Museum. At the same time, they revere Saint Sava, born in 1175, as the greatest of Serbs. He was a member of the royal family, a patriarch in the Serbian Orthodox Church, and a statesman, lawgiver, scholar, teacher, and humanist.

The Serbs, like members of other small nations, have a tendency to stretch their admirable history beyond its true dimensions. More than one Serb has told me, "My ancestors were eating with golden forks while the French were still using their fingers." Serbia from the twelfth to the fourteenth century was a feudal society. The royal residence was often moved around, like those of many medieval monarchs. One imagines the insalubrity of Macbeth's dank and drafty castle more than the amenities of the French court. Still, Serbs enjoyed a civilization surpassed by no other in the Balkan peninsula, not even by medieval Greece, the center of whose culture had moved east to Constantinople.

The defining historical event for all Serbs is the battle of Kosovo. It was fought on June 28, 1389, by the Serbian Prince Lazar against the invading Turks, who were moving up from Bulgaria. The Serbs lost; there is a beautiful Serbian folk myth that explains their defeat. On the night before the battle a gray falcon flew from Jerusalem to the Kosovo field where Prince Lazar was encamped. It told him that he must choose between a heavenly and an earthly kingdom. He chose the heavenly kingdom, and the Serbs lost the battle.

For Serbs the Battle of Kosovo defines their nationhood, their Christianity against the infidel, and their self-styled role as Europe's protectors. Dozens of Serbs have asserted to me that the Serbian stand at Kosovo saved Europe from barbarism, a position somewhat difficult to reconcile with the fact that the Turks won the battle and ultimately reached the gates of Vienna. June 28 is a national holiday for Serbs, the only people I know who celebrate a defeat. In 1989, the six hundredth anniversary of the battle, the bones of Prince Lazar were carried on a winding route from one Serbian church to another to their resting place in the monastery he founded at Ravanica in the Morava Valley. I could follow in the Serbian press every stage of that journey.

The true story of the Battle of Kosovo, though dimmed by centuries, is different from the myth. Some Serbian historians now call the battle more of a draw, since both Lazar and Sultan Murad were killed. There's also evidence that it wasn't even the decisive battle between the Serbs and the Turks; that had taken place eighteen years before at Maritsa in Bulgaria. Kosovo was a typical feudal battle, complete with mercenaries and shifting alliances. Serbs fought on the Turkish, as well as on the Serbian, side, a fact indirectly recognized by the account in the folk epics of the treason of the Serb warrior Vuk Branković, who was alleged to have gone over to the Turks on the eve of the battle. Most inconvenient for Serbian nationalists is the view of one Serbian historian that Muslim Albanians, Christian Bosnians, and Catholic Croats fought on the Serbian side.

The evidence of history has not shaken the general Serbian conviction, derived from Kosovo, that Europe owes the Serbs something for defending it and that valiant Serbian warriors are always betrayed, either by treason in war or by an unjust peace. Thus, the argument goes, Serbs deserve special treatment. This mind-set is important for understanding why Serbia remained aggrieved after World War I despite receiving royal authority over the new state of Yugoslavia; why Serbian nationalists hate Tito for not having given them a dominant position after World War II; and why the Bosnian Serbs so long resisted a political settlement to the Bosnian war that gave them more territory per capita than it gave the far more numerous Muslims.

Serbia's tragic flaw is an obsession with its own history. Serbian hearts are in their past, not their future. As a foreigner, I patiently sat through interminable recitations by Serbs from all walks of life about the boundless ways in which they have been victimized through the centuries. This potted history—it never varies in its content—is a ritual that Serbs must go through in justifying the current actions of Serbian politicians or soldiers.

Unfortunately, there is a tendency, particularly among nationalistic Serbs, to assume that their paranoid view of the past excuses, or at least explains, any atrocity committed in the present. It was with genuine hurt as well as reproach that Serbian friends would ask, "How can you Americans criticize our actions against the Kosovo Albanians when they have discriminated against us so much in the past? Don't you remember that Serbs and Americans fought side by side in two world wars?"

When I arrived in Belgrade in early 1989, Kosovo was on everybody's mind. Two years before, Milošević had used the Kosovo issue to claw his way to power as head of the League of Communists of Serbia. He had accused his predecessor, patron, and friend of twenty-five years, Ivan Stambolić, of tolerating discrimination against Serbs by the Kosovo Albanians and had engineered Stambolić's removal. For reasons that go back to 1389, Kosovo remains an emotive issue for Serbs. Many of the great Serbian monasteries are there; the patriarchate of the Serbian Orthodox Church is in the Kosovo city of Peć; and of course Kosovo is the site of the historic battlefield. Kosovo is to Serbs what Jerusalem and the West Bank are to Israelis—a sacred ancestral homeland now inhabited largely by Muslims.

After the defeat of Turkey in 1912, Kosovo fell under Serbian control for almost the rest of the twentieth century. But Tito's 1974 constitution gave the province considerable autonomy from Serbian rule. As a result the Albanian population of Kosovo—currently about 90 percent of the total—had carved out a dominant position. In the process there was undoubtedly discrimination against Serbs, just as I remember discrimination against Albanians when the Serbs had the upper hand in Kosovo in the 1960s. But there was nothing to justify the ruthless methods by which Milošević wrested back control. Working through the intimidating powers of the communist apparatus, he took over or suspended Kosovo's governing bodies and replaced them with Serbs or pliant Albanians. Then he got the Serbian parliament to pass legislation to prevent an Albanian return to power. Individual Albanians who got in the way were subjected to arbitrary arrest and imprisonment.

By the time of my return in 1989 Kosovo had become the most serious European human rights problem west of the Soviet Union. Nowhere was there more concern than in the United States. Important members of Congress, led by Senator Robert Dole (Republican of Kansas) and Representative Tom Lantos (Democrat of California), were warning that Milošević's approach to Kosovo would damage U.S. relations with Yugoslavia. Eagleburger's own strong testimony on the issue had been a way of assuring the Congress that the administration shared this concern.

On March 21, 1989, I presented my credentials to the president of the Yugoslav presidency, Raif Dizdarević. In keeping with Yugoslavia's proletarian pretensions, we wore suits, not morning coats. Dizdarević was a communist and ex-partisan from a prominent Muslim political family in Bosnia and a strong proponent of Yugoslav unity. I used the fifteen minutes allotted to me on this formal occasion to convey the hope—time-honored for all new ambassadors in all countries—for constructive bilateral relations. I also stressed U.S. support for the independence, unity, and territorial integrity of Yugoslavia, a policy of nine successive American presidents. I said that the United States would support economic and political reform in Yugoslavia but expressed concern about the human rights situation in Kosovo.

Dizdarević, who had no love for Milošević or his policies, nevertheless volunteered that the Yugoslav government had been compelled to go along with the Serbian requests that a state of emergency be declared in Kosovo and that the Yugoslav army be sent there to maintain order. The alternative, Dizdarević said, was an Albanian general strike that would threaten Yugoslavia's stability. I left the meeting with an appreciation of Milošević's ability to blackmail weaker politicians.

In subsequent meetings with federal Yugoslav officials in Belgrade I made clear that, in raising our Kosovo concerns, we had no intention of meddling in Yugoslavia's internal affairs. Just a few months earlier, the Vienna review meeting of the Conference on Security and Cooperation in Europe—a two-year-long negotiation devoted to human rights and arms control and involving the European and North American states—had concluded with a document reaffirming that a government's treatment of its own citizens was a legitimate subject for international scrutiny.

I had been the head of the U.S. delegation at that negotiation and could attest that we weren't picking on Yugoslavia. In fact, Yugoslavia's record had gotten off lightly at Vienna, especially in comparison with other Eastern European countries like Czechoslovakia, Romania, or Bulgaria, not to mention Mikhail Gorbachev's Soviet Union. My point to Yugoslav officials was that, if Yugoslavia wanted to continue its close relations with the United States, it would have to curb the human rights abuses in Kosovo. The choice was Yugoslavia's to make.

The response of federal officials to these comments gave me an early taste of Yugoslav political reality. I met frequently with Foreign Minister Budimir Lončar, a canny Croatian veteran of the Tito era, who moved with catlike tread through the minefields of conflicting republican nationalisms. When I mentioned Kosovo, as I often did, Lončar, a former ambassador to Washington and a friend of the United States, spread his hands and said, "I absolutely agree with you. It's a difficult situation in Kosovo. I can well understand the concern in Washington. But I'm counting on you and my friend Larry Eagleburger to keep it in perspective. The congressional resolutions against Serbia's actions in Kosovo are one-sided and counterproductive. They won't change Serbian policy because they don't accept that the Serbs who live in Kosovo also have rights. Only the Serbian government can affect this issue. We in the federal government can do nothing about it. Your job, and mine, is to see that it doesn't poison our bilateral relations."

I reminded Lončar that the federal government hadn't been exactly passive—it had approved martial law and sent the army to the province. He smiled his feline smile. "You have to understand what's happened to Yugoslavia since you were last here. With Tito gone we have become a completely decentralized country. The federal government has very little influence, and no control, over the six republics. Whatever the constitution says, nobody is going to stop Milošević from doing what he wants in Kosovo. The army can maintain order, but it isn't going to prevent Milošević from establishing Serbian political control. Of course we can talk to him"—here Lončar's face made it clear that such "talk" wasn't his idea of fun—"but it isn't going to do any good. He doesn't particularly care about the international reaction to Kosovo or its effect on Yugoslavia's relations with Western countries."

What this pragmatic diplomat was saying was that Tito, through the 1974 constitution, which took full effect upon his death in 1980, had effectively destroyed the center in Yugoslavia. The old dictator's reasons can only be guessed at. Possibly he didn't want any more Titos, possibly he wanted to deny Serbia the opportunity to reestablish its pre–World War II dominance over Yugoslav political institutions. The result of Tito's short-sighted decision was that power flowed down to the republics where, in the hands of republican leaders, it could be used to foment nationalism. This is what Milošević was doing in Serbia. He was free to do it because—thanks to Tito's legacy—the Yugoslav government was too weak to stop him.

In fact, the government of Yugoslavia was constitutionally the weakest in Europe—a condition that contributed critically to the rise of the republican nationalisms that killed it. In one of my first cables I cautioned Washington not to equate decentralization with democracy or centralism with authoritarianism. Those equations might have described the Soviet Union, a ruthless dictatorship from the center. But they didn't describe Yugoslavia.

During my first few weeks in Yugoslavia I found that Milošević's trampling on Albanian rights was almost universally popular among Serbs, and not just among those with a limited grasp of political issues. Members of the Serbian Academy of Sciences had written a memorandum in 1986 that cataloged real or imagined Serbian grievances throughout history. It was a potpourri of paranoid thinking, castigating the other republics for forming an "anti-Serb coalition" and for believing that "a weak Serbia makes for a strong Yugoslavia." On no subject were the complaints more vociferous than on Kosovo. Most dismaying was the way the memorandum dehumanized the Albanians of Kosovo, treating them as if they were no more than a Muslim army single-mindedly dedicated to the destruction of Serbian culture. The memorandum stressed that righting the wrongs done to Serbs in Kosovo was vital for the Serbian nation.

There was no use dismissing these crackpot ideas as the maunderings of intellectuals; they were prevalent throughout Serbian society, from shopkeepers to peasant farmers to journalists. I remember meeting an art historian at a dinner party. A tall, attractive, and sensitive woman, she had been to New York many times and loved America and its culture. After a wide-ranging and fascinating conversation on a variety of subjects, I asked her how she would deal with the Kosovo problem. "Simple," she said. "Just line all the Albanians up against a wall and shoot them."

While getting my bearings, I kept my remarks on Kosovo private. I gave no press interviews. Following discussions with Lončar and other federal officials, I took Eagleburger's advice and immediately established contact with the republican governments, which wielded the real power in Yugoslavia. In the pre-election year of 1989 these governments were all under the control of communists. But these were communists who rejected the Leninist principle of democratic centralism. They paid no attention to instructions from the central party organs; in fact, they made sure there were no such instructions. Their power base was in their respective republics, and as political animals they acted accordingly. All but one of the republican presidents were glad to meet the new American ambassador, and early visits were arranged to Slovenia, Croatia, Bosnia-Herzegovina, Macedonia, and Montenegro.

The one exception was Milošević. He had undoubtedly seen the accounts of my meetings with federal officials in Belgrade, so he knew of the deep American concern over Kosovo. But that wasn't the reason his protocol flaks gave. They said that bilateral relations were handled by the Yugoslav Ministry of Foreign Affairs; as president of Serbia, Milošević was too busy to meet with ambassadors. Since Milošević wasn't going to give me the chance for a quiet discussion—which would include, but not be limited to, Kosovo—I got Washington's clearance to try some public diplomacy. *Borba,* an independent and objective newspaper, had been asking for an interview.

In an on-the-record discussion in June with Slobodan Pavlović, who was later to become *Borba*'s first-rate Washington correspondent, I described our support for the country's nascent economic reform, our hopes for continuing a close relationship with Yugoslavia, and our sense of the changing post–cold war geopolitical environment. Pavlović gave me my opening by asking whether I saw any problems. I answered that Kosovo had unfortunately become a serious concern, since our bilateral relationship was no longer based on an external threat to Yugoslavia but on more specific factors like human rights. Picking my words carefully, I said that "it would be unfortunate if the rights of one nationality were advanced at the expense of the rights of another nationality." At the end of the interview, Pavlović, a Serb, closed his notebook and said quietly, "I agree with the American position on Kosovo."

Later in June all the embassies in Belgrade got a peremptory note from the Serbian "Foreign Ministry" (all Yugoslav republics, just like all the republics of the old Soviet Union, had nominal foreign ministries). It said that on June 28 on the Kosovo battlefield there would be a mammoth commemoration of the 600th anniversary of the Battle of Kosovo. The collective presidency of Yugoslavia would be there, as would the Yugoslav prime minister; the main speech would be delivered by Slobodan Milošević. The presence of the heads of all the diplomatic missions was requested; a special train would be provided for the three-hour trip to Kosovo.

Not pausing to wonder why the Serbian government had reversed its view that it shouldn't deal directly with foreign governments, I called in my senior staff. It didn't take us more than a few minutes to decide that I should not attend that ceremony. The other ambassadors and I would be props in Milošević's theatrical performance, by our presence giving credence and approval to whatever he might say about Kosovo and its Albanian population. If Milošević intended to use the occasion to heal the rift he had provoked with the Kosovo Albanians, who were after all citizens of Serbia, there might have been a reason to attend. But Serbian officials provided no such assurances. The decision not to attend was so obvious that we didn't even ask Washington for instructions.

The European Community's ambassadors, who met regularly, took a similar decision not to attend Milošević's rally. Some of them called me in advance to find out what I was doing, and I told them. But I made no effort to influence their decision. As I recall, Turkey was the only Western government that chose to go. My Turkish colleague chuckled that, as the victor at the Battle of Kosovo, Turkey took a somewhat different view of its commemoration than other countries.

The Western no-shows hardly crimped Milošević's extravaganza. He drew a million people to the battlefield, some twenty-five times the number of soldiers who had fought in the battle. My reasons for not attending proved valid. Milošević made no direct reference in his address to the two million Albanian inhabitants of Kosovo, in itself something of an insult. But he did lace his speech with veiled warnings and threats against those who would block Serbia's national aspirations. For the first time he raised the specter of war, saying: "Six centuries later, again we are in battles and quarrels. They are not armed battles, though such things should not be excluded yet."

Shortly after this apotheosis of Serbian nationalism I got word from Serbian journalist friends that Milošević was incensed with me. He believed, I was told, that I had organized a Western boycott, thus exposing myself as anti-Serb. Milošević had access to evidence that this wasn't true, since the Serbian secret police would have seen the taps made by Yugoslav intelligence of my phone conversations with diplomatic colleagues. Nevertheless, Milošević refused to see me until I had been in the country nearly a year. After our initial meeting, in January 1990, he was generous in receiving me; in all we had over a dozen long conversations. My impressions of his character recounted below are drawn from those meetings.

A law graduate of Belgrade University, Milošević began his career as a communist apparatchik with an authoritarian personality already noticed by schoolmates. He was too young and too junior to have been close to Tito, but he was old enough (thirty-eight when Tito died) to have prospered in the Titoist system. I never saw in him the personal animus against Tito that many other Serbs felt. In fact, on my first visit to his office I noticed a large painting of Tito behind his desk; significantly, he took it down in 1991, the year Yugoslavia fell apart.

As he cultivated a nationalist persona, Milošević dropped the external aspects of his communist formation. He purged himself of the wooden language that makes communists the world over such hapless communicators. He dropped all references to communism. And he renamed the League of Communists of Serbia the Serbian Socialist Party.

In two ways, however, Milošević failed to break the ties. The first was his continued reliance on communist techniques of control over his party, the Serbian police, the media, and the economic sector. The second was his highly visible wife, Mirjana Marković, a Belgrade University professor and frequent author of turgid Leninist essays in glossy Serbian magazines. Marković flaunted her communism; in fact, she cofounded a communist party in 1990. She was thought to have the influence of a Lady Macbeth over her husband, particularly with regard to his frequent abrupt dismissals of hitherto trusted subordinates. Liberal Serbs described her variously as flaky, crafty, amoral, or vicious.

Whatever his real views of Tito, Milošević was nevertheless the vessel for the Serbian claim that Tito had denied Serbs the role to which destiny had entitled them. The charge may have been partly true, but it was certainly exaggerated. Serbs were a major element of Tito's partisan army during World War II, including its first two elite units, and played a prominent role in the Yugoslav army and police afterward. At his death, however, Tito left Yugoslavia so decentralized that no ethnic group—and certainly not the Serbs—could possibly dominate it. Given Serbian messianism, it became inevitable that a Serbian nationalist would rise up to redress the imagined wrongs dealt his nation. It was a tragedy for Serbia, its neighbors, and Europe as a whole that this nationalist turned out to be Slobodan Milošević.

The Serbian leader makes a stunning first impression, particularly on foreigners who don't have the background or the information to refute his often erroneous assertions. He is competent in English, and he speaks forcefully and clearly. While his handshake is limp, his eye contact is steady. When you're talking, he really listens. His appearance doesn't comport with the "strongman" image. His cherubic cheeks give him a baby face; one imagines a lot of practice at the mirror so that he can glower in his public appearances.

His dress is Western; he made many visits to New York as a banker before he became a Serbian party official. His visible vices are clubby. He drinks scotch on the rocks (I never counted more than a glass or two) and smokes Italian cigarillos. His manner is unfailingly affable; while all our conversations were contentious, none were shouting matches. Many's the American politician who has reeled out of his office exclaiming, "Why he's not nearly as bad as I expected!" One congressman even invited him to a White House prayer breakfast. All this is the light side of Milošević. Unfortunately, the man is almost totally dominated by his dark side.

Milošević deploys his arguments with force and apparent conviction. They're always internally consistent, even when based on fallacies or delusions. "You see, Mr. Zimmermann," he would say, "only we Serbs really believe in Yugoslavia. We're not trying to secede like the Croats and Slovenes, we're not tied to a foreign country like the Albanians in Kosovo, and we're not trying to create an Islamic state like the Muslims in Bosnia. They all fought against you in World War II. We were your allies."

On Kosovo, Milošević painted a picture without shadings: "Kosovo has always been Serbian, except for a brief period during World War II [it was actually under Turkish rule for 523 years]. Yet we have given the Albanians their own government, their own parliament, their own national library, and their own schools [all of these assertions had ceased to be true at the time he

made them to me]. We have even given them their own Academy
of Sciences. Have you Americans given your blacks their own
Academy of Sciences?"

Milošević was always expansive when it came to his democratic qualities: "You Americans criticize us Serbs for the way we
deal with the Albanians in Kosovo. But don't you realize that
they're trying to take our Serbian homeland out of Yugoslavia
and unite it with Albania? How do you expect us to respond to illegal acts of secession? We don't have anything against Albanians
as a people. Did you know that 80,000 of them live in Belgrade,
as doctors, professors, laborers, and shopkeepers? Go and talk to
them, you'll find that they have no complaints about Serbian
democracy."

Milošević himself would have been the last person to "go and
talk to them." A recluse, he almost never put himself into an informal personal situation that he couldn't control. But if he *had*
talked to the Albanians in Belgrade—or to the Hungarians, Muslims, Croats, Slovaks, or other minorities living in Serbia—he
would have heard a litany of complaints of discrimination rather
than the contented mouthings of satisfied subjects. Since
Milošević's rise to power, Serbia was not a happy place to be if
you belonged to the one-third of its population that was non-
Serbian.

Milošević had a curious attitude toward people. While he could
be an electric speaker, as he was June 28 in Kosovo, he shunned
public exposure. He rarely gave speeches, even during election
campaigns. When he did venture forth, his tendency was to keep
his distance from crowds through the obtrusive use of bodyguards, rather than plunge into them. He did make an exception
of journalists on unstructured occasions; he would answer any
question a reporter would manage to shout at him. A master of
media manipulation, he himself appeared rarely on television and
almost never gave interviews. His personal life, his whereabouts,

what he liked to do on weekends—all were kept behind a veil of secrecy, just as with the leaders in the former Soviet Union.

Despite his undeniable charm, I found him a man of extraordinary coldness. Except in saying hello or goodbye, I seldom saw him smile. Rarely would he illustrate an argument with a personal reference. Once with me he used photographs of mutilated Serbs and Serbian funerals to buttress his allegations about Albanian crimes in Kosovo. For the most part, however, people were groups ("Serbs," "Muslims") or simply abstractions to him. I never saw him moved by an individual case of human suffering. Nor did I ever hear him say a charitable or generous word about an individual human being, not even a Serb.

This chilling personality trait has made it possible, I believe, for Milošević to condone, and even encourage, the most unspeakable atrocities, such as those committed by Serbian citizens in the early days of the Bosnian war. It also accounts for his habitual mendacity, as in his outrageous distortion of Serbian behavior in Kosovo. For Milošević, the truth has a relative and instrumental rather than an absolute value. If it serves his objectives, it is put to use; if not, it can be discarded.

Milošević can be ingratiating when he wants to be, but his character is authoritarian. He is a bully on a grand scale. The embassy's able and outspoken political counselor, Louie Sell, once took a group of American religious leaders to meet him. Milošević treated them to an amazing analysis of American policy that was based on our alleged support of Albania as an "unsinkable aircraft carrier." He claimed that, moving up from Albania, the United States intended to turn the Balkans into a sphere of influence, sharing domination with Germany.

As an American official, Louie felt compelled to set the record straight, so he went up to Milošević after the meeting and told him that his analysis was wrong. Milošević recoiled as if he had been physically struck, a look of horror on his face, and had to be led away by one of his aides. This is not a man who enjoys or welcomes criticism, and it's clear from the flunkeys with whom he surrounds himself that he doesn't hear it very often.

In my view, Milošević is an opportunist rather than an ideologue, a man driven by power rather than nationalism. In the late 1980s he was a communist official in search of a legitimation less disreputable than communism, an alternative philosophy to help him consolidate his hold on Serbia, and a myth that would excite and energize Serbs behind him. He calculated that the way to achieve and maintain power in Serbia was to seize the nationalist pot that Serbian intellectuals were brewing and bring it to a boil.

I don't see Milošević as the same kind of ethnic exclusivist as Croatia's President Franjo Tudjman, who dislikes Serbs, or Bosnian Serb politician Radovan Karadžić, who hates everybody who isn't a Serb. Milošević felt no discomfort in bragging to me, no matter how fraudulently, about Serbia as a multiethnic paradise. Nor, I'm sure, did it disturb his conscience to move ruthlessly against Serbian nationalists like Karadžić when they got in his way. He has made a compact with nationalism as a way to bring him power. He can't break the compact without causing political damage to himself, but it has a utilitarian rather than an emotional value for him.

I can't recall ever seeing a cooler politician under pressure than Slobodan Milošević. In March 1991 he lunched with me and six other Western ambassadors. The meeting came during one of the most explosive crises of his political career. The week before, he had weathered the largest street demonstration ever mounted against his rule, had lost a bid to overthrow the leaderships of Slovenia and Croatia, and was in the process of trying to destroy the presidency of Yugoslavia.

He had come to our lunch from a four-hour meeting with hostile Belgrade University students. Yet he looked and acted as if nothing gave him greater pleasure than to sit down for a long conversation with us. He addressed all our questions with equanimity, asserting with good humor that the Kosovo Albanians were the most pampered minority in Europe, that street demonstrations (which had brought him to power) were wrong, and that Serbia had the freest media and the freest election system in Yugoslavia.

As I pondered the surreal quality of Milošević's remarks, I couldn't help admiring his imperturbability. I went back to the embassy and wrote a facetious cable saying that I had finally penetrated the mystery of the man. There were really two Milošević's. Milošević One was hard-line, authoritarian, belligerent, bent on chaos, and wedded to the use of force to create a Greater Serbia. Personally, he was apoplectic, he hated Westerners, and he spoke in Serbian. Milošević Two was polite, affable, cooperative, and always looking for reasonable solutions to Yugoslavia's problems. He was calm, he liked to reminisce about his banking days in New York, and he spoke good English.

I did note that Milošević One and Milošević Two had several traits in common: they disliked Albanians, they were strong in the defense of Serbian interests, and they seemed to believe that the world was ganging up against Serbia. Milošević Two, I wrote, would often be summoned to repair the horrendous damage caused to Serbia's reputation by Milošević One, who would be sent back to the locker room. There his handlers would salve his wounds and get him ready for the next round. The one sure thing, I concluded, was that Milošević One would always be back.

The strategy of this schizoid figure was based on the fact that Serbs were spread among five of Yugoslavia's six republics. Slovenia was the only exception. At the foundation of Yugoslavia after World War I, Serbia's chief interest was that all these Serbs live in a single state. Before Tito, Serbia had dominated that state. Now, after Tito, Milošević wanted to restore that dominance. His chief obstacle in the late 1980s was Slovenia, ironically the only republic without large numbers of Serbs. The Slovenes were the first to challenge the unity of Yugoslavia.

Milošević, no supporter of Yugoslav unity except as a vehicle for Serbian influence, wrapped himself in the mantle of unity as he sharpened his duel with the Slovenes. His concept of unity was Serbian nationalism buttressed by communist methods of control. It tolerated neither democracy nor power-sharing with other national groups. Because it was unacceptable to all Yugoslavs who wanted real unity or real democracy, or both, it was bound to be divisive. In fact, Milošević's pursuit of a narrow Serbian agenda made him the major wrecker of Yugoslavia.

REFORM

One of the few admirable figures in a landscape of monsters and midgets.

The year 1989 was a year of souring relationships. The sourest of all were between Slovenia and Serbia. This was not a natural enmity, for both republics had profited from their membership in Yugoslavia. The Serbs had used Yugoslavia to unite their scattered populations in a single state. The Slovenes had used it for security and economic purposes. Ever since World War I, Italy has claimed parts of Slovenian territory; even today neo-fascists in the Italian parliament assert those claims. Following World War II the Yugoslav army (JNA in its Serbo-Croatian acronym) won for Slovenia territory that Slovenes claimed had been unfairly assigned to Italy after World War I. Today, independent Slovenia owes one-third of its current area to the JNA's military actions against Italy. Yugoslavia also gave Slovenia a protected market for its finished products (skis, furniture, crystal), which were only barely competitive in Western Europe.

While the Slovenes may have had much to thank Yugoslavia for, their gratitude was not conspicuous. As the country's most prosperous republic, with a per capita gross national product 60 percent above the national average, Slovenia complained that its wealth was being drained south into such ne'er-do-well areas as Macedonia, Montenegro, Bosnia-Herzegovina, Serbia, and Kosovo. This argument was true but not surprising—all Western countries redistribute wealth to their poorer regions. The Slovenes also argued that the development strategy worked out in Belgrade was extremely wasteful; here they had a stronger point. In Kosovo, for example, one of the poorest regions in Europe, funds were plowed into such prestige items as soccer stadiums and garish public buildings, with no discernible effect on the standard of living of the Kosovo Albanians.

The Slovenes' quarrel with Yugoslavia was political as well as economic, and it gathered force with the rise of Milošević in Serbia. The last thing the Slovenes wanted was to be a cash cow tethered to Serbian nationalism. They had nothing in common with Milošević and his expansionism, even though as Yugoslavia's only Serbless republic Slovenia wasn't directly threatened by Milošević's determination to unite all Serbs. The Slovenes saw their republic as a Western democracy in embryo. They were already sliding away from the kind of communism that Milošević was using to consolidate his control in Serbia. Their strategy for dealing with this new challenge was a pugnacious one. Rather than wait Milošević out, they decided to take him on.

By 1989 it was clear that Serbia and Slovenia were the main antagonists in Yugoslavia and that the issues they were contesting went to the heart of Yugoslavia's continued existence. A few weeks after my arrival in Yugoslavia I traveled to Ljubljana, Slovenia's capital, to take the measure of the sharpening debate. If there's a prettier small capital city in Europe than Ljubljana, I have yet to see it. Set in the Ljubljanica River valley with snow-capped mountains visible from the center of town, Ljubljana provides a miniature medieval setting for the modern bridges and buildings designed by its brilliant turn-of-the-century architect Jože Plečnik, who trained in the Jugendstil in Vienna.

Most of the Slovenes I met on that first visit gravitated, like Plečnik, toward Western Europe. If you had put a weather vane on them, it would have pointed northwest—to Italy, Austria, and Germany. The ebullient Slovenian prime minister, Dušan Šinigoj, was full of ideas and projects for economic cooperation with western countries; never once in our meeting did he refer to Belgrade. There's a geographical irony in Slovenia's western yearnings. The Sava, Yugoslavia's longest river (named for the Serbian Saint Sava), rises in Slovenia and flows east, not west—past Ljubljana; through Croatia; along the Croatian-Bosnian border; thence to Belgrade, where it joins dramatically with the Danube to continue east to form the borders between Serbia and Romania and between Romania and Bulgaria, finally emptying into the Black Sea.

I got a fuller sense of Slovenia's eastern attachments from the president of the League of Communists of Slovenia, Milan Kučan, whom I didn't meet on that first visit but saw many times thereafter. Kučan was all politics, and the words rat-tatted from his squat form as if he were a human AK-47. One of the major political figures in Slovenia's recent history, he was the animator of the "Slovene spring," a conscious effort by the Slovene communist party to turn the republic into a Western democracy, with free elections that the party was prepared to lose. The Slovenia I saw was the only republic in history to have prospered under communism. It was also the closest any communist state has ever come to being a democracy. Elections were being prepared for the next year, and Kučan swore to me that there would be no turning back.

Although Slovenian was one of the official languages of Yugoslavia, Kučan, a pragmatist not an ideologue, had no hang-up about speaking with me in Serbo-Croatian, our only common language. In fact, he seemed intent on setting a speed record in it. He expressed a strong commitment to the concept of Yugoslav unity and to Slovenia's commitment to it. But the main purpose of his staccato delivery was to excoriate Milošević and Serbia in the sharpest tones.

"He's a demagogue with a gangster attitude," Kučan said. "He's destroying everything good that Yugoslavia has stood for, especially the tolerant attitude that has made it possible for all of us to coexist. Nobody here seeks a future for Slovenia outside Yugoslavia. But Milošević's imperialist arrogance can only make Slovenes wonder whether this is the kind of Yugoslavia they can live in. We're moving toward democracy and Milošević is moving away from it, toward a kind of 'Serbo-slavia.'" Kučan was careful not to condemn Serbs in general; in fact, he emphasized the traditional friendship between Serbs and Slovenes as well as their natural trading relationship. But he warned that Slovenia was on a collision course with Serbia: "We have no alternative to continuing straight ahead."

Kučan was particularly vehement on Kosovo—oddly, since one of Slovenia's major grievances was the financial assistance it was compelled to contribute to Kosovo. "This is the worst human rights problem in Europe," he charged. "It's giving all of Yugoslavia a bad name. How are we going to get into the European Community or the Council of Europe with this Kosovo albatross around our neck? If we have to go through Belgrade to join Europe, we'll never make it. There's no justice in Milošević holding us all hostage to his crazy schemes. We have a right to demand changes in his policies, because they're dragging us all down. I've explained all this to the Serbs, and they accuse me of high treason. Still, to the extent we can affect the situation, we will—that's why we're pulling our Slovenes out of the Yugoslav police forces serving in Kosovo. We don't want any part in that dirty operation."

The Slovenian leader told me that, personalities aside, the key dispute between Slovenia and Serbia was constitutional. "For Serbia," he said, "authority flows down to the republics from the central government of Yugoslavia. For Slovenia, it moves from a consensus of the republics up to the central government. That was the deal we made in 1918; it's still the deal." He asked for American understanding of Slovenia's position. "We don't want your money, but we do want your moral support for an image of Yugoslavia that can be a part of democratic Europe."

During my first visit to Ljubljana I met two memorable political figures. The first was Janez Stanovnik, the venerable president of Slovenia, who sported a spectacular handlebar mustache and radiated the air of a bon vivant. Stanovnik had spent two decades in Geneva as a senior United Nations civil servant and knew the West well. He represented the best of the Central European tradition: he was courtly, articulate, generous, and wise. He also had an unshakable conviction that Slovenia must become a Western democracy. Stanovnik was an unabashed admirer of Kučan, who was young enough to be his son. He told me that, following his return from Geneva, Kučan had talked him out of retiring and into taking the position of president (even in Slovenia the communist party still controlled all major appointments). While Kučan was the power in Slovenia, Stanovnik exerted considerable moral authority.

Stanovnik and I had lunch with our wives at an outdoor restaurant on a hill overlooking the city. I found the president preoccupied with the future of Yugoslavia. "I fought as a partisan with Tito," he said, "and I remember the price we paid to bring this country together. My own wife is a Serb from Montenegro. Our future must be in Yugoslavia. Secession would be suicide for Slovenia. We may look rich from a Serbian point of view, but we're too small and too poor to make our way alone into Europe. But to survive, Yugoslavia has to be democratized, a market economy has to be created, and the rights of all nationalities have to be respected."

Like Kučan, Stanovnik felt great concern about the direction in which Milošević was trying to take Yugoslavia. He saw the Serbian leader as an unscrupulous opportunist who had made what Stanovnik called a "Faustian pact" with nationalism and was now stuck with it. This marvelous old Slovene, trained as a diplomat in the art of compromise, still believed that things could be worked out, that Yugoslavia could stay together, and that Slovenia could lead it by example. But he admitted to fears. "Slovenes call me up and ask, 'How long are we going to stand for what's happening? The country is going to pieces.' I try to reassure them, but I have the premonition that those of us in favor of keeping Yugoslavia together are swimming against the stream."

There was another Slovene at our lunch, a young economist in his late thirties named Janez Drnovšek. Stanovnik had asked to bring Drnovšek, saying he wanted us to get to know someone who stood for the political future of Slovenia. Drnovšek, improbably, was about to become the next president of Yugoslavia. At lunch he didn't have much to say; in fact he seemed painfully shy behind a pencil-thin mustache and lively eyes. Stanovnik explained how his young friend had achieved his sudden new eminence. "As you know," he said, "Yugoslavia's chief of state is a collective presidency composed of representatives of the six republics plus Kosovo and Vojvodina. You may think an eight-person presidency is a bit bizarre, and it is. But it protects small republics like Slovenia from being intimidated by bigger ones like Serbia." I knew that the president of the presidency changed every year on a rotating basis and that in a few weeks—mid-May—it would be Slovenia's turn. Drnovšek would take over from Dizdarević, to whom I had presented my credentials.

"Normally," Stanovnik continued, "the communist party in each republic selects the representative it will send to the presidency. But we Slovenes of course had to do it differently. We decided to have a republic-wide election. Of course we didn't expect that our party's candidate would have any serious opposition. But Drnovšek ran against him and beat him. He won the first free election in Yugoslavia. Now, if he's confirmed by the Slovenian parliament, a formality, you can say that you were the first foreign ambassador to meet the next president of Yugoslavia."

During this recitation Drnovšek looked more and more uncomfortable. But by now I had an entirely different picture of this man who lacked all the defining features of a politician. However shy and reticent, he was a person who had shown the courage and the ability to challenge the power structure and win. Once he moved to Belgrade, I came to know Drnovšek well as a politician of toughness and judgment. He served both Yugoslavia and Slovenia with distinction.

As Teeny and I got in our car for the six-hour drive back to Belgrade, an incident happened that turned out to be a harbinger. My driver, Neša Janković, a competent and infectiously friendly young Serb, told me that he'd been refused service at the main gas station in Ljubljana. When I asked why, he said, "They saw the Belgrade license plate and heard my Serbian accent." For Neša this wasn't so much a blow to his pride as an omen about the Yugoslavia he loved. Over eight years Neša had driven two of my predecessors all over Yugoslavia; he had close friends in every republic, including Slovenia. Now he and I had to deal with this omen: the politics of hate had reached the point where even gas was sold according to racial criteria.

When I returned to Belgrade, my colleagues in the embassy and I began to think seriously about how different parts of the country viewed Yugoslavia's preservation or breakup. Milošević and his Serbian minions were giving lip service to Yugoslav unity but were actually exploiting that unity to further their hegemonic goals. Kučan and Stanovnik, leaders of the most anti-Serb republic, were also arguing for the importance of a united Yugoslavia, but their vision was of a looser and more democratic confederation in which the six republics could enjoy maximum autonomy.

The most genuinely pro-Yugoslav republics were the two weakest—Macedonia and Bosnia-Herzegovina. Macedonia, parts of whose territory were claimed by all four of its neighbors—Greece, Bulgaria, Albania, and Serbia—had gained its republican status from Tito just after World War II and needed Yugoslavia above all for self-preservation. Bosnia-Herzegovina, elevated by Tito to the status of a republic, was a mixture of Muslims, Serbs, and Croats whose stability depended on the stability of Yugoslavia, of which it was a multinational microcosm. The Kosovo Albanians also owed much to Tito's Yugoslavia; he had given them the autonomous status that so rankled the Serbs.

By 1989 Yugoslavia's opponents were beginning to organize. In Slovenia and Croatia anticommunist dissidents, liberal journalists, and nationalists were raising their voices against Yugoslavia. In the spring of 1989 none of these groups was yet represented in the power structure, which was still entirely communist. But the ones I had met in Ljubljana were looking to the first Slovenian elections to bring their anti-Yugoslav views to power.

As communist parties began to fracture in Eastern Europe and the Soviet Union, we in the embassy began to question the staying power of Yugoslav communism. It had been the product of unique historical forces. Tito had become a communist as a young man after World War I, when he had been on the fringes of the Russian Revolution as a captured Austrian soldier. He had carried out purges for Stalin in Yugoslavia in the 1930s on his way to the leadership of the Yugoslav Communist Party. But his wartime liberation of Yugoslavia from the Germans and Italians was accomplished without much support from Stalin, except at the end, when the Red Army helped retake Belgrade. Tito succeeded in removing the Soviet brigades to Hungary, leaving Yugoslavia with no Soviet troops on its soil. This unique independent power base enabled the Yugoslav leader to survive Stalin's expulsion of the Yugoslav party from the communist movement in 1948. Thenceforth Yugoslav communism proceeded on an entirely different track from that of its neighbors.

Tito consciously sought ways, however artificial, to make Yugoslavia distinct from the Soviet bloc. Against the Leninist principle of "democratic centralism" the Yugoslavs created the political concept of self-management, by which economic and political decisions were to be taken (theoretically at least) by citizens at the grass roots level. As a counter to the Moscow-ruled Warsaw Pact, Tito joined Egyptian President Gamal Abdel Nasser, Indian Prime Minister Jawaharlal Nehru, and Indonesian President Sukarno in founding the nonaligned movement, an unfocused Third World pressure group whose main feature was an aversion to blocs. The Communist Party even changed its name to League of Communists of Yugoslavia, in an effort to show collegiality and rejection of the iron-clad discipline of Soviet-style communist parties.

There was a good deal of fakery in all this. As long as Tito was alive, Yugoslavia remained a dictatorship. But it was a dictatorship with a difference. Yugoslav communists were themselves different. The accident of war had brought to Tito's cause all kinds of people who would never have been communists under normal circumstances. For Yugoslavs who wanted to fight the Germans, Tito's partisans were their only recourse. "If it hadn't been for the war, I would have been a normal Catholic boy," Stane Južnić, a moon-faced, myopic, and broad-minded professor of history in Slovenia, told me back in 1967. "Now I'm a communist, having nothing in common with communists from any other country."

From top to bottom of the party, Tito had exceptional human material to work with. Together with the time-servers, there were people with independence of thought, liberal views, and a self-confidence sometimes bordering on arrogance. Buoyed by their leadership of the nonaligned movement, Yugoslav statesmen strode the world stage, dispensing advice on all the issues of the day from development assistance to nuclear disarmament. In the choppy waters of the cold war they navigated skillfully between the Scylla of NATO and the Charybdis of the Warsaw Pact, coaxing favors from both. It was exhilarating to sit under the chestnuts in a dusty cafe in the most Balkan of capitals and listen to a subtle and penetrating analysis of some global problem from the mouth of a Yugoslav diplomat, political scientist, or journalist. Rarely since World War II has such a brilliant mandarinate elevated such a small country to global importance. Yugoslav communists had extraordinary charm.

The result of these human and political factors was a relatively open political system. To relieve unemployment and generate hard currency, Tito opened the borders and allowed Yugoslavs to work in Western Europe. This action alone created a sophistication within the populace that made the standard propaganda about the superiority and achievements of communism not even worth trying. Nikita Khrushchev in his memoirs spoke admiringly and with envy of Yugoslavia's open borders. In the arts, in journalism, and in information policy generally, the softer touch applied by Yugoslav communists spared their people the sense of oppression felt elsewhere in communist Europe.

Not least important, during almost all of the Tito period the Yugoslav economy rode a rising curve; people's lives were getting better, and they knew it. I can remember in the 1960s seeing tourists from Czechoslovakia, one of the better-off communist countries, stealing fruit from the orchards along Croatia's Dalmatian coast. The Czechs may have been driving Skodas (by then the Yugoslavs had Fiats), but they were too poor to pay for a meal at Yugoslav restaurants.

Yugoslav communism—home-grown, independent, successful, and smug—never carried among the Yugoslav people the domestic stigma that blackened communism for people in the rest of Eastern Europe, where the regimes were clones of the Soviet party and dependent on its direction and influence. This fact may explain why communism was never really swept away in Yugoslavia, in contrast to some Eastern European countries where it was seen as a colonial imposition by an alien power. It may also have been one of the reasons why Yugoslavia turned from communism to nationalism, rather than democracy. Not having a wholly malevolent communist system to despise, Yugoslavs didn't have a wholly democratic alternative to embrace.

Until 1990 communists were in charge in all six Yugoslav republics. Even in 1996, after elections, secessions, and wars, former communists are still at the helm in five out of the six. Alija Izetbegović, the president of Bosnia, is the only republican leader who has never been a member of the League of Communists of Yugoslavia. These peculiar Yugoslav conditions led to two distinct strains of communism after Tito's death. The first tended toward Western democratic values, the second toward the more primitive traditions of ethnic hostility.

Paradoxically, many Yugoslav communists, particularly intellectuals, were closer to the culture of Western political moderation than members of many noncommunist Yugoslav political groupings. These communists wanted to see Yugoslavia copy the democratic institutions and practices of Western Europe. They also wanted to keep the country together and take it into the European Community as Yugoslavia. Fearing violence, they rejected the nationalist appeals for secession. This was even true of most Slovenian and Croatian communists; Kučan and Stanovnik were examples. The main impetus for secession in those two republics came from anticommunists.

Srdja Popović, a Belgrade lawyer, human rights leader, founder of the liberal newsmagazine *Vreme,* and outspoken critic of Yugoslav communism, once said to me in exasperation, "I never thought I'd see the day when most of the people whose views I agree with are communists or former communists." He could have been talking about his own magazine, still the most distinguished in the entire territory of the former Yugoslavia. Most of its writers had been members of the party.

These communists took seriously the watchwords of the Tito era: "brotherhood and unity." This mantra was reproduced ad nauseam in the typical style of communist propaganda; the road between Belgrade and Zagreb was named the "Brotherhood and Unity Highway." The slogan was often ridiculed as a crude effort to manipulate; it even became the butt of black humor. Nevertheless it contained a home truth. Of the million or so Yugoslavs killed during World War II, probably more than half died at the hands of other Yugoslavs.

Ethnic peace was fragile; to preserve it took special efforts. Yugoslavs had to stay together and practice toleration toward each other. Tito backed this message with hard-fisted measures. People convicted of sowing ethnic hatred went to jail. Franjo Tudjman, now president of Croatia, did time for nationalism. So did Jože Pučnik, who was to engineer the defeat of the communists in the Slovenian parliamentary elections of 1990. So also did the mad Serbian racist Vojislav Šešelj. Bosnia's Muslim president Izetbegović was imprisoned for writing his dreamy "Islamic Declaration," wrongly thought to be a Muslim call to arms.

After Tito's death in 1980, "brotherhood and unity" lost a lot of its luster. Some of this loss was Tito's own fault. Via his 1974 constitution, he unwittingly stimulated nationalism by destroying the central government's viability, empowering the republics, and creating the ludicrously feeble collective presidency. If power now resided in the republics, then republican issues would dominate the agenda. More and more, these issues became nationalist rather than Yugoslav in their focus. The main pressure was on how to improve the position of one's republic or nationality within Yugoslavia, not on how to make Yugoslavia itself a more effective state. In parallel, the 1980s was a period of the first prolonged downturn in the Yugoslav economy since the early 1950s. In the economic as well as the political sense, "brotherhood and unity" were beginning to look counterproductive.

These conditions produced the second and more vicious strain of Yugoslav communism. Communists of this type, whether opportunists or nationalists, or both, were ready to exploit the national discontent now being felt in the republics. They practiced a particularly virulent nationalism that derived its force from hostility to other ethnic groups. The aggressive and authoritarian nationalism of Slobodan Milošević in Serbia, and later of Franjo

Tudjman in Croatia, was a classic case of this nationalism-as-racism. The two leaders combined the worst features of communism and nationalism. They took the management skills that are a part of standard communist training, plus the instruments of communist power—a large and intrusive party apparatus, control of key elements of the press, an intimidating secret police, and a centralized economic structure—and put them at the service of the demagogic advancement of narrow national interests.

It may seem strange that in Yugoslavia the ideology of communism, a doctrine that from its conception had always professed internationalist principles, should have slipped so easily into the dogma of nationalism. Yugoslavia was not the only site of this phenomenon. In several states of the former Soviet Union—Ukraine, Azerbaijan, Armenia, Georgia, Uzbekistan, Tajikistan, and Turkmenistan—communists reinvented themselves as nationalist leaders. The similarities between orthodox communism and aggressive nationalism have proved greater than once imagined. Both ideologies are collectivist, setting the group over the individual. Both are exclusivist, branding outsiders as enemies. And both are militant, insisting that those enemies be eliminated, preferably by force. The decline of communism unleashed a particularly dangerous form of nationalism, as communists scrambled to find a new source of legitimacy. The Polish philosopher Adam Michnik once said, in parody of Lenin, that nationalism was the final stage of communism.

It is too simple to say that the problem in Yugoslavia was communism by itself or even that the main struggle was between communism and democracy. The real problem was nationalism, which some communists, former communists, noncommunists, and anticommunists were trying to appropriate for their own ends. Regrettably, the Yugoslavia that Tito bequeathed wasn't equipped to deal with nationalism. Tito left his country two poison gifts. The first, paradoxically, was nationalism itself. During his lifetime Tito never really removed nationalism. Instead, he trapped it in a pressure cooker. With his death, the steam began to escape until finally things blew sky-high.

The second gift was a bogus democracy rather than the real thing. A genuinely democratic system might have filtered and attenuated the militant nationalism that arose after Tito's death. In the United States, France, the United Kingdom, and Germany racist demagogues have been politically active, but they have rarely been able to clear the hurdles and obstacles thrust in their way by the need to win and hold the support of electorates. Yugoslavia had no such democratic obstacle course. A clever political manipulator like Milošević could exploit the nondemocratic elements of Yugoslav communism for his own nationalistic purposes.

As the embassy surveyed this scene toward the end of 1989, it was apparent to us that the threat to Yugoslavia's unity had changed. Now that the Soviet Union was collapsing, Yugoslavia was no longer threatened from outside. The threat came from within, from aggressive nationalism. I pressed the talented and professional group of political and economic officers in the embassy in Belgrade and the consulate general in Zagreb (Croatia) to consider "worst-case" scenarios for Yugoslavia. The "worst case" we could think of was the breakup of the country under nationalist pressures. We believed, and reported to Washington, that no breakup of Yugoslavia could happen peacefully. Because of the ethnic hatred sown by Milošević and his ilk, and because of the mixture of races in every republic except Slovenia, the shattering of Yugoslavia would surely lead to extreme violence, perhaps even war.

It was only reasonable to seek to prevent such violence. I outlined the dangers of dissolution and my belief that it had to be prevented at a U.S. ambassadors' meeting called by Secretary of State James A. Baker in Brussels in December 1989 to discuss European issues. There was surprisingly little concern among the attending U.S. ambassadors to European countries, two-thirds of whom were nonprofessional political appointees. Most of the time at the meeting was understandably taken up by the more immediate issue of Germany's reunification. Nevertheless, Baker's deputy, Lawrence Eagleburger, the State Department's Office of East European and Yugoslav Affairs, and the Central Intelligence Agency were all alive to the growing dangers in Yugoslavia.

The embassy was convinced, and Washington agreed, that the United States should support a combination of unity and democracy. The two had to go together. If we encouraged the breakup of Yugoslavia in support of Slovenian (and later Croatian) democracy and self-determination, then democracy as well as unity would be lost. Serbia and the Yugoslav army would fight to prevent secession, and no program of civil liberties could survive such an ethnic conflict. The Slovenes might escape unmarked, but nobody else would. Bosnia, as the most ethnically mixed republic, would be most at risk.

On the other hand, if we backed the coercive unity that Milošević was advancing as a cover for Serbian hegemony, real unity would become impossible because the Slovenes and Croats would resist. Thus unity without democracy meant Serbian or military dictatorship; democracy without unity meant war. Democracy and unity were the inseparable Siamese twins of Yugoslavia's fate. The loss of one meant that the other would perish.

How was this union of unity and democracy to be embodied in Yugoslav political life? In the seething cauldron of ethnic rivalries, Yugoslavia needed a leader who could deal with the growing economic crisis and at the same time appeal to Yugoslavs to stay together and build a democratic society. Amazingly, a man who represented all these qualities found himself the new prime minister of Yugoslavia in March 1989. Ante Marković, a politician of great ability and determination, had been voted into office by the Yugoslav parliament with a mandate to curb the runaway inflation and institute a radical economic reform. In his political and business careers, Marković had known nothing but success. In this, his biggest job, he became the embodiment of Yugoslavia's final failure, the confirmation that genuine reform in a unified Yugoslavia was impossible, and the ultimate proof that the country was doomed.

Historians look backward to the past. Diplomatic analysts, seeking to lay a basis for policy, must try to map the future. In hindsight, Marković represents an experiment in reform that was too little and too late. Like Aleksandr Kerensky, the last Russian prime minister before the Bolsheviks came to power in 1917, Marković was a good man contending with powerful forces beyond his power to influence. Milovan Djilas, the famous dissident and political seer, called him Yugoslavia's first modern statesman. At another time and place Marković would have been a major catalyst of reform. He was one of the few admirable figures in a landscape of monsters and midgets.

History is hard on also-rans. Without hindsight, fifteenth-century Burgundy had a more important trade, industry, and agriculture than France; sixteenth-century Antwerp was Europe's foremost commercial and financial center, surpassing London; and the Socialist Revolutionary Party of Russia was the winner (with a majority of parliamentary seats, over twice the number of Lenin's Bolsheviks) in the Soviet Union's first and last democratic election in November 1917. Looked at from the perspective of 1989, Ante Marković had assumed office in a time of troubles, yet a time when leadership and reform still had a fighting chance.

Marković was impossible to dislike. A good-looking silver-haired man in his mid-sixties, he radiated good humor and ebullience. He laughed easily—not a trait of Slavic officials and certainly not of Yugoslav communists. He had a can-do attitude and an unbounded conviction that he could overcome what was now universally called "the Yugoslav crisis." A man of large ego, he saw himself as a messiah for Yugoslavia; it was "my policy," "my reform," "my ability to save the country." Marković had earned his spurs in the tough school of Croatian communist politics. He had run a large heavy machinery enterprise, then had become in succession prime minister and president of Croatia.

In a republic of lackluster politicians he had stood out as a strong believer in such capitalistic reforms as privatization. After he became Yugoslav prime minister, his dynamism and supreme self-confidence impressed visiting Westerners. The financier-philanthropist George Soros, a shrewd judge of Eastern European politicians, told me after a visit to Belgrade that Marković was one of the most remarkable leaders he had met.

P. J. Nichols, the embassy economic counselor, and I had many discussions with Marković. We would meet him in the immense modern federal building, erected as a tribute to Tito's capacious ambitions, across the Sava River from the old part of Belgrade. Marković's office was one of the largest I had ever seen; his anteroom alone was nearly as big as the oval office in the White House. As P. J. and I sat with Marković at his gigantic conference table, I wondered whether there was some law of nature by which the size of an office is inversely proportional to the political power of its occupant.

Marković at least didn't seem discomfited by his surroundings. In his soft Croatian accent he made sure we understood the sweeping nature of his chosen task. "Yugoslavia is in a crisis of politics, of economics, and of relations among republics and nationalities," he said, adding grandly, "but for the first time there is combined in the prime minister's office a concept for resolving that crisis with a dynamic man representing that concept."

Immodestly but accurately, Marković described the obstacles to his reform as "the greatest economic challenge a Yugoslav leader has ever confronted." "Do you realize," he asked, "that each of the six Yugoslav republics has to have its own steel mill, its own oil refinery, and all the other heavy industry dinosaurs? Because every republic must have prestige industries that even some middle-sized countries do without, we have to sacrifice the efficiency of our whole economy. As for the banking system, do you know how that works? Banks exist to provide loans to favored industries on political, not economic criteria. They're really subsidiaries of the enterprises they lend to." I asked him whether that were true of the bank Milošević had run. "That's one of the worst," he said. "It makes regular loans to the Smederevo steel works, the biggest money loser in Serbia, if not in all of Yugoslavia."

The new prime minister was quite specific about his intentions. "I started with the idea of modernizing socialism," he said, "but now my plan is to go far beyond that. The role of the state has to be reduced. There must be structural changes. Yugoslavia has to become a Western democratic country with a capitalist system. The 'socialism' of Eastern Europe, even if it reforms itself, isn't good enough for us. I'm pressing for legislation that will remove the limits on private ownership, liberalize trade by allowing imports to come in freely, reduce our swollen government expenditures, promote small and medium-sized industries, and restore real banking functions to the banking system. Most important of all, I have to stop the runaway inflation. I intend by 1990 to have a strong and fully convertible Yugoslav dinar."

One of Marković's constant complaints was how little power the prime minister had in the Yugoslav system. "I was mandated by republics all over Yugoslavia to launch a serious reform. But do you think any republic would give up even some of its economic authority to let me do it? In the end the Yugoslav reform will focus economic power where it should be—on the individual firms. But I need the political powers to make that possible. The only clear powers I have are over the federal budget—but that goes mainly to the Yugoslav army—and over monetary policy. Even in those areas I have to operate through the force of my character and through persuasion."

"But everyone knows that inflation has to be stopped," he continued, "and I intend to stop it. Yugoslavia now has the highest inflation rate in the world, over 3,000 percent on an annual basis.

That's nearly as high as Germany in the 1920s." I thought of the wad of Yugoslav dinars in my pocket, still moist from the printers. They would have to be spent that day or their value would drop 10 to 20 percent by the next day.

Marković could be accused of bravado, but he knew that he had few assets beyond himself. He had to convince people in fractious Yugoslav republics that he could serve their interests better than their own nationalist politicians. His optimism, his conviction that anything could be done and that he was the only man who could do it, and his energy and competence were assets that he exploited skillfully. No doubt it helped that he actually believed everything he said; nobody with less egotism could have lasted a month in his job.

What Marković wanted most of all was support from the West. He saw the United States as the key country. He wanted to visit Washington to meet President Bush. He wanted clear statements of American support for his programs. And above all he wanted money. How much? "Well," he said with his infectious smile, "I'm playing a big game, and that requires big money. I think four billion dollars would be a good start to help a reform that's going further than anything in Eastern Europe." Swallowing hard, I told him I'd report his request to Washington. I knew what the answer would be. U.S. policy in Eastern Europe was heavily focused on Poland and Hungary, countries that were moving on the reform path faster than Yugoslavia and without the baggage of divisive nationalism. Yugoslavia would be seen as a poor risk and therefore a low priority.

Marković got his trip to Washington in October 1989. I had lobbied hard for it, and, with the support of Eagleburger and the European Bureau of the State Department, the White House agreed to a meeting with President Bush. We then filled in additional meetings with Secretary of State Baker, Defense Secretary Richard B. Cheney, Treasury Secretary Nicholas F. Brady, and Commerce Secretary Robert A. Mosbacher, as well as a visit to

Congress and a trip to New York for talks with bankers and businessmen. I accompanied Marković to all his meetings and could
see he was a bit bemused by Washington's way of handling foreign dignitaries. Like most other leaders of small countries, he
expected earnest attention, respectful deference, and lavish hospitality—a guest suite, an official car, lunches and dinners in his
honor, full coverage in the American press.

He got none of these. The U.S. government paid for nothing
during his visit. In fact, the only meal for which Marković himself didn't have to pick up the tab was a breakfast roundtable at
the Council on Foreign Relations in New York. His discussions
with members of the Foreign Relations and Foreign Affairs com-
mittees of the Congress were marked by the typical pattern of
members wandering in and out. Some, like Lee Hamilton of Indi-
ana and Tom Lantos of California, were attentive and informed,
while others read pompous texts their staffs had written for them
or else exposed their uncertainty as to what country they had
come to be briefed about.

Marković was a good sport about his rude experience of a no-
frills official visit to the United States. It certainly showed him
that Yugoslavia was not in the center of Washington's universe.
But he did get a taste of the importance of the Kosovo issue for
the Congress. Several members blamed his government for the
iniquities of the Serbian position. The visit may have sown
doubts within him that he could launch an economic reform without involving himself in the political and human rights issues that
he had hoped to keep at arm's length. Marković was hampered by
his lack of English; working through interpreters always makes a
personal relationship hard to establish, especially with a person as
dynamic as the Yugoslav leader. Still, he did a good job of explaining the breadth of the reform he had initiated; Baker, with
his quick intellect, understood immediately.

The short meeting with President Bush was something of a dis-
appointment, mainly because the conversation centered on the

Soviet Union rather than Yugoslavia. Bush asked for Marković's views on Soviet leader Mikhail Gorbachev's staying power, a subject on which Marković was only too happy to expatiate. The two never got down to the key Yugoslav issues. At the end of the allotted half-hour Marković was cordially ushered out, with most of his appeal for economic assistance unuttered. The meeting did produce a clear public statement of U.S. policy toward Yugoslavia. The president reaffirmed his strong support for Yugoslav independence, unity, and sovereignty and welcomed Marković's commitment to market-oriented economic reform and building democratic pluralism.

Back home, the Yugoslav prime minister scored some initial successes in pushing his economic reform through the Yugoslav parliament, although he often had to use procedural loopholes to do it. During the autumn of 1989, at the urging of the Slovene Janez Drnovšek, by now president of the Yugoslav presidency, he consulted Jeffrey Sachs, the young Harvard economist and expert on inflation. Sachs persuaded him to take a radical step—make the Yugoslav dinar immediately convertible to hard currency, thus eliminating the incentive to spend dinars and drive their value down.

As a result, skyrocketing prices fell. Marković had dramatic success in early 1990 in bringing inflation down to zero from the by-then 25,000 percent on an annual basis—"the 14th highest inflation in the history of the world," said Sachs, who then proceeded to describe the other thirteen at a dinner at my house for economists. In less than a year in office the prime minister quadrupled Yugoslavia's foreign exchange reserves. And he began the process of opening the economy to imports, to investors, and to the competition of the private sector.

Marković was embarked on the most radical economic reform program in Eastern Europe. Unfortunately, the social and political costs of his "shock therapy" were too great. Inefficient Yugoslav producers didn't want to compete with liberalized imports; they persuaded their republics to shield them. Wage-earners were not keen to accept a ceiling on wage rates, whose upward spiral had been a major cause of inflation. And, most important, political leaders in the Yugoslav republics saw his reform as a threat.

Marković claimed with some justification that the Yugoslav reform was a model for the reforms in Poland and Czechoslovakia (Hungary's approach was different). Why then did the other reforms succeed while the Yugoslav reform failed? The key reason is that those countries had strong central governments; Yugoslavia did not. The fragmentation of power among the republics left the prime minister with little influence. Marković was forced to operate by persuading and cajoling. To get something, he often had to give away elements of the reform that were necessary to its effectiveness. Nothing could be done without the agreement of all six republics, and agreement was not an abundant commodity in the waning days of Yugoslavia.

The problem was structural. Each of the three strongest republics had special and often contradictory reasons to combine against him. Slovenia, though reformist itself, didn't want any reforms coming out of Belgrade. Croatia, even before the nationalists came to power and still more after, rejected both the Belgrade origin of the reform and its threat to the old-style command economy that exists to this day in Croatia. Milošević's Serbia had no interest in an economic reform that might dissipate its own powers. It also rejected Marković's appeal to Yugoslav unity, since it wasn't the Serb-dominated unity Milošević fancied.

Marković tried to parry the opposition of the republican governments by going over their heads and appealing directly to the people. He was good at people-to-people politics. His upbeat message and his kinetic energy made a positive contrast to the Slavic gloom of most Balkan oratory. He stood consistently high in the opinion polls; in fact, he was the most popular political figure in Yugoslavia. But he couldn't get a pulpit. The media outlets were almost all controlled by republican governments, which had no interest in giving exposure to a rival politician. Marković even failed to get television time for his annual "State of Yugoslavia" message to the parliament.

In frustration, he tried to acquire shares in *Borba,* an independent Belgrade daily, and he founded a Yugoslavia-wide television channel, YUTEL. During its short life YUTEL was the most objective and informative source of television news in Yugoslavia. Its professionalism attracted to its staff first-rate television news reporters and anchors from all over the country. But republican regimes refused to carry it, except at two or three o'clock in the morning after their regular programming and their audience were both exhausted. "To be a liberal in Yugoslavia," a friend of mine said, "you have to be an insomniac."

There were no illusions either in the State Department or in our embassy about Marković's prospects. P. J. Nichols, who knew the Yugoslav economy well from a previous tour in Belgrade, rated the chances of Marković's success at less than 50 percent. But what was the alternative? The probable consequences of Marković's failure would be the breakup of Yugoslavia, the victory of nationalism, and war. Janez Stanovnik, my reflective Slovenian friend, called Marković's reform "the alpha and omega for Yugoslavia." If it failed, he told me, there was no hope for Yugoslavia as a united country. I personally had no doubt about the right U.S. policy. It was better to support reform and unity than to concede victory to the cancer of nationalism. I cabled Washington in September 1989: "Whatever the odds—and they are probably against—it is profoundly in our interest to help the Yugoslav economic reform succeed."

Beset by the intractable problems of Yugoslavia's political realities, Marković harbored extravagant hopes that the West would somehow bail him out. From time to time he would explode in frustration. Once, at a point when the Yugoslav reform was showing tangible success, he complained to me that Western governments had refused to roll over Yugoslavia's debt. "You Americans tell us that you support our reform," he said. "You say you favor our efforts to establish convertibility, to introduce financial discipline, and to eliminate inflation. You tell us we can be a model for Eastern Europe. And then you say that, because all the things you want us to do are actually proving successful, you can't give us help, because we don't need it. In fact, you say that only if we fail will you consider helping us."

We in the embassy worked as hard as we could on Marković's behalf and did achieve a high public level of U.S. political support for the embattled prime minister. The Washington view was that a large infusion of dollars was out of the question, partly because of Yugoslavia's poor human rights record (which was due to Milošević, not Marković) and partly because it wouldn't have worked just to throw money at the problem. This was understandable, but I couldn't fathom why Washington wouldn't help Marković on his more modest requests, like debt rollover.

The main obstacle was the U.S. Treasury Department, which took an ideological view of Eastern Europe: only if a country moved on a straight line toward capitalism would it qualify for exceptional American attention. Yugoslavia, with its unique nationality problems, was too complex for this rigid model. U.S. support for Yugoslavia's reform suffered in comparison with our help to Poland, Hungary, and Czechoslovakia. Treasury, which wielded great power in George Bush's Washington, had a tin ear for political considerations, even when they meant that Yugoslavia might fall apart.

There was a more general reason for Washington's hesitancy. The very difficulty of Marković's problems, which should have made assistance imperative, caused people to shy away. Compared with other countries in Eastern Europe, Yugoslavia didn't look like a good bet. Politicians would rather back a winner than a loser, and, despite Marković's heroic efforts, Yugoslavia looked like a loser. This view didn't prevent the U.S. government from helping Marković. In fact, no country supported his reform more than the United States. But it made our support less than it should have been.

In the late summer of 1989, while I was in New Jersey for my daughter Lily's wedding, I paid a call on George Kennan at Princeton. I revered Kennan as the most incisive thinker and writer among American professional diplomats of this century. He had been ambassador to Yugoslavia in the early 1960s under President John F. Kennedy; I was interested in his current views. Kennan received me in his office at the Institute for Advanced Study, a stiff but not austere presence at age eighty-five.

After recalling his immersion in Balkan affairs during his time in Belgrade—he had set the embassy staff to writing a complete history of Yugoslavia—Kennan made a stunning prediction. "You know," he said, "the first major war in this century started in what is now Yugoslavia. Today, with the Cold War ending, people think Yugoslavia isn't in a position to do any damage. I think they're wrong. There's a fault line of instability running through the Balkans. I think events in Yugoslavia are going to turn violent and to confront the Western countries, especially the United States, with one of their biggest foreign policy problems of the next few years."

As if in response to Kennan's warning, the year 1989 drew to an ominous close. Milošević, stung by Slovenian attacks on his Kosovo policy, decided to hold a mass rally in Slovenia's capital. Hundreds of thousands of Serbs were organized in special trains and buses supplied by their enterprises to travel to Ljubljana and teach the Slovenes the "truth" about Kosovo. Of course, the real purpose of this "Meeting of Truth" wasn't educational. The Serbian leader had used mass rallies to dispose of anti-Milošević governments in Kosovo, Vojvodina, and Montenegro. The tactic was right out of Hitler's and Mussolini's play books. The goal was to destabilize, perhaps even overthrow, the Slovenian leadership.

The Slovenes took a tough line—they banned the meeting and threatened to stop the procession at the border. In the end only a few Serbs made it to Ljubljana. Later I asked Stanovnik why the Slovenian government had taken this action against the principle of freedom of assembly. He replied that the Serbs had been offered a roundtable discussion in an auditorium, plus free television time and newspaper space to make their case. "They refused all this," he said. "They insisted on a demonstration. And we had reliable information that they were bringing guns and intended violence. Even the Yugoslav army urged the Serbs to abandon the confrontation—in fact, the army played a helpful role. In those circumstances, what would you have done?"

Milošević, furious at the rebuff dealt his campaign against the Slovenes, slapped an economic embargo on Slovenia—an act that, to say the least, cast doubt on his professions of support for the unity of Yugoslavia. It was as if Massachusetts had imposed economic sanctions against Maine in the name of the unity of the United States. In December 1989, with Kennan's prophecy in mind, I sent Washington a gloomy assessment, noting that Milošević's efforts to destabilize the Slovenian leadership had sharply exacerbated ethnic tensions throughout the country—"the fabric of ethnic tolerance, never very strong in Yugoslavia, has been badly torn"—and that the odds against Prime Minister Marković's success were lengthening.

Whatever Milošević may have contributed to the restoration of Serbia's self-confidence, I wrote, "he has done major damage to the unity of Yugoslavia, to tolerance among its peoples, and to the Serbian democratic tradition itself. . . . Milošević seems compelled to move by creating crises in which he defines his own security and that of his republic by the insecurity of everybody else. . . . In Slovenia, more people now seem to be thinking of secession—whether in fear or anticipation—as a real option." I concluded, "In the longer—and perhaps not too much longer—term, it's becoming possible to think the unthinkable—that Milošević's divisive tactics could encourage Slovene separatism and Croatian nationalism and ultimately split the country."

DEMOCRACY

*The elections helped snuff out the very flame of
democracy they had kindled.*

On January 24, 1990, the League of Communists of Yugoslavia
became the first ruling communist party in the world to commit
suicide. The occasion was the fourteenth extraordinary party congress that the main centralizers in Yugoslavia—Serbia, Montenegro, and the army—had insisted on holding. Their aim was to
arrest the trend toward decentralization that had dominated the
country since Tito's death. Instead, they accelerated it. As usual,
the problem began with Slovenia.

The congress met in Belgrade's cavernous Sava Center, which
a few months before had been the site of the summit conference
of nonaligned countries featuring, among other circusy adorn-
ments, Muammar al-Qaddafi's hard-eyed, well-armed female
bodyguards. The Yugoslav communist party got no such protection. The Slovenes came to the congress with a scathing denunci-
ation of Serbian policy in Kosovo and a take-it-or-leave-it
insistence on an "asymmetric federation" in which the republican
parties would be virtually autonomous. When Milošević and oth-

ers refused to go along with this assault on communism's tradition of centralized rule, the Slovenes walked out. Milošević tried to keep the congress in session without them, but the Croats objected. The congress broke up, never to meet again.

Prime Minister Marković, a communist all his adult life, shed no tears at the demise of the party. Marković was at the flush stage of his economic reform and of his personal popularity in the country. Against the disarray of the party's demise, he positioned himself at the Sava Center as dapper, confident, and in control. He told journalists with his trademark smile that the end of the party was not the end of Yugoslavia, that his government would go right on working. Marković was undoubtedly right that his efforts to wrap himself in the fraying Yugoslav flag didn't depend on a viable communist party. But they did depend on the strengthening of other Yugoslav institutions, especially his government and the federal parliament, whose support he needed. Marković told me repeatedly that his strategy depended on a newly elected, modernized federal assembly to replace the communist-dominated dinosaur that had been in place since the mid-1980s.

The prime minister was the first political figure in Yugoslavia to come out for the first countrywide democratic elections in postwar Yugoslav history. In a stark and tragic irony, his attempt to initiate a democratic process in Yugoslavia was blocked, not by undemocratic Serbia, but by relatively democratic Slovenia. Milošević in fact went along with Marković's desire to hold elections. The Serbian leader favored direct elections for the lower chamber, combining the democratic principle of "one-person, one-vote" with the less altruistic desire to exploit the numerical plurality of Serbs throughout Yugoslavia.

The Slovenes, on the other hand, opposed direct parliamentary elections; in fact, they didn't want a lower chamber at all. They weren't interested in anything that strengthened Yugoslavia, even if it was in the direction of democratic and economic reform.

Slovenia's blockage prevailed. In the end, Yugoslavia perished without its citizens ever being permitted to cast their votes as Yugoslavs.

A day after the collapse of Yugoslav communism in ethnic enmity, an incident at my house recapitulated that enmity in personal terms. Teeny and I were giving a small dinner for Katharine Graham, chairman of the Washington Post Company, and several of the *Post*'s senior correspondents. We had thought to show them a cross section of Yugoslav opinion and had invited, among other guests, President Stanovnik of Slovenia and Professor Mihajlo Marković (no kin of the prime minister), a Serbian philosopher who had suffered under Tito for his liberal views of Marxism.

Both Stanovnik and Marković had spent years in the West; both were highly civilized, decent men. Yet, when the subject of Serbian policy in Kosovo came up, both lost their tempers and started shouting at each other across the dinner table. The commotion went on from soup to dessert. For our visitors from the *Post,* it was a fascinating picture of what was happening to Yugoslavia. For our staff, who were serving the dinner, it was a tragedy. Verica Borić, our partly Serbian housekeeper who had worked in the house for over two decades, told Teeny in tears that she had never felt such shame and sorrow for her country.

A few days later, Milošević sent word that after ten months he was now willing to receive the American ambassador. I would finally have a chance to make a personal evaluation of the leader who had caused so much controversy. I asked Louie Sell to accompany me to the meeting; I wanted both a note-taker and a witness. Milošević on this occasion, as at most future meetings, was alone. His secretiveness and lack of trust in subordinates sometimes made it necessary for me to brief the Serbian foreign minister on my meetings with his boss, a practice both of us found unpleasant.

This first meeting with Milošević was a study in contrasts. Having ignored me for nearly a year, he had apparently decided that it wasn't good politics to keep the United States at arm's length. He began by trying to please. He brushed aside my nonattendance at the anniversary of the Battle of Kosovo with neither an apology nor an accusation. "It was impossible to receive you after the June 28 celebration," he said, "but now we're in a new year." He then set out to establish his credentials as an economic reformer by means of extravagant praise, backed by questionable details, of Serbia's economic performance.

Milošević's ugly side finally came out. He stubbornly defended his economic blockade against Slovenia. When I questioned the economic grounds for his action, he said brusquely, "There were no economic grounds. The Slovenes opposed us over Kosovo, so they had to pay a price." Paradoxically, he accused the Slovenes —the strongest advocates of multiparty democracy in Yugoslavia —of having a "Bolshevik" conception of the role of parties. In a semithreat, he said, "If it comes to secession, Serbia is a lot bigger than Slovenia. In fact, we're bigger than a lot of European countries. The United States should look to where its interests lie."

Kosovo was Milošević's hottest button. He was unyielding, emotional, pugnacious, and full of invective for its Albanian inhabitants. "Kosovo is Serbian," he asserted, with no reference to the fact that 90 percent of its population was Albanian. I asked him what his strategy was for winning Albanian support. He had no answer; the question had obviously never occurred to him. In the car going back to the embassy, Louie and I couldn't make up our minds whether Milošević believed everything he said or whether he was cynically exploiting nationalist symbols. We agreed that he was either an unhinged fanatic or a clever manipulator. I wasn't sure at the time. I'm quite sure now—he is a manipulator.

In the conditions of early 1990—an embattled prime minister fighting for reform against the odds, growing secessionist pressures from Slovenia, and a regime in Serbia that was showing fascist tendencies—it seemed important to increase the visibility of U.S. support for Marković. Washington decided, with my strong concurrence, that Deputy Secretary Eagleburger should visit Yugoslavia.

During his first year in office Eagleburger had kept himself out of direct involvement in Yugoslav affairs as a result of the baseless concern expressed by Senator Jesse Helms (Republican of North Carolina) that he had an important financial stake in the country. In fact, Eagleburger was on the board of one Serbian and one Slovenian firm. Both were trying to modernize the economy and introduce Western business practices; his remuneration was next to nothing. He had mixed emotions about a reimmersion in Yugoslav affairs, but his knowledge and judgment were too valuable to waste. He was also the U.S. government's coordinator for assistance to Eastern Europe; it would be natural for him to make a personal assessment of Yugoslavia's needs and qualifications.

Eagleburger, who arrived in Belgrade on February 25, met with Prime Minister Marković and told the press that he had been very impressed with Marković's reform program. He added pointedly that Yugoslavia's political issues would be easier to solve if the economy were healthier. He also met with his old friend, Foreign Minister Lončar, and with Slovenian President Stanovnik, who did him the courtesy of traveling to Belgrade from Ljubljana to accommodate Eagleburger's schedule. Stanovnik told him that Yugoslavia would pass through a tough period "but will not easily fall apart." On specifics the Slovene president seemed less optimistic. He lamented, "Yugoslavs are abandoning class thinking only to replace it by nationality thinking." For Slovenia he predicted that the April elections would produce a noncommunist government there that would work for secession. From his lips we heard for the first time a word soon to take on a nightmarish reality: "Lebanonization."

Eagleburger admitted to me a certain trepidation about renewing his acquaintance with Milošević, whom he had known in the late 1970s when he was U.S. ambassador to Yugoslavia and Milošević was a banker. "I thought he was a liberal; he talked so convincingly about westernizing Yugoslavia's economy. I just must have been wrong." I don't think Eagleburger was wrong. In his prenationalist phase Milošević probably did sound like an economic liberal; indeed, he continued to pass himself off as an economic reformer even after Serbian nationalism had pushed economic issues off his agenda. It was his ability to remake—in the modern cliché "reinvent"—himself that made him so impressive. What Eagleburger saw on his return to Yugoslavia was a new color on the skin of the most artful chameleon in the Balkans.

In his meeting with Milošević the deputy secretary made a strong case for Prime Minister Marković's economic program. Milošević feigned surprise that his own devotion to economic liberalization could be questioned in any way. He said that Marković had actually borrowed the essence of his reform from the Serbian reform program of two years before. He boasted that three thousand private enterprises had been created in Serbia during the past year, neglecting to point out that not a single state-run industry was among them.

Eagleburger expressed concern that Yugoslavia was lurching toward nationalism, separatism, and major violations of human rights. "Why are you blaming Serbia for this? Are you saying that we're the only ones responsible?" asked Milošević. "My impression is that all of you are responsible," Eagleburger countered. Milošević challenged Eagleburger's emphasis on human rights. The deputy secretary answered, "The United States has a legitimate commitment to defending human rights. Beyond that we have a right to decide how we use our taxpayers' money or which countries to advise our businesses to invest in. If we choose to give priority to countries with good human rights records, that's our choice to make."

The conversation turned to Kosovo. Eagleburger said that Serbia's strong-arm tactics were hurting Yugoslavia's relations with the United States. Milošević bristled. He conceded no wrongdoing; Serbs had to defend themselves against "Islamic fundamentalism" and the "narco-Mafia" in Kosovo. "The Albanians are carrying out systematic murders and rapes of Serbian women and children—and this doesn't even take into account the mental murder of the 200,000 Serbs who live in Kosovo. This Albanian strategy is being supported by the Slovenes, who are trying to use the Kosovo issue to destabilize Serbia." The garishness of Milošević's language on Kosovo—"mental murder" was a new addition to his Orwellian lexicon—contrasted oddly with the reasonable pose he had struck in his defense of the market system.

On political issues, Milošević argued that a unified Yugoslavia was the only political formation that made it possible for all Serbs to live in one country. His formula for unity was uncompromising—a tight federation with minimal autonomy for the republics. He professed not to have anything against a multiparty system but stressed that it had to operate on a Yugoslav and not a republican basis—"It wouldn't work in Serbia." What emerged was a defense of the preservation of Yugoslavia, but in a rigid mold defined by Serbian interests as interpreted by Milošević. He made one comment that was soon to take on ominous overtones: "Serbs live all over Yugoslavia. The unity of Yugoslavia is the only way they can live in one country."

On the second night of Eagleburger's two-day visit, I invited to my house about fifteen members of opposition groups from all over Yugoslavia. With Yugoslavia's first free elections scheduled for the spring in Slovenia and Croatia, Eagleburger wanted to meet opposition figures from those and other republics. No such meeting had ever been held under official American auspices. So fragmented had Yugoslav politics become that most of the politicians had no contacts outside their own republics; in many cases they were meeting each other for the first time. Just sponsoring such a meeting was an important signal that the United States no longer based the bilateral relationship exclusively on our links to Yugoslav communists.

Eagleburger heard a variety of views, most expressed with clarity and passion. Liberal politicians from Macedonia, Montenegro, and Bosnia argued for support for Prime Minister Marković, urged that Yugoslavia stay united, and predicted civil war if it broke up. From Serbia, Tanja Petovar, the courageous head of a leading human rights group, told the deputy secretary that Milošević's communist leadership was seeking to survive by encouraging nationalism as a way to block democratic change. Petovar urged maximum pressure on Serbia over the Kosovo issue. The group from Kosovo was impressive and articulate. Ibrahim Rugova, leader of the Albanian party in Kosovo, said that Kosovo should be autonomous within a confederal Yugoslavia. To get away from Serbian control, he favored a dialogue with Marković's federal government. Veton Suroi, a young Albanian with perfect English, said that the people of Kosovo didn't accept Serbian rule but didn't favor independence, a view that was soon to change.

The voices from Croatia and Slovenia sang a different tune. Slavko Goldstein, an intrepid Jewish human rights advocate from Zagreb, said he was not for continuing Yugoslavia at any price, but he wouldn't break it up at any price either. His Croatian colleague, Vladimir Šeks, representative of a new nationalist party (the Croatian Democratic Union) headed by Franjo Tudjman, struck the first chilling note by arguing for the expansion of Croatia. He said that his party was ready to recognize the republic's internal borders, but if any borders in Yugoslavia were redrawn, "Croats should not be left outside the republic's influence." Eagleburger asked if Šeks would give the same rights to Serbs living in Croatia. "No," he answered.

From Slovenia, Peter Jambrek, representing the anticommunist coalition DEMOS, had only one thought on his mind: independence. He predicted that DEMOS would win the Slovenian elections and would quickly move the republic toward secession (he was right on both counts). Jambrek was the only one in the room who answered yes when Eagleburger asked if anyone favored the end of Yugoslavia as a unified country. When others argued that a breakup would produce bloodshed, Jambrek insisted that there would be no bloodshed in Slovenia, which would be able to escape by walling itself off from the rest of Yugoslavia.

The deputy secretary resisted offering policy prescriptions to this disparate group of republican nationalists, human rights advocates, and pro-Yugoslav democrats. He did make two comments—both true and both unexceptionable—that set off shock waves in Slovenia. First, he expressed the view that human rights, freedom, and a market economy would be best advanced if Yugoslavia remained united. Second, he said that the United States would not advocate the breakup of Yugoslavia, but—if it happened—would have no choice except to live with it.

Mike Einik, the U.S. consul general in Zagreb, who followed developments in Croatia and Slovenia, later heard that many Slovene politicians were annoyed at Eagleburger's defense of Yugoslav unity. They had hoped for an assertion that a loose confederation represented the only viable future for Yugoslavia. More important, some Slovenes took the deputy secretary's remark that the United States could live with the breakup of Yugoslavia as a green light to push a secession program. All Eagleburger had implied was that the United States and NATO would not use force to keep Yugoslavia together—a conclusion any informed observer could have drawn. What the Slovenes heard for the first time was that the United States was not going to fight for the unity of Yugoslavia.

Before he left Belgrade, Eagleburger did what he always did on trips abroad—he stopped by the embassy to talk to the staff. A professional foreign service officer for three decades, he had a deep understanding of the strengths and weaknesses of the foreign service and an instinctive sense of how to get the best out of it. He knew that no foreign policy could succeed without the expertise, the dedication, and the continuity supplied by the first-rate men and women who devoted—and sometimes gave—their lives, with small compensation and even less recognition, to the service of their country abroad. In the Baker State Department, the secretary ran policy with a small, close-knit coterie of gifted outsiders: Bob Zoellick, Dennis Ross, and Bob Kimmitt. Eagleburger, the only senior insider, was the link to the professionals. Though he grumbled about this role, he also enjoyed it, never more than when he was visiting embassies abroad and especially now, back at his old embassy.

As he rolled his bulk through the embassy compound toward the makeshift auditorium set up near the snack bar in the American Club, he had a gruff greeting for the veteran Yugoslav employees who had come to see him. I found myself thinking what an extraordinary group they were. Some had come to work shortly after the war when it was politically dangerous for Yugoslavs to associate with Americans. Most of them were Serbs, and they were perplexed about our strong opposition to Milošević. But, for the most part, they remained dead loyal to the United States.

One Yugoslav in particular, the language teacher Marija Andjelić, a small and stylish woman, still looked as elegant as when she had first reported to work forty years before. She had taught Serbo-Croatian—as well as how to behave, what to wear, what not to say, and all the other essentials under the underrated rubric of "protocol"—to nearly every American ambassador since World War II, and to lots of junior officers as well. She counts them all as her friends and maintains a vivid correspondence with George Kennan, who is the godfather of her now grown-up son. A martinet in a profession of perfectionists, she was the best language instructor I ever had in a career of learning five foreign languages from dozens of teachers.

Mrs. Andjelić seemed delighted to see Eagleburger, who in his time had undoubtedly mangled her fastidious verb endings in the earthy populism of his convivial encounters with Yugoslav friends. He managed to resurrect for her benefit a long-dormant greeting in Serbo-Croatian. He then turned to John O'Keefe, the innovative embassy administrative counselor who had served with him in Belgrade ten years before. "This was a very well-organized visit, O'Keefe," he said. "The embassy did a very good job." As the glow from the compliment spread across John's face, Eagleburger added with a malevolent grin, "Of course, I'm sure you had nothing to do with it."

As we drove to the airport where his U.S. Air Force plane was waiting, Eagleburger told me that the visit had confirmed his fears that Yugoslavia was in bad shape. "I'm going to make some waves when I get back to Washington," he said. "I've got to get people to focus on how dangerous this situation can become. Marković is doing the best he can, but he needs help." As I suspected, Eagleburger didn't think it realistic to pour financial assistance into Marković's economic reform; the Kosovo albatross, for which Marković bore no blame, precluded large-scale support. But the deputy secretary did see value in alerting the European countries to our concerns and urging them to lend international political weight to Marković's beleaguered efforts.

On his return Eagleburger found ready allies in the White House for internationalizing the Yugoslav problem. Brent Scowcroft, President Bush's national security adviser, a former air force general, had served as a young major in Belgrade from 1959 to 1961 as assistant U.S. air attaché and maintained a special interest in Yugoslav affairs. David Gompert, Scowcroft's able senior deputy for Europe, inspired an instruction to U.S. embassies in Western and Eastern Europe to make their host governments aware of American concerns about the growing tensions in Yugoslavia.

The U.S. representatives were instructed to convey Washington's conviction that a breakup was in the interest neither of the

Yugoslav people nor of Europe's security and to urge the Europeans to avoid actions that could encourage secession. Washington didn't commit itself on the form of government Yugoslavs might choose—the tight federation advocated by the Serbs or the loose confederation favored by the Slovenes and Croats—but stated neutrally that it was up to the citizens of Yugoslavia to decide. The United States asked the Europeans in their public statements to express support for unity and democracy in Yugoslavia and for Marković's reform program.

The American message was greeted in Europe with a yawn. The Europeans simply couldn't believe that Yugoslavia was in serious trouble. There had been too many cries of wolf in the decade after Tito's death in 1980, when practically everybody had predicted that the country would fall apart. When it didn't, Europeans blinded themselves to the cataclysm that was now imminent. The French and British governments were particularly dismissive of American concern, putting it off to a fevered Congress and an overwrought executive branch. The Europeans did begin to pay more attention to Marković as an agent of democratic change. But their approach to Yugoslavia was without any of the urgency with which they acted fourteen months later, when the breakup they said couldn't happen was upon them.

The State Department's instruction cable to the European capitals took note of the republican elections that were to begin in Slovenia in April 1990. In supporting Yugoslavia's first venture in democracy, Washington also warned that the elections might bring to power those advocating confederation or even the dissolution of Yugoslavia. Since Marković had failed to win support for federal parliamentary elections, there would be no opportunity to vote on a Yugoslav basis. Unity was therefore likely to suffer in electoral campaigns stressing national republican issues. These prophetic thoughts highlighted the paradox of the Yugoslav elections of 1990—in bringing democracy to birth, they helped strangle it in its cradle.

The motivation for elections was mixed. In part they were inspired, as Susan L. Woodward points out in her comprehensive survey *Balkan Tragedy,* by "politicians seeking more political power over their territories and opposition intellectuals seeking more political influence over the course of events." Popular enthusiasm for elections visible in countries like Poland and Czechoslovakia, which had undergone serious repression, was less apparent in Yugoslavia. In Slovenia and Macedonia the impetus came from reformist communist parties that were prepared to risk their hold on power. In Croatia, the communist leadership was panicked into a hurried scheduling of elections by the fear of mass demonstrations similar to those Croatian television viewers had seen in Prague a few months before. In Bosnia-Herzegovina, a complacent communist party marched to the polls in the serene but erroneous conviction that it would breeze to victory. And in Serbia, followed by Montenegro, Milošević—despite his oft-expressed contempt for multiparty democracy on the republican level—scheduled elections in full assurance that he could either win them or rig them.

Ante Marković surveyed a scene in which the republican election campaigns were being dominated by parties making blatantly nationalistic appeals, which would undercut his reform. Marković's instinct and experience were economic, but he continued to enjoy political popularity in the polls—he registered a 79 percent approval rating among Yugoslavs in one poll in the spring of 1990. He recognized that economic and political reforms were linked, and he expected his economic reform to lead to political reform, rather than the other way around. This had been the case in the Soviet Union and even more strikingly among some of the "tigers" of East Asia, notably South Korea and Taiwan. But Marković, an impatient man, didn't expect a Western-style economy to take hold in Yugoslavia for years.

The prime minister was also aware of the pattern in Eastern Europe, where the engine of reform had been political, not economic. There reformist political movements had won support on a countrywide basis. But in Yugoslavia, which was plagued more by virulent nationalism than all the Eastern European countries put together, there was no reformist party with a Yugoslav orientation. With his incandescent popularity, Marković decided that he was the man to create such a party. It was a disastrous decision.

Marković called his new party the Alliance of Reform Forces. It was formed too late to catch the high tide of his personal popularity or to contest the elections in Slovenia and Croatia. But it did compete in the other four republican elections in the fall. While few political campaigns in these first elections were particularly well run, Marković's efforts set an early record for incompetence. His activists were primarily intellectuals, journalists, and economic managers. There was no effort to tap into the sympathetic reserve, reflected in the polls, among workers and peasants. An air of dilettantism prevailed. Teeny and I ran into Mirko Klarin, an outstanding liberal journalist and Marković's campaign manager, at a dinner party during the summer. Teeny, who had worked in political campaigns in the United States, asked Klarin what he was doing at dinner. Why wasn't he working dawn to dusk on the hustings? Klarin had no answer; he clearly didn't understand the question. "Campaign manager" was a title, not a job.

The 1990 republican elections were a triumph for local nationalisms almost everywhere. In Slovenia, the anticommunist DEMOS coalition, led by strong advocates of independence, took control of the parliament, though Milan Kučan, the popular communist leader, won the race for president, replacing his friend Stanovnik. In Croatia, Franjo Tudjman's aggressive Croatian Democratic Union swept to power. In ethnically mixed Bosnia-Herzegovina, where the largest number of pro-Yugoslav and pro-democracy parties were in the race, 84 percent of the parliamentary seats went to the three ethnic parties: Muslim, Serb, and

Croat. Marković's nonethnic appeal brought his party only 5.4 percent of the seats in Bosnia. The Yugoslav prime minister did slightly better in Macedonia with 9.2 percent of the seats, then got a lucky break when a political compromise brought his ally, the veteran communist and economic reformer Kiro Gligorov, to the Macedonian presidency. In Serbia and Montenegro, where Milošević and his young Montenegrin protégé Momir Bulatović had few scruples about manipulating the campaigns, the ruling communist parties won comfortable majorities.

In bringing nationalism to power, the elections helped snuff out the very flame of democracy they had kindled. They were democratic in one sense, antidemocratic in another. By and large they represented the choice of republican electorates, with the important caveat that people were given no chance to vote as Yugoslavs. But they put no curbs on the potentially nondemocratic behavior of those elected. Nationalism is by nature uncivil and antidemocratic because it elevates and empowers one ethnic group over all others. Even if nationalism arrives by democratic means, it accepts no obligation to conduct itself democratically. As the elections weakened the democratic element so necessary for Yugoslavia, they also weakened the equally necessary unifying element. The stronger the nationalism in a republic, the greater was its inclination toward separatism.

Why did Yugoslavs vote the way they did, so differently from the moderate voting patterns apparent in the first free elections in Czechoslovakia, Hungary, and Poland? One answer lies in bad luck—there were no Yugoslav Havels or Walesas, no political leaders capable of rallying their citizens behind great democratic ideas. Perhaps, given the fragmented nature of the political system bequeathed by Tito, this was too much to ask. In frustration, I titled one of my cables to Washington: "Josephine Baker Was Right about Yugoslavia." I recalled the story of the famous Folies Bergères star who was scheduled to go on stage right after a midget act. As she waited in the wings, the electricity failed, the lights went out, and the midgets started to scamper around in panic. After a few seconds, Josephine Baker's voice could be heard above the confusion: "Turn on the goddam lights—I'm up to my ass in dwarfs!"

A second reason for the triumph of nationalism was that, in half the republics (Slovenia, Bosnia, and Macedonia) the most democratic alternative to the nationalists was the communists, of whom people had simply had enough. In states emerging from dictatorship, the first election is often a referendum on the past. So it was in Yugoslavia. Many Yugoslavs vented their pent-up frustrations by voting for nationalist politicians who hammered on ethnic themes.

Third, many Yugoslavs are susceptible to ethnically based appeals. Yugoslavia was, after all, a young state, dating back only to 1918. For most of its life it was seen from within as a Serbian and then a communist dictatorship. Moreover, World War II was also a Yugoslav civil war, with half the dead killed by other Yugoslavs. When nationalist demagogues appealed to the worst in people's characters, making the elections a test of ethnic loyalty, they all too often got a response.

A final reason for the nationalists' victories was that Tito had left no democratic traditions or institutions for winnowing nationalism out. Extremists in democratic countries have difficulty in capturing control of governments. In Yugoslavia there were no democratic filters, baffles, or obstacles to slow their ascent. The elections took them on an express train from purdah to power.

As the nationalist leaderships took office in the republics, Yugoslavia became the battleground for two competing principles of sovereignty, two legitimacies. There was the federal legitimacy based on Tito's 1974 constitution. While this legitimacy didn't provide for a strong central government, it did establish clear federal competence in such important areas as foreign affairs and defense. Now, after the elections, a new republican legitimacy coexisted with the older federal legitimacy. It was defined by republican leaders who for the most part held the federal government in contempt and who immediately set out to give their republics the attributes of independent states. Republican constitutions were written, foreign relations established, armies formed.

What we were seeing, the embassy wrote Washington in the aftermath of the republican elections, was a highly inflammable transition from a federal legality, which was in decline but not dead, to a republican legality, which was on the rise but not yet predominant. This fissionable transition dominated and embittered the final days of Yugoslavia, ending only with the destruction in violence of the federal state and the governing principles it represented.

With the 1990 elections, the age of naked nationalism had begun. In my discussions with the new republican leaderships, it quickly became evident that the forms of nationalism were as varied as the ethnic groups themselves. The Slovene variety was certainly the most democratic of the Yugoslav brands, at least for Slovenes. The driving force behind the parliamentary victory of the anti-Yugoslav, anticommunist DEMOS coalition in Slovenia was Jože Pučnik, who had lived for several decades in Germany after imprisonment by Tito. Pučnik's hatred for Yugoslavia was visceral. The first time I met him, he refused to speak Serbo-Croatian with me, although it was our only common language. Pučnik was more guarded about secession than his ally Peter Jambrek had been. He told me that the views of DEMOS members were "between confederation and secession."

Another of Pučnik's coalition allies, France Bučar, was the new president of the Slovene assembly. A distinguished philosopher who had suffered under Tito for publishing heretical articles challenging communism, Bučar minced no words in supporting Slovenia's independence. For him Belgrade was Sin City. He couldn't imagine that anyone could live there without indelible tarnish; he even confessed to distrusting Slovenes who had represented Slovenian interests while living in Belgrade. Bučar told me, "We Slovenes have to be able to choose our destiny independently of Belgrade. We might choose Yugoslavia. But to make the right choice, we have to be independent. Not forever. Perhaps only for one day or one hour. Perhaps only for one minute!" Mike Einik and I attended the opening session of Bučar's new assembly. No other diplomats were there, but to us it was an occasion not to be missed—the opening of the first democratically elected parliament in Yugoslavia.

Slovenian nationalism was unique—it had no victims and no enemies. While the Slovenes hated Slobodan Milošević, they built no ideology against him. They practiced a "Garbo" nationalism—they just wanted to be left alone. Their virtue was democracy and their vice was selfishness. In their drive to separate from Yugoslavia they simply ignored the twenty-two million Yugoslavs who were not Slovenes. They bear considerable responsibility for the bloodbath that followed their secession.

No Yugoslav republic was more transformed by the elections of 1990 than Croatia. The communists in power had devised a nonproportional electoral system intended to maximize their representation in the new parliament. But they failed to reckon with the outside money that flowed from Croatian emigrants, mostly in the United States and Canada, to Franjo Tudjman's Croatian Democratic Union or with the highly effective nationalist electoral campaign it enabled Tudjman to run. The communists' electoral strategy boomeranged: Tudjman's party, with 42 percent of the vote, won two thirds of the seats in the legislature. I first met Tudjman in Zagreb, the pretty, tidy medieval capital of Croatia, on the morning of his victory. I had avoided him before then because of the extreme nationalism of some of his campaign statements. We talked for several hours over the breakfast table at Mike Einik's residence.

Tudjman, who had fought as a partisan under Tito in World War II and had risen to general in the Yugoslav army, was later expelled from the communist party and imprisoned for Croatian nationalism. At our meeting he was clearly savoring his remark-able change of fortune. Even in his jubilation there was some-thing of the martinet about him. If Milošević recalls a slick con man, Tudjman resembles an inflexible schoolteacher. Prim steel-rimmed eyeglasses hang on a square face whose natural expres-sion is a scowl. His mouth occasionally creases into a nervous chuckle or a mirthless laugh.

In our first meeting the new president displayed all three quali-ties that mark him as a politician: authoritarianism, impulsive-ness, and intolerance. He treated the two subordinates who had accompanied him with extreme disdain. Then on the spot he ap-pointed one of them, Žarko Domljan, president of the Croatian parliament. Domljan's evident surprise could only have been aug-mented by the fact that this battlefield promotion took place over the scrambled eggs at the breakfast table of the American consul general.

I asked Tudjman to describe his political orientation. He said, "Forty-five years of communist rule have destroyed the moral values of Croatian society. People don't know how to accept responsibility for their own future. The one-party system has created disillusion everywhere. The best people have left. Corruption has become a way of life. The idea of Yugoslavia has been a negative influence. You Americans don't understand Yu-goslavia; it can't be looked at from an American perspective. To us Croats, Yugoslavia was built on an illusion. Croats, Serbs, and Slovenes are products of different civilizations, different cultures. Croats are Catholics and Europeans; Serbs are not. Croats and Serbs never even lived together until 1918; the longer they've lived together since then, the more difficult their relations have become. In fact, the only thing holding the country together has been the one-party totalitarian communist system."

Barely drawing breath, Tudjman launched into a description of his plans for Croatia. "We're going to have a new constitution, with full civil rights and guarantees for the rights of minorities, including Serbs. We're also going to create a Western-style market economy. Yugoslavia must be turned into a confederation, an alliance of sovereign states. In the past, any powers given to the central government have just meant additional powers for Serbia. Croatia has paid heavily for the so-called economic reforms so far. Tito let the Serbs discriminate against us. We don't even have a highway from Zagreb to the coast—something essential for our tourism. In the future the central Yugoslav government can set a framework for reform, but all decisions on resource transfers must be decided by the republics by consensus. What's needed is a new agreement between Croatia and the rest of Yugoslavia. If we can't get it, then Croatia will have to take an independent path into Europe."

I asked Tudjman about Prime Minister Marković, his fellow Croat. Tudjman showed no affection. He replied that Marković's goals of market reform and political pluralism were the right ones but complained that the prime minister stood for an unacceptable level of centralization. The Marković government, he said, "is one of the last communist governments in the world. Why does the United States support him?" I answered that we didn't support Marković because he was a communist but because he was a reformer with a good plan. I told Tudjman that the U.S. government favored the unity of Yugoslavia but wouldn't support the preservation of unity through force. Tudjman said he was relieved to hear that. I continued that we had no problem with Tudjman's idea of a Yugoslav confederation, but we did feel that the central government ought to have considerable economic powers on, say, the Swiss model.

The conversation moved into choppy waters when I asked Tudjman about his much-quoted remark during the election campaign that he was glad his wife was neither a Serb nor a Jew. His temper flared and he launched into a highly defensive ten-minute justification of his ethnic humanity, climaxed by the straight-faced assertion that some of his best friends were Serbs. "But," he said, "you must understand my problem as the new leader of the Croatian people. Serbs are 11 percent of the population of Croatia, but they make up 40 percent of government employees. In the police and the media the situation is even worse. Seventy-five percent of the police are ethnic Serbs, and so are six and a half of the seven top editors. They give our news an anti-Croatian slant." I couldn't resist asking about the half an editor. Tudjman replied gruffly that his father was a Serb and his mother a Croat.

The president-elect left no doubt about his intentions. "These people can't stay in control of our vital institutions. They will have to be dismissed. Apart from this, however, we guarantee that there will be no persecution or discrimination against any minorities." I wondered how Tudjman's professions of political pluralism squared with his intention to carry out a wholesale purge of the press, but deferred my questioning to later meetings.

On the subject of Jews, Tudjman didn't claim any Jewish "best friends." But he charged angrily that any allegations of anti-Semitism in Croatia were the product of Serbian propaganda—a considerable distortion of the historical record. Tudjman's own writings had downplayed the importance of the Holocaust. At Mike Einik's suggestion, I asked him if he would be willing to make restitution to the Zagreb Jewish community for the destruction of their synagogue by the Croatian fascists during World War II. To our surprise, he promised to do this. He kept that promise.

The most troubling part of our conversation concerned Bosnia. Tudjman stated flatly (and with no evidence): "Bosnia has historically been a part of Croatia and has always been in Croatia's geopolitical sphere. Not only do Croats live in Bosnia, but most Muslims in Bosnia consider themselves Croats." Taken aback by these ludicrous assertions, I asked Tudjman what he intended to do. "If there's pressure from the Serbs in Bosnia, we will defend our interests. If there isn't, it's fine with us if Bosnia remains an independent republic." Our memorable breakfast ended on that disquieting note.

Unlike Milošević, who was driven by power, Tudjman betrayed an obsession with Croatian nationalism. His devotion to Croatia was of the most narrow-minded sort, and he never showed much understanding of, or interest in, democratic values. He presided over serious violations of the rights of Serbs. They were dismissed from work, required to take loyalty oaths, and subjected to attacks on their homes and property. I sat several times at Tudjman's lunch table and listened to his ministers revile Serbs in the most racist terms. He didn't join in, but he didn't stop them either. He also stifled the independence of the press as much as, maybe even more than, Milošević.

There is a tragic subtext to the racist attitude toward Serbs that Tudjman tolerated within his party. During World War II Croatia was a Nazi puppet state under Hitler's control. Many Croats, including Tudjman, joined Tito's partisans. But the Croatian fascists of that period—the Ustaše—committed unspeakable atrocities against Serbs in Croatia and Bosnia. In this Yugoslav civil war, Serbs, Croats, Muslims, Gypsies, and Jews were all victimized, but no group suffered more than the Serbs. By changing street names that had previously honored victims of fascism and reviving the traditional Croatian flag and coat of arms last used during the 1941–45 Ustaše dictatorship, the Croatian government contributed to the resurrection of this grotesque period in the minds of Serbs. Tudjman always gave me reasons why these symbols of the new Croatia were politically neutral—"Don't you know, Mr. Ambassador, that the checkerboard pattern on the Croatian flag goes back to medieval times?"—but no such arguments could dispel the anxieties and fears, fed by Milošević's propaganda, among Croatia's Serbs.

I tried repeatedly to get Tudjman to show more sensitivity toward the Serbian population, many of whose families had lived in Croatia for three centuries. Mike Einik and I raised with him or his aides every piece of information that came to us about abuses of the civil rights of Serbs, in hopes that his government would crack down on the offenses and bring the offenders to book. With a few individual exceptions, he was unresponsive. I urged him to visit Jasenovac, the notorious World War II Croatian concentration camp where tens of thousands of Serbs and others had perished, as Willy Brandt had gone to Yad Vashem in Israel in an act of contrition for the Holocaust. He refused, preferring to attend the opening of the Holocaust Museum in Washington than to pay a visit to the death camp in his own republic.

My entreaties seemed to make Tudjman more defensive. He reminded me that he had fought against the Ustaše (true) and as president would therefore do nothing to support their revival (questionable). But toward Croatia's Serbian population he rejected any gesture that smacked of reconciliation, cooperation, or healing. Tudjman's accession to power completed the drawing of the lines between Yugoslavia's classic antagonists, Serbia and Croatia—republics now led by nationalists who are the very embodiment of the past ethnic enmities of their peoples.

In personality, Tudjman vacillated between the grandiose and the narrow-minded. He loved to entertain in high style, offering several kinds of wine even at working lunches. His passion for display caused him to write his own pompous speeches and to concoct ceremonial events at which, resplendent in military uniform, he would be the central figure. For a former general, he seemed curiously impervious to staff work, briefings, or position papers. His preparation was slapdash compared with that of Milošević, who was always on top of his brief.

Also unlike the loner Milošević, he surrounded himself with aides. Rarely, however, were they invited to speak, and his volatile temper may have set a Balkan record for the number of dismissals of high-level officials. He advertised his militancy in the cause of nationalism in a way the more devious Milošević would never have done. At the same time, he could call himself a "pacifist" with no sense of irony, as he did once to me. Tudjman always seemed to me on the brink of becoming a slightly ridiculous operetta figure. But this impression was contradicted by the ruthlessness with which he pursued Croatian interests as he saw them.

Tudjman's saving feature, which distinguished him from Milošević, was that he really wanted to be seen as a Western statesman. He listened to Western expressions of concern and—except on issues he considered vital, like the treatment of Serbs in Croatia—he often did something about them, even when he saw no clear interest. While not subservient, he was susceptible to Western pressure, as when in 1994 he agreed against his instincts to form a federation with the Muslims in Bosnia. But he seemed to me incapable of transcending the constricting nature of his nationalism. His inherent intolerance, and that of his party, helps explain why so many Serbs in Croatia have rejected Croatian rule and why the core hostility in former Yugoslavia is still between Serbs and Croats.

During 1990 Serbian nationalism under Milošević became even more aggressive. No longer was it enough for Serbs living outside Serbia to have their rights protected. They also had to own and control the territory they inhabited, regardless of prior sovereignty. These Serbian claims had no consistent principles behind them. Where Serbs were a minority, as in Kosovo, they asserted a historical, rather than a numerical, right to rule. Where no such historical right was plausible, as in the Krajina area of Croatia, they claimed self-determination on the majority principle. Where even those claims didn't work, they found others, for example, asserting Serbian sovereignty from the fact that Croatian genocide during World War II had turned Serbian majorities into minorities. Revealingly, Milošević was unwilling to give the Albanians in Kosovo the same right of self-determination that he demanded for the Serbs in Croatia and Bosnia.

In the Serbian elections of December 1990, Milošević made nationalism the litmus test: if you didn't vote for him, you weren't a good Serb. The Serbian opposition, overwhelmed by the superior organization of Milošević's still-intact communist apparatus and a near-total media blackout, foundered on whether to play the nationalist game or reject it. Milošević won in a tainted but convincing landslide. The one-party system, beloved by the Serbian leader, survived. Milošević simply modernized it by giving it multiparty trimmings.

To the different faces of nationalism in Yugoslavia—reclusive in Slovenia, aggressive and expansionist in Serbia and Croatia— was added, in Kosovo, a third face. The model for Albanian nationalism in Kosovo was not Balkan; it was the struggle by the nations of Africa and Asia for independence from colonial rule in the 1950s and 1960s. The Albanian strategy of passive resistance against Serbian domination drew on Mahatma Gandhi for its inspiration.

I first visited Kosovo in July 1989 and returned often. The province had a colonial air about it. Serbian officials were arrogant and often abusive. Albanians were nervous, lowering their voices as if listening devices were everywhere. I got used to the experience of being conducted to some Potemkin economic project by Serbian hosts. Lower-level Albanian officials would trail silently and sullenly behind, only to spring to life the minute the Serbs were gone to vent their anger to me over Serbia's imperial policies.

For an American ambassador, even setting foot in Kosovo carried political risks, just as failing to go there would have. U.S. policy didn't question Serbian sovereignty in Kosovo, the heart of medieval Serbian kingdoms and the site of some of the loveliest small churches and monasteries in Christendom. Yet the Albanian majority in Kosovo, whose heritage goes back nearly as far, was being systematically deprived of its political and civil rights. In all my visits I made a point of dividing my time equally between the authorities—Serbs and pliant Albanians—and the Albanian dissidents.

As my car crossed into Kosovo for the first time, I asked Neša to drive me to the battlefield. The two of us stood at the monument and looked down on the vast plain that had easily accommodated the million Serbs who had come to hear Milošević a few weeks before and that must have swallowed the two tiny armies on that fateful June 28 six centuries earlier. I read Prince Lazar's warning to his fellow Serbs, engraved on the marble of the monument, and took note of its contemporary ring:

> Let him who fails to join the battle of Kosovo
> Fail in all he undertakes in his fields.
> Let his fields go barren of the good golden wheat,
> Let his vineyards remain without vines or grapes.

The first impression I had of Priština, the derelict capital of Kosovo, was of people—thousands of Albanians, mostly young, walking up and down the dusty streets. In fact, this impression was statistically important, for the Albanians of Kosovo had one of the highest birth rates and one of the highest unemployment rates in Europe. In a seedy government building I talked with Rahman Morina, a burly Albanian police officer elevated by his Serbian masters to Kosovo party chief; as such he was the principal Uncle Tom.

Morina recited, as if by rote, the standard Serbian propaganda about the wonderful freedoms enjoyed by Albanians. But he looked extremely nervous doing it; he was sweating profusely. He did make one proposal that didn't seem to follow the script (and wasn't enacted)—amnesty for all Albanian youths arrested for nationalism. I noticed that one of his Serbian "aides" was watching him closely, presumably to ensure that he didn't make a slip. Morina didn't strike me as a very enthusiastic spokesman for the Serbian cause in Kosovo. By the time of my next visit he had died of a heart attack. His successor was a Serb.

In sharp contrast, the Albanian dissidents were impressive— disciplined, articulate, and rigidly opposed to accepting Serbian authority. Their leader, Ibrahim Rugova, was one of the most out-standing political figures I met in Yugoslavia. A modest, almost a gentle, man, he looked like the poet he was. He smiled frequently and with warmth and always wore a wool scarf, even in the hottest weather. When I asked him why, he looked embarrassed and said he had read somewhere that everybody needed a signature piece.

Rugova clearly had the affection of Priština's Albanians. When we walked down the street together, people of all types came up to say hello to him. When he took me to Albanian restaurants, bills were never produced. During times of great Serbian provocation, he managed to keep his two million compatriots on the course of peaceful resistance. When the authorities introduced a Serbian curriculum into the schools—with the Serbian, but not the Albanian, language mandatory—the Albanians quietly boycotted, starting schools in their homes. When the Serbs imported doctors to staff the state-run hospitals, the Albanian doctors set up private clinics of their own.

I had been warned by American journalists not to believe anything I heard in Kosovo, so I decided to give Rugova a truth test. Referring to the Serbian abuses against Albanians, no aspect of which was ever conceded by Serbian officials, I asked him how Albanians had treated Serbs when they held the upper hand before the Milošević period. "Unfortunately," he answered without hesitation, "there were many crimes committed against Serbs."

Albanian nationalism as shaped by Rugova may have been nonviolent, but it was determined. It had to be, since it was primarily a reaction to Milošević's aggressive tactics. As the Serbs pressed, the Albanians stiffened. I worked hard to convince Rugova to take his party into the Serbian elections of 1990, arguing that rejecting elections would not help his democratic credentials. I cited examples of how a well-disciplined, elected minority could hamstring parliaments, as the Irish had done in the nineteenth-century British House of Commons and as the Algerians had done in the French Chamber of Deputies in the 1950s. I stressed that it was possible for the Albanians to advance their cause in a hostile political environment.

Rugova was intransigent. He made it clear that he would not last a single day as Albanian leader if he took such a step. He said that Kosovo Albanians would never again recognize Serbian authority. It was clear that Milošević's strong-arm approach was pushing the Albanians onto a path of no return toward complete independence from Serbia.

By December 1990 there were few Kosovo Albanians who didn't insist either on an independent Kosovo or on a Kosovo linked with Albania, where the democratization process was beginning. On their side, the Serbs who governed Kosovo were inflexible to the point of caricature. One of them told me with a straight face that the only political role of the Albanians was to implement the laws and regulations that the Serbian parliament passed for them. The psychological break was complete. Any provocation launched by either side had the potential to blow the province apart. In these volatile circumstances, I urged Milošević to meet with Rugova. I had secured in advance Rugova's agreement to a meeting. Milošević refused, saying of the leader of some two million citizens of Serbia, "Who does he represent?"

During that pivotal year of 1990, when democracy came and went through the same nationalist door, Teeny and I received a visit from close Russian friends. We had known Misha and Flora Litvinov during our posting in Moscow in the early 1980s. This remarkable couple stood for much of what we loved about Russia. Misha had had a favored childhood as the son of a Bolshevik who became one of Stalin's post–World War II foreign ministers, before being fired for insufficient rigidity toward the West. Misha and Flora's son Pavel demonstrated on Red Square in 1968 against the Soviet invasion of Czechoslovakia and was sent to Siberia; he later emigrated to America. Misha and Flora took great risks in helping the victims of Soviet repression. They numbered among their close friends Andrei Sakharov and other champions of human rights. Now, profiting from Gorbachev's easing of travel restrictions, they were able to visit us in Yugoslavia in 1990.

We took Misha and Flora everywhere we went during their three-week stay. They visited most parts of Yugoslavia and had a chance to see the attractiveness of its people and the relative prosperity of the country. They also got a picture of the chaos that impended. They were able to compare Yugoslavia with Gorbachev's Soviet Union on the availability of food and consumer goods, prices, public services, and other issues affecting ordinary people. Naturally, I was anxious to know what this wise and experienced couple thought, but I restrained myself until their last day with us. As I was putting them on the train back to Moscow, I asked them for their impressions of Yugoslavia. Flora thought for a moment, then her intelligent face broke into a broad smile. Without a trace of irony, she exclaimed, "Paradise!"

CONTRADICTIONS

*"They're creating republican armies in direct
challenge to Yugoslavia. . . . How many armies
does the United States have?"*

The postelection weather in Yugoslavia was heavy with storm
clouds. The elections had widened the gap between those who
wanted to preserve Yugoslavia and those who wanted to destroy
it. The handicappers in the U.S. government, the embassy included, began to predict disaster. We cabled in late September
1990 that Yugoslav unity was decaying and that Yugoslavia as we
knew it was dying. Marković was running out of steam: the elections were not helping him; the republican consensus behind him
had collapsed; his shock therapy had stiffened opposition to the
economic reform; and the Yugoslav institution he had sought to
revive—the Federal Assembly—was paralyzed. We had detected
some pro-Yugoslav sympathy in Slovenia and Croatia but cautioned that if Serbia didn't abandon its aggressive approach, both
republics would secede.

In an October message, I expressed the concern that Milošević
would lash out in Bosnia. And in a November cable, I pointed out
that the secession of Slovenia and Croatia would leave the rest of
the country to the untender mercies of Serbia, with its irresistible

propensity to hegemony. The resulting cycles of violence would make democracy the first casualty.

The Central Intelligence Agency (CIA) came out with an even starker analysis during the autumn of 1990. In an estimate that quickly leaked to the *New York Times,* the CIA forecast that Yugoslavia would cease to function within one year and would probably dissolve within two. The agency predicted that Serbia would block Slovenian and Croatian attempts to form a Yugoslav confederation, that there would be a protracted armed uprising by the Albanians in Kosovo, and that Serbia would foment uprisings by Serbian minorities in Croatia and Bosnia. The CIA noted the danger of a slide from ethnic violence to organized civil war between republics but considered this unlikely within two years. It concluded flatly that there was nothing the United States or Europe could do to preserve unity.

This prescient analysis erred only on Kosovo, which remained tense but quiet, and on the timetable for civil war, which unfolded even faster than predicted. In its main elements, the estimate proved dead accurate. I didn't disagree with its findings—the embassy had been warning about breakup and violence for a year—but I saw its air of inevitability, in the perfervid atmosphere of Washington, as a major problem. I worried that its bald assertion that nothing could be done might take the heart out of American efforts to stave off the worst. It's always easier in large bureaucracies to heed the counsel of inaction than to take the risks that action requires. Even though the odds were heavily against, I believed that the high cost of failure warranted continued American efforts to seek a formula for unity. "This game can be won," I argued in a piece of inflated advocacy in November. "Dissolution is not inevitable."

Within half a year, however, the actions of the main Yugoslav players had removed all hope of peace, democracy, reform, and unity. The first postelection friction occurred between the Yugoslav army and Croatia. No battle before the outbreak of the

Bosnian war was waged with more bad faith, viciousness, and sheer malevolence than the test of wills between the JNA and its former general, Franjo Tudjman.

The Yugoslav Peoples' Army enjoyed a proud tradition with roots in Tito's partisans, who had fought the Germans to a standstill in the Second World War. After Tito and Stalin parted ways in 1948, the United States became a significant military supplier to Yugoslavia; the equipment included 155-milimeter howitzers to be used decades later in 1991 against Croatia. On my visits to republican capitals I could still see Korean War–vintage F-86 Saber-Jets rusting on the far outskirts of the local runways. Following Tito's reconciliation with Soviet leader Nikita Khrushchev in the mid-1950s, the Soviet Union became the JNA's chief arms supplier. Yugoslavia also had a domestic arms industry of its own, even producing fighter aircraft. Much of it was positioned in Bosnia, in line with Tito's guerrilla strategy of reacting to an attack by giving up Belgrade and northern Serbia and taking his stand in the mountains. Because of the army's unassailable reputation in Yugoslavia, the perceived threat of invasion from east or west, and plain inertia, the JNA had become one of the ten largest armies in Europe.

The toughness of the JNA undoubtedly protected Yugoslavia from Stalin's wrath and may also have discouraged his successors from taking on Yugoslavia after their suppression of Hungary in 1956 and Czechoslovakia in 1968. It also saved Tito from at least one major internal challenge to his rule—by his Serbian vice president Aleksandar Ranković in 1966. A conscript force, the JNA brought together enlisted men from all parts of Yugoslavia. In this sense it was the most genuinely Yugoslav institution of all.

It demonstrated pride in its fighting heritage in all sorts of ways, not least in a wild derring-do. The president of Yugoslav Airlines (JAT) told me that he resisted hiring former JNA pilots because they were too reckless. The first time Teeny and I invited JNA generals to our house, they brushed aside the California wine on offer and filled their wine glasses to the brim with straight scotch. Once, while traveling in one of the JNA's Soviet-made helicopters with a Yugoslav air force general, I noticed with horror that he was lighting matches on the fuel tank, then dribbling cigarette ashes down its side.

The JNA's officer corps was over 50 percent Serbian. There was nothing inherently nefarious behind that fact, though Serbian and Montenegrin candidates for officers and noncommissioned officers probably got preferential treatment over candidates from other ethnic groups. Serbs have a heroic military tradition, going back to the battle of Kosovo and including distinguished service in both world wars. Austrian emperors in the late seventeenth and eighteenth centuries brought Serbs to the Croatian marches to defend the Habsburg frontier—the *krajina*—against the Turks to the southeast. The Serbs of the Krajina, mostly dispersed in 1995 by Croatian arms, owe their ancestry to those rugged border guards of three centuries ago. For Serbs and Montenegrins, more than for the other ethnic groups, the military was an envied and honorable profession.

In my first encounters with the JNA, I didn't detect a pro-Serbian bias in the high command. The air force chief of staff, General Anton Tus, was a Croat; the deputy defense minister, Admiral Stane Brovet, was a Slovene; and the chief of staff, General Blagoje Adžić, was a Serb. General Veljko Kadijević, the defense minister, came from Croatia and had a Serbian father and a Croatian mother. Factors such as these encouraged me to report in late 1989, before the republican elections, that the army was a stabilizing and thus a positive force. It was not long before the JNA's actions caused me to revise that opinion.

With the collapse of the League of Communists, the JNA became the last standard-bearer of Tito's communism. In return for its loyalty Tito had rewarded the army with sumptuous perquisites. Military clubs and spas dotted the countryside, surpassed in luxury only by Tito's numerous villas. I once stayed in a military hotel near Dubrovnik on the Dalmatian coast; it was as grand as Dubrovnik's most elegant tourist hotel. Tito also provided the JNA a swollen defense budget for weapons and equipment. As the glory days of the partisan struggle receded into the past, the army grew sloppy and corrupt. The conscript sons of our Yugoslav friends complained of incompetence, drunkenness, insubordination, and ethnic intolerance.

Now, with Tito's death in 1980 and the death of the communist party in 1990, the army was cut adrift with a rigid ideology and nobody to control it politically—a deadly combination. The concurrent ending of U.S.-Soviet hostility deprived the JNA of its primary mission to keep the balance between the two superpowers and left it free to indulge its anti-German, anti-Western fantasies. In counterweight to its vaunted military tradition, the army was becoming doctrinaire, narcissistic, paranoid, flaccid, and unruly.

I had my first meeting with the defense minister on July 6, 1990. General Kadijević was a somber, brooding officer in his mid-60s with beetling eyebrows and a sepulchral way of expressing himself. Contemporaries remembered him in his youth as a brave, dashing, and arrogant partisan warrior. Now nearly a half-century of soldiering had given him heavy jowls and a weary, humorless mien. He liked to pontificate in a low, rumbling voice, weighing his words as if they were lumps of gold.

He had done a stint, class of 1963, at the U.S. Army's Command and General Staff College at Fort Leavenworth, Kansas, in contrast to his chief of staff, General Adžić, and others who had gone to the Soviet Union for military training. My first duty was to present Kadijević a framed certificate recording his induction into the Fort Leavenworth "Hall of Fame," an honor reserved for foreign graduates who had reached the highest pinnacles of their armed forces (apparently irrespective of their ideology).

Kadijević's Leavenworth experience, plus his obsessive desire to attract Secretary of Defense Cheney to Yugoslavia, made him willing to drop a few favors in America's direction. During a visit in the spring of 1989 General Robert Herres, the vice chairman of the U.S. Joint Chiefs of Staff, was given a tour of Yugoslav military installations, topped off by a half-hour in the cockpit of a Soviet MIG-29—the first time an American had gotten that close to the newest Soviet fighter-bomber. Herres, an air force pilot, had the technical expertise to appreciate what he had been allowed to inspect; he could hardly believe the good fortune that Kadijević had put in his way.

Despite his background, Kadijević was no friend of the United States. He consistently expressed to me distrust of American motives and doubt that our actions were contributing to Yugoslavia's unity. He was less coy in his memoirs, published in 1993, in which he charged the United States (and me personally) with being in league with Germany to destroy communism everywhere, break up Yugoslavia, and rule the region. Nor was he impressed with American efforts to help bring democracy out of the shards of Eastern European communism. I felt he hankered for the old ways, a belief strengthened by the JNA's support for the coup against Gorbachev in the Soviet Union in 1991. Nor was Kadijević a supporter of the U.S. stand against Saddam Hussein, especially after I was instructed to raise with him our evidence that the JNA was violating the United Nations' arms embargo against the Iraqi dictator.

I was pretty sure that the bugging of our residence—standard practice in communist countries—was being carried out by the JNA rather than the normal organ, the secret police. Occasionally, JNA officers would let slip to one of our military attachés a piece of information that could have been heard only at our dinner table. We were quite used to this; we'd had five years of it in the Soviet Union. In any case, the embassy had a secure room for classified conversations. Besides, U.S. policy was no secret, and the bugging allowed us to communicate to people we wouldn't ordinarily get to see. There were amusing moments. Once Teeny heard a high whine in our living room chandelier—obviously a defective listening device. When she called Vlada, the embassy electrician, he took pains to explain that it was just an electric light. "Light bulbs often whine like that when they blow out," he explained.

In our discussions Kadijević expressed an almost mystical view of Yugoslavia and the JNA's mission to defend it. His analysis of the external threat to Yugoslavia was, to say the least, odd. He told me with fire in his eye that the danger came from Germany, which was spreading its economic and political tentacles around the Balkans in an effort to dominate the area. In the heat of his hostility he might have been back in the World War II bunkers battling the panzers and the Luftwaffe. This long-dead history was as alive for him as yesterday's news.

The Germans had been defeated then; now they had to be kept permanently down. In his view, the Federal Republic of Helmut Kohl was no different from the Third Reich of Adolf Hitler; today's Germans were bent on incorporating all the Balkans from Albania to Hungary into a Fourth Reich. "How can you Americans have such good relations with a people whom you fought so fiercely as our allies?" he wondered aloud to me. Kadijević offered no evidence for this bizarre analysis, but the visceral nature of his convictions was unmistakable.

The defense minister identified two major JNA objectives—to defend Yugoslavia against foreign aggression and "to protect the constitutional and social order." With the end of the cold war, the army was thrown back on the second objective, an internal mission for which it had no training and, as it turned out, no talent. Kadijević made clear to me that protecting the social order meant protecting communism and its achievements—including, I assumed, the JNA's perquisites. Protecting the constitutional order, he stressed, involved combating nationalism and holding Yugoslavia together at all costs. I have little doubt that he was sincere about nationalism as the force threatening to destroy

Yugoslavia. Once, when we were discussing a mutual passion, soccer, he brightened unexpectedly when I remarked on the multiethnic nature of Belgrade's Red Star team, with its Romanian Serb fullback, its Macedonian and Bosnian wings, and its Croatian striker.

Nationalism may have been a minus for Kadijević, but democracy wasn't a plus. From the very beginning, I detected a reserve in his treatment of Prime Minister Marković. No doubt it came in part from the fear that Marković's economic reform would cut into the nearly two-thirds of the federal budget that went to the JNA. Even more important, I believe, he despised Marković's intention to turn Yugoslavia into a Western state. That meant capitalism, a dirty word for Kadijević, who told me that even Gorbachev had gone too far with *perestroika*. Despite his protests of support for economic reform, the general didn't accept that an improvement in living standards was a better way to deal with nationalism than the JNA's chosen instruments—intimidation and force.

His choicest vitriol was reserved for the new leaders in Croatia and Slovenia. The anti-Yugoslavism of the new republican governments was compounded by the presence of officials who hated the JNA. The new Slovenian defense minister, Janez Janša, had been jailed by the JNA for exposing military secrets while a journalist. Even worse, the new Croatian president, Franjo Tudjman, was a renegade JNA general who was looking for opportunities to humiliate his former comrades. Kadijević's voice dripped with venom when he spoke of those two, particularly Tudjman, whose rejection of the JNA and its culture he could neither forgive nor forget.

After the elections Kadijević grumbled in his lugubrious way, "You like to praise democracy, Mr. Ambassador, but in Yugoslavia democracy has revived the Ustaše and other forces that we defeated in World War II. Democracy is leading to bloodshed and to an abyss for our people." He complained that Croatia and

Slovenia were calling on their young men to desert from the JNA and were trying to weaken the JNA's control over the republican territorial defense forces, a civilian militia similar to the U.S. national guard.

"They're creating republican armies in direct challenge to Yugoslavia and in direct violation of its constitution. Can't you understand why we can't allow this? How many armies does the United States have?" Kadijević would storm at me. He and his army displayed serious disorientation at these root-and-branch challenges to the concept of Tito's Yugoslavia in which they were among the last true believers. No longer threatened from outside Yugoslavia's borders, they turned to face their enemies within. And they resolved to destroy them.

Looking around, Kadijević saw few political allies to help the JNA prevail over Slovenia and Croatia. Marković was, at least for a while, sympathetic to the army's pressure on the two republics, but the generals wrote the prime minister off as an anticommunist and a liberal. The republican leaders in Macedonia and Bosnia-Herzegovina, Kiro Gligorov and Alija Izetbegović, were wary of the JNA. With the collapse of the League of Communists of Yugoslavia, there was no political outlet for military officers, virtually all of whom were communists.

The JNA, which was hemorrhaging non-Serbian soldiers who were returning to their republics, made a conscious or unconscious choice in the autumn of 1990. It would support Slobodan Milošević's concept of Yugoslav unity as the only way to win its showdown with Slovenia and Croatia. From that point on, Milošević and the JNA were close allies. The JNA was a step away from becoming a Serbian army.

Milošević was in the meantime refining his tactics for achieving hegemony. The death of the communist party and the stunning electoral victories for nationalism in Slovenia and Croatia had killed his dream of dominating all of Yugoslavia. He therefore fell back on an alternative approach. He would fashion a strategy around the Serbian populations that inhabited five of the six republics of Yugoslavia. In Montenegro, Montenegrins who saw themselves as Serbs were safely in control. In Macedonia, Serbs constituted too small a minority to exert political pressure. And in Slovenia, they were virtually absent. That left Croatia and Bosnia, where Serbs made up about 12 and 31 percent of the population, respectively. Milošević would declare himself the protector of the Serbian minorities there, and they in turn would become fifth columnists for his interests.

The goal would be a "Greater Serbia"—an objective Milošević always publicly denied—in which the Serbian minorities would be incorporated with generous pieces of territory into a Serbia-centered "Yugoslavia." Milošević never dropped his verbal support for the unity of Yugoslavia, but his actions increasingly contradicted his lip service to unity. In December 1990, for example, Serbia stole $1.8 billion from the National Bank of Yugoslavia, presumably to ensure that the Serbian elections came out right.

Milošević had a seductive argument for his changed tactics. "You have to understand our history, Mr. Zimmermann," he would say. "Serbia helped to found Yugoslavia because we saw it as the way to bring Serbs from the defeated Turkish and Austrian empires into a single state. That's why Serbia gave up its own sovereignty to join with the Croats and Slovenes, who didn't have states of their own. It was a big sacrifice for us. Now these same Croats and Slovenes are trying to break up Yugoslavia and endanger Serbs. We want to preserve Yugoslavia. But if we can't do that, the right of self-determination must be respected for Serbs outside Serbia. If they choose by democratic referendum to remain in Yugoslavia, then they should be able to remain. If the Croats and Slovenes have the right to leave Yugoslavia, then Serbs have the right to stay. All Serbs have the right to live in the same state."

I told Milošević that the United States also wanted to preserve

Yugoslav unity but added our view that his own actions were disrupting unity and destroying confidence that Serbia would be a cooperative partner in an integral Yugoslavia. I noted, for example, the military equipment that was flowing from Belgrade to defiant Serbs in the Krajina. As for his view of "all Serbs in one state," it might seem reasonable as philosophy, but in a world of multiethnic states it was a dangerous doctrine.

I argued from analogy: "If the right of self-determination is universal, extending all the way down to the county and even village level, then the current map of Europe would have to be redrawn. There would be hundreds of independent countries and dozens of wars to establish them or prevent them from being established. The multinational compromises that have made Western Europe so prosperous and peaceful would be threatened." I pointed out that a million Germans lived in France, that Belgium was living space for both French and Flemish, and that Switzerland was a successful mixture of French, Germans, and Italians. "Even if different ethnic groups can't learn to live together," I said, "separating them is no solution, because it will only result in violence."

Milošević was unfazed. He had found a simple formula for ethnic apartheid that would bewitch most of the Serbian people, would send them to war for despicable objectives, and would lead to unspeakable atrocities. I thought about where I had first heard the doctrine that all Serbs have the right to live in a single state. It was in the writings of Dobrica Ćosić, a Serbian novelist whom I saw from time to time. Ćosić had written a tetralogy celebrating Serbian heroism and agony during the First World War. Now in his seventies, he was a Serbian nationalist and, according to the polls, the most popular figure in Serbia.

His comfortable house in Dedinje, an affluent section of Belgrade where Tito had lived and where there were many embassy residences (including ours), was a lodestone for Serbian nationalists of all stripes, as well as for curiosities like Teeny and me.

Ćosić would preside, fussed and clucked over by a hovering wife whose hospitable smile didn't quite conceal beak and claws. I found him on the surface unfailingly sympathetic and courteous, though many antinationalist Serbs saw him as vain, ambitious, and scheming. His nationalism seemed tempered by sympathy for the concerns of other ethnic groups.

But Ćosić had a frequent failing of intellectuals—he combined messianic tendencies with the certainties of one who had never had to put his views into practice. He never discussed with me his relationship with Milošević; many believed he was the Serbian president's intellectual mentor. It was hard to imagine two more different personalities—both ambitious, but one naive and the other ruthless. Yet together they provided the ideology and the muscle for the perpetration of some of the most horrendous crimes Europe has witnessed since the Holocaust.

Milošević's growing tactical cooperation with the Yugoslav army found its first expression in an attempt to prevent the Slovenes and Croats from creating their own military forces. The JNA, assisted by the Serbian political apparatus and by the Milošević-controlled press, launched a public campaign against the two republics and their efforts to build up paramilitary units. The JNA's concerns were not imaginary. Yugoslavia was still one country, with one constitutionally approved army. Federal law was on the JNA's side. Moreover, the growing republican armies gave every indication of being hostile. The new Slovene government held a referendum in December 1990 in which the Slovene people voted overwhelmingly for independence in six months. A Slovene army would be an intimidating asset in a bid for secession. The Croatian challenge was even greater. Croatia's president Tudjman had promised to take Croatia out of Yugoslavia if Slovenia seceded; that meant taking 670,000 Serbs out with it.

The problem of Serbs in Croatia was intractable and dangerous. Tudjman's anti-Serb rhetoric during the 1990 electoral campaign had further radicalized the already belligerent Serbian population of the Krajina region. In the summer of 1990 Serb militants, supported and armed by Milošević's people, drove the Croatian police out of Knin, the capital, making the Krajina virtually autonomous and threatening access to the lucrative tourist areas of the Dalmatian coast. Tudjman was itching to use his growing Croatian army against these rebellious Serbs. Here was a problem with the complexity of a nesting Russian doll. While Milošević and the Yugoslav army saw a Croatian rebellion against the state of Yugoslavia, Tudjman saw a Serbian rebellion against the democratically elected government of Croatia. It was a rebellion within a rebellion.

In the autumn of 1990 someone from Tudjman's office came to Mike Einik with a request for "technical assistance for police improvements." Behind the bureaucratic language, the Croats acknowledged that what they really wanted was arms. I had no hesitation in recommending to Washington that we do nothing to increase the Croatian government's capacity to oppress its Serbian population. By then the roster of Croatian Serbs whose civil, property, or job rights had been infringed was long and growing. The Croatian actions against Serbs were systematic, and the Croatian authorities, when they were not actually complicit, were doing virtually nothing to stop them. In December 1990 the U.S. government decided to deny the Croatian request.

The Yugoslav army had a point in its desire to prevent the proliferation of armies in the still-sovereign state of Yugoslavia. After all, the United States had fought a rebel confederate army to maintain its unity, as Kadijević never tired of reminding me. (Not surprisingly, he was less enamored of the example of the American revolution.) But the repugnance of the JNA's chosen methods undercut any international support it might have attracted. The army began with a smear campaign against Croatia that was ham-handed even by JNA standards. Assisted by the Serbian political apparatus and the Milošević-controlled press, the JNA spewed bile against Tudjman and his government. In describing Croatian officials, the generals refused to acknowledge that they had won an election; they referred to Tudjman as the "so-called president."

Kadijević himself took the campaign to a new level of intimidation the day before the Serbian elections in early December 1990. In a press interview clearly designed to help Milošević at the polls, he threatened to use the JNA to disarm the Croats and Slovenes by force. Furious, the two republican governments demanded that the defense minister be reprimanded. On December 10 I took Kadijević a strong message of Washington's concern. Its sharpest point was the assertion that the proper role of a military is to defend the country, not engage in domestic politics.

Kadijević was sarcastic in rebuttal. He asked me why I hadn't told Washington that there was no need to question the JNA's commitment to democracy and legality. He wondered what had happened to American professions of noninterference in Yugoslav affairs. He asked the grounds for our conclusion that the JNA might violate the constitution and laws. And he wondered aloud what the United States would say if Yugoslavia's neighbors were illegally smuggling arms to Croatia and Slovenia. I replied that this was a serious charge and asked for evidence. He told me to inform Washington that foreign aggression had already begun in Yugoslavia and that we would soon get all the facts.

The "facts" weren't long in coming. The JNA produced and distributed broadly a television documentary attacking Croatia in the most abusive terms. While mostly propaganda, it contained authentic footage filmed by hidden cameras. One devastating scene depicted an incident, secretly and at night, of arms being smuggled from Hungary across the border to Croatia. Another showed Martin Špegelj, the Croatian defense minister and a former JNA general, trying to persuade a Croatian JNA officer to defect. On camera he told him, "We are at war with the JNA."

Tudjman branded the film a forgery but ignored my suggestion that he invite an impartial international group to test its authenticity. Whatever the propriety of the JNA's methods, it had caught the Croats red-handed in an attempt to build up their military forces for the purpose of targeting the Yugoslav army. Ignoring American and all other voices of moderation, the JNA was preparing the Yugoslav people for an attempt to dismantle the Croatian and Slovenian armed forces, an act whose certain result would be civil war. I cabled Washington that Yugoslavia was in a "permanent crisis."

The JNA began the showdown by seeking legal cover. Its chosen instrument was Borisav Jović, the Serbian member of the eight-man Yugoslav presidency and a close ally of Milošević's. For the year between May 1990 and May 1991—the period of republican elections, followed by the JNA's challenge to the republican armies—Jović was president of the presidency, a position that gave him power over the convening and closing of meetings and over their agenda.

Like Milošević, Jović pursued a narrow Serbian nationalist agenda, but, unlike his boss, he never quite transcended the communist style or ideology in which both had been raised. During the Yugoslav election period he asserted to me with finality that the United States was so anticommunist that it would never respect any election in Yugoslavia that communists won—"You Americans are interested in democracy primarily so you can destroy communism." I learned later that in his first report to the presidency in May 1990, Jović attacked me for allegedly heading and coordinating the activities of foreign intelligence services in Yugoslavia.

Jović was a small man in ways beyond size. Short in stature, freckled, and pugnacious, he reminded me of Soviet communist apparatchiks I had known in Moscow in the pre-Gorbachev period. He loved the cut and thrust of cold war debates. His positions betrayed a deep suspicion of the West and of its pluralism and disorder. I enjoyed tangling with him. He was honest in the rigidity of his views and in the myopic self-assurance with which he advanced them. Unlike Milošević, Jović made no effort to pretend he was anyone but who he was.

In one of our jousts, he revealed his mind-set on human rights by praising the violent suppression of a pro-democracy demonstration by the post-Ceauşescu government in Romania. He waxed so lyrical at the bashing of demonstrators' heads in the interest of protecting the authority of the state that an aide had to whisper in his ear that the Romanian government's brutality had been condemned all over the world (he used the English words "lynch mob").

On freedom of the press, Jović couldn't understand why people needed anything more than the official sources of information. Once, in a flash of inspiration between the halves of a soccer game, he shared with me an idea that he promised would fully satisfy Western concerns about press objectivity—"We'll have two television channels, one run by the government, the other by the opposition!" He was chagrined and confused by my explanation that two biased viewpoints were not much better than one.

Jović's vocabulary was laced with the language of conflict and militancy. In our first meeting in the spring of 1990, long before violence had broken out, he referred to "war" eight or ten times, curiously interspersing this bellicose talk with pleas for more foreign investment. His adversaries in the presidency, particularly the Slovenian, Croatian, and Macedonian members, resented the high-handed duplicity with which he sought to manipulate the institution. It was this pit bull of a politician to whom General Kadijević turned for help against Croatia and Slovenia.

In a presidency meeting January 9, 1991, Jović sought a majority in favor of authorizing the JNA to use force against the two republics. Thanks to Milošević's purges in the late 1980s, Jović could count on four of the eight votes—Serbia's, Montenegro's, Vojvodina's, and Kosovo's. Slovenia and Croatia were automatic noes, leaving Macedonia and Bosnia-Herzegovina. The Macedonian representative, Vasil Tupurkovski, opposed Jović and the army. Tupurkovski was a Rabelaisian figure weighing close to 300 pounds, but he was nimble enough to weave his massive way through Jović's barricades. Young, U.S.-educated, dynamic, and clear-headed, Tupurkovski cultivated a common touch. His trademark casualness—he was always tieless and in a sweater—won him fans throughout Yugoslavia.

Tupurkovski often made common cause with Janez Drnovšek, who had preceded Jović as president of the presidency and was still its Slovenian member. Both men, like Marković, wanted to preserve, reform, and democratize Yugoslavia. Their political skills made them natural allies but otherwise they were an odd couple—the ebullient, gargantuan Macedonian and the introverted, wraithlike Slovene. Even in retrospect this Mutt-and-Jeff pair stand out as major democratic figures against a background of opportunists and fanatics.

The swing vote on the presidency rested with Bogić Bogičević, the Bosnian representative, a tall, well-favored young politician who had done nothing particularly outstanding. He was a Bosnian Serb, and one can imagine the pressures applied on him to vote the Serbian line. Rarely is a politician's career marked by his vote on a single issue, but this was to be Bogičević's moment of truth. He did the courageous thing; he voted no, and Jović failed to get his majority.

A week later I was in Jović's office with an instruction to urge settlement of the paramilitary issue through negotiations rather than force. There was tremendous concern in Washington that the JNA was looking for an excuse to crush Tudjman, and we wanted Jović to be aware of it. I emphasized our view that the use of force or intimidation by the JNA would hasten disintegration rather than promote unity. Those who used force would be isolated and would damage American efforts to help Yugoslavia's economy. I made clear that we were giving Tudjman exactly the same message, as we were.

Jović disclaimed any intention to use force, though he didn't admit that the reason was his failure to get the presidency to authorize it. He expressed resentment at pressure by "the biggest power in the world" against "the legal head of the Yugoslav state." Tudjman told me several weeks later, and Jović confirmed years later, that Milošević and the JNA were considering moving against the Croats and Slovenes without the presidency's authorization and that the strong U.S. opposition to force was a major factor in restraining them. Henceforth the JNA would continue to browbeat the presidency, with its four automatic Serbian votes, in search of the decisive fifth vote. The failure of Milošević and his cohorts to seize control of a presidency he himself had rigged says something about the tenacity of democratic feelings in a crumbling Yugoslavia.

During this period of contradictions in early 1991, I thought that some extracurricular activity on my part might help cool passions. I had a line of communications with Kadijević, who professed to be antinationalist. Why not try to make contact with nationalist elements in the army as well? Their leader was reputed to be General Blagoje Adžić, the JNA chief of staff, whom I had gotten to know during the 1989 visit of the American General Herres. Adžić had the physique and ferocity of a grizzly, though his bluff manner was eased by a ready smile. He made no secret of his political orientation. "I'm a communist, I've always been a communist, and I'll be a communist till the day I die," he told me. As a child he had witnessed the mass murder of most of his family by the Croatian Ustaše, and he was considered a virulent Croat-hater. He also had no affection for the Slovenes or the Albanians—"separatists in one part of the country joining separatists in another," he once described them to me.

Still, I thought of something that might help us build a dialogue. In 1989 during the Herres visit we were staying at the JNA's elegant resort of Kupari, just outside Dubrovnik on the

Dalmatian coast. Adžić came up to me at breakfast on June 5. "Did you hear the news?" he asked. I had. The Chinese army had killed hundreds of students demonstrating on Tiananmen Square. "That's terrible," Adžić said, "terrible that an army should be used against civilians." Remembering that brief conversation, I put in a request through JNA protocol to see Adžić alone. After several weeks of masticating this unusual, out-of-channels application, the military bureaucracy gave me an appointment.

Sitting alone with Adžić in his Defense Ministry office dominated by a large map of Yugoslavia, I recalled to him the long cooperation between the JNA and the U.S. military, the public American support for Yugoslav unity with democracy, and my sympathy for the personal tragedy his own family had suffered in a previous civil war. Then I told him that the JNA was in danger of losing its favorable image in my country. The threat of force against Croatia was going down badly; so was the JNA's growing nationalist alliance with Serbia and its insistence on maintaining a communist Yugoslavia. The JNA had a case to make, but the way the army was doing it could only lose it friends in the West. I urged a reasonable dialogue, without accusations and smear tactics. I assured Adžić that we were pressing the same approach on Tudjman.

As Adžić listened to this, his face grew redder and redder, his bushy gray mustache began to twitch, and his already enormous bulk seemed to expand and ascend in his chair. When I had finished, he exploded into a deluge of invective against Tudjman and the Slovenes, a defense of the JNA's actions on behalf of Yugoslavia's unity, a flat denial of any complicity with Milošević, and a scolding of me for putting him in an awkward position ("Why didn't you see Kadijević on this!?"). He repeated an accusation I had heard several times from Kadijević—that the United States wasn't really in favor of unity. He added ominously: "The JNA will not allow Yugoslavia to be destroyed by force, and make no mistake—the Croats and Slovenes are using force. The nonuse of force is an important principle, but the preservation of unity is an even more important one."

After a few unsuccessful efforts to splice the severed line of communication, I gave up. As I rose to leave, I reminded Adžić of our mutual horror at the Chinese army's attacks on civilians. "Yes," said Adžić coldly, "It's terrible what a state must do sometimes in order to preserve its existence." I departed, saluted out by the usual clutch of colonels and majors, no doubt more eager than normal to learn what had gone on. I had made my point but in the process had discovered that there was an important element of the JNA that seemed determined to carry the duel with Croatia to the point of war.

The army's efforts, backed by Milošević and Jović, culminated in the second week of March in a dramatic JNA attempt to force the presidency to vote its way. As the members of the presidency gathered at their Belgrade offices March 12, they were whisked in a JNA bus to a military headquarters in another part of the city. Kept on and off for three days in a freezing meeting room, they were importuned by Kadijević and Jović to give the army the authority to crush the Croats and Slovenes. The attempt failed again. Again Bogičević held firm, to Jović's fury, and the plotters came up short of a majority for military intervention.

Milošević's reaction was electric. He withdrew Jović from the presidency and secured the resignation of the other three members under his control. One of them, a prominent Albanian economist representing Kosovo, had ignored the script and voted against Serbia; the Serbian parliament dismissed him and replaced him with a bingo hall operator ready to do what he was told. Milošević alerted a hastily summoned group of 200 Serbian local politicians to the prospect of war: "If we have to fight, we'll fight. . . . If we don't know how to work and do business, at least we know how to fight." In a dramatic television address the same day, March 16, he announced that "Yugoslavia is finished" and that Serbia would no longer respect federal Yugoslav authority. In effect this was secession, well before the Croats and Slovenes were to declare independence. It was also an attempt to clear the way for the JNA to move against the rebel republics; with no presidency, the army had no civilian authority to rein it in.

The stakes were high. During that climactic week of March 11–17, Kadijević made a secret trip to Moscow to seek the support of the Red Army in the event of Western intervention against the JNA's power play. But the coup attempt failed. The Macedonian Tupurkovski rallied the four presidency members left—the Croat, the Slovene, and the Bosnian, plus himself. They met as the Yugoslav presidency, with Prime Minister Marković's support. Milošević backed down, and Jović and company returned to the presidency. This near-miss was another proof of Milošević's contempt for Yugoslavia. He would support unity as long as it served his purposes; when it didn't, he was quite prepared to try to tear the country apart.

The scrimmaging between civilian and military leaders in Belgrade and Zagreb, none of whom had visible democratic credentials, obscured a phenomenon that was as much a result of the 1990 elections as nationalism was. This was the rise of Yugoslavs who were prepared to fight for individual freedoms—opposition politicians, independent journalists, victims of ethnic intolerance, human rights advocates, union organizers, and ordinary people who just hated what they saw around them. The last thing they had in common was unity among themselves. But the sum of their voices represented an alternative to the nationalist slogans sounding down the corridors of power.

Of course they were powerless against the ethnic demagogues who controlled the apparatus of governments and media, but Vaclav Havel, Lech Walesa, and Nelson Mandela were once powerless as well. The United States made a large investment in these courageous people, beginning with our speaking out on Kosovo and with Eagleburger's unprecedented meeting at my house with opposition groups from around the country.

I can remember when the American embrace of Tito persuaded us to look the other way on human rights. I was a junior officer in the U.S. embassy in 1966 when Milovan Djilas was released from his second prison term. Djilas had been one of the three most powerful partisan figures under Tito during the Second World War. In Montenegro, his native republic, he had a reputation for ruthlessness in putting down Yugoslav opposition to Tito's plans.

After the war, Djilas turned in a democratic direction. In 1957 his book *The New Class* exposed all communist systems as corrupt, intolerant, and dictatorial. He followed with a memoir containing candid and embarrassing first-hand glimpses of Stalin. His heretical writings earned him a total of nine years in Tito's prisons. With Djilas now out of jail, it would seem natural for somebody in the embassy to make contact with this historic figure. Nothing doing—the word went out that nobody in the embassy was to approach him. He was a pariah as far as the U.S. government was concerned.

When I returned to Yugoslavia as ambassador in 1989, I resolved to redeem that mistake. After I had made my official calls, I invited Djilas and his wife Stefanija to lunch with Teeny and me. They accepted with alacrity. As these two elderly people came through the front door on a beautiful June day, I could see Djilas looking around with curiosity. "You know," he said, "this is the first time I have ever been in the American ambassador's residence." Having made his point, he turned out to be the most delightful of guests. He had a cherubic smile, an ironic wit, and—even at his age—a flirtatious eye for the pretty waitress who was serving his lunch.

I had several long talks with Djilas in his book-filled Belgrade apartment. His readings of the Yugoslav situation were acute and pessimistic. Early on, he had identified nationalism as the proba-ble grave-digger of both Yugoslavia and the Soviet Union. He greatly admired Ante Marković but didn't see how he could sur-vive against the growing nationalisms. On the other hand, he pre-dicted correctly that Poland and Hungary would succeed on the democratic path. He was one of the first to see the dangers for Bosnia. He reveled in paradoxes. As the man who had done more than anybody to destroy the moral basis for communism, he en-joyed pointing out that Milan Kučan and his Slovenian commu-nist party were the least nationalistic group in Slovenia.

In listening to Djilas, I felt in the presence of a man both serene and wise. I gained the impression that prison had had a cathartic effect on him, had transformed the hot-headed and ruthless revo-lutionary into a person with some of the qualities of a saint. You could see that he and Stefanija adored each other—she was a Croat, he a Serb—and that each gave the other a depth of suste-nance that perhaps only Slavs can understand.

Djilas was Yugoslavia's first famous human rights hero, but in the age of nationalism there were many more. Groups and indi-viduals bold enough to lean against the nationalist gales appeared all over the country. In Belgrade Srdja Popović, whose Serbian credentials went back centuries, plowed his law office profits into *Vreme,* a newsmagazine whose commitment to unbiased report-ing attracted some of the best journalists in Yugoslavia. In Zagreb Slavko Goldstein, a Croatian Jew, founded a human rights organi-zation and risked arrest by organizing a group of intellectuals to demand Tudjman's resignation. And Ivan Zvonimir Čičak, a bookish intellectual, infuriated Tudjman by cataloguing Croatian crimes against the Serbian minority in Croatia. In Ljubljana Jurij Gustinčić, who had sparked controversy in the 1960s by arguing that Yugoslavia should opt for Europe rather than nonalignment, was still writing lucid commentaries for both Slovenian and Ser-bian media.

In Sarajevo a Muslim editor, Kemal Kurspahić; a Serbian

deputy editor, Gordana Knežević; and the heroic multiethnic staff of *Oslobodjenje* put out a decent daily newspaper throughout the Bosnian war from the cellar of their bombed-out office building. And in Montenegro, a Milošević stronghold, Miodrag Perović started a scathingly antiregime magazine called *Monitor,* publishing it on a desk-top printer in his house on a quiet street in Podgorica. As I was giving him an interview at his kitchen table, I noticed a gaping hole in his roof. "Oh," he said off-handedly, "the police told me a stray mortar had landed accidentally."

In particular, three women stand out in my memory for their bravery in championing the rights of others. Tanja Petovar, the daughter of a Slovenian general in the JNA, represented Human Rights Watch, the New York–based organization with a distinguished record for energy and fairness in publicizing human rights violations. Tanja was fearless in her even-handed exposure of Serbian abuses in Kosovo and Croatian abuses in Krajina. Vesna Pešić, a slight, attractive Belgrade University professor, chose a more political route. As ethnic tensions mounted, she founded a peace movement that set up branches in all the Yugoslav republics. Cyrus Vance made a point of attending its New Year's Eve vigil in 1991.

Gordana Logar, a correspondent and later editor-in-chief of *Borba,* helped to transform the paper from the communist party's boring official journal into the only independent daily in Serbia. Gordana refused to flatter Milošević in print and insisted on publishing foreign news critical of his policies. She looked the image of meekness with her small frame, slight limp, and huge, owl-like glasses, but she took on Milošević's press and police apparatus in 1994 when it tried to close *Borba*—and won.

All three women were constantly subjected to intense intimidation. Each routinely received death threats; in Gordana's case, her college-age daughter was threatened as well. Vesna's peace committee office was broken into and ransacked. The message was passed around that they were anti-Serb and anti-Yugoslav, that they were in the pay of foreign intelligence services, that they were traitors. I saw them and others like them differently—as a long-term investment in freedom and the core of a democratic revival that must one day replace the hysteria of nationalism.

The 1990 elections produced a whole crop of young people who had never been in politics before. They sprang up to found political parties and human rights groups. Some were outright nationalists, some were antinationalist, and some were on a journey of self-discovery. One of these last was Vuk Drašković, the most interesting opposition figure in Serbia. A flamboyant novelist, Drašković leapt onto the political stage as a Serbian extremist, complete with old testament beard, racist ideas, and the persona of a Serbian peasant. At first he was a bit of a trickster. When I invited him for a get-acquainted lunch, he looked suspiciously at the main course. "What is this meat?" he inquired. "It's beef," I said. He pushed it away, saying, "I eat only goat." When I told this story months later to Drašković's wife, Danica, she laughed and said, "He's never eaten goat in his life."

I felt there was more to Drašković than he displayed on first impression. When he found his political sea-legs, he turned into a staunch defender of an open political system and a free press. Danica, a formidable political figure in her own right, undoubtedly helped. With her long black dress, gorgeous features, and shoulder-length chestnut hair, she looked like a fleshier version of Morticia in the Addams Family. She had extraordinary courage, as she was to show when she and Vuk were arrested and beaten by Milošević's police in June 1993. She taunted her captors, challenging both their virility and their Serbianness, and, after her release, defiantly vowed to keep fighting against Milošević.

On March 9, 1991, Vuk Drašković staged a mass rally in Belgrade against Milošević's control of the press. Clumsy handling by the police and the army led to two deaths—a student demonstrator and a policeman—and to Drašković's arrest and brief detention. A tape released later captured the voice of General Adžić

—the man who had expressed revulsion to me at the Chinese army's brutality against the students in Tiananmen Square—urging the police to "beat the demonstrators till you're exhausted."

Drašković's demonstration took place on the Saturday before the fateful week in which Milošević, Jović, and the JNA tried to hijack the Yugoslav presidency. Perhaps the experience of nearly 100,000 hostile demonstrators unhinged the Serbian leader and brought him to his televised assertion a week later that Yugoslavia was finished. Whatever its effect on Milošević, the March 9 demonstration testified to the courage and democratic feeling of many ordinary Serbs. It was the most serious challenge so far to Milošević's power in Serbia.

I knew many Yugoslavs, mostly middle class, who opposed nationalism and yearned for democracy. Most of them supported Marković and what he stood for. Gavro Altman, a Jew and former communist editor, was typical of many who moved from the liberal wing of Yugoslav communism to the embrace of Western political values. Many Serbs were notable in this group. Živorad Kovačević, the tall and erudite Yugoslav ambassador to Washington, won enormous popularity among his American hosts, but it didn't save him from being fired at Milošević's demand for having opposed the rising communist politician in Belgrade politics years before.

Saša Nenadović, a famous journalist of the prenationalism days, moved to *Vreme* because it rejected the nationalist extremism of his former paper *Politika*. Zoran Kojić, a graduate of New York University's business school, managed to maintain sound business practices in running the Intercontinental Hotel in Belgrade in an atmosphere of urban corruption. His reward was getting his arm broken by a gang of Radovan Karadžić's toughs when the Bosnian Serb leader, a frequent guest at the Intercontinental, took umbrage at Zoran's efforts to keep Karadžić's rowdy crew from annoying the other guests.

Both Milošević and Tudjman were bemused or irritated when I emphasized the importance of people who made civil rights or political opposition their concern. Neither could understand why the U.S. government cared so much about people who were murdered, tortured, abused, or harassed. Milošević would listen patiently, then ask, "Why do you waste time on these individuals, who are mostly criminals anyway, when Serbs as a nation have been abused for years?" Tudjman would often erupt in fury when I had the temerity to suggest that Croatian authorities were not always model democrats in the treatment of their own citizens.

As it became clear to Milošević and Tudjman that the U.S. government and its representative in Yugoslavia were not fans of their authoritarian rule or their treatment of minorities, they unleashed their minions in the media. In Croatia the criticism was limited primarily to carping at U.S. support for Marković, to complaining that I lived in Belgrade where I couldn't help but be brainwashed by Serbian and Yugoslav propaganda, and to occasional distortions of my public statements.

The Serbian attacks amounted to a hate campaign. The U.S. government had fallen under the influence of the "Albanian lobby," led by that notorious Albanian (*sic*), Senator Robert Dole. The U.S. ambassador "hated Serbs" and traveled frequently to Slovenia and Croatia to consort with other Serb-haters. The ambassador treated Yugoslavia as his "ranch," to dispose of as he wished. Worst of all, Zimmermann often went to Kosovo to give instructions to the "Shiptar" (a racist word for "Albanian") separatists bent on the destruction of Yugoslavia and Serbia. The headlines were often spicier than the stories. I remembered with amusement how similar the metaphors were to the hack journalism I was compelled to read as a political officer in Brezhnev's Soviet Union—"What New Dishes Are Being Concocted in the Imperialist Kitchens?" or "Strange Journey: Why Is the American Ambassador in Slovenia?"

When I was given the opportunity, I would explain our policy in print or on television, sometimes in the same newspapers or on the same channels that were leading the campaign. Among people prepared to be fair-minded, this helped to break down the extreme insularity that resulted from the rise of nationalism. Virtually nobody in Belgrade read the Zagreb press and vice versa—an enormous advantage for local demagogues. Milošević's propagandists always found ways to impute sinister designs to my visits to Kosovo. Once, when I opened a U.S.-sponsored cultural event in Priština, speaking in English to an ethnically mixed audience, the interpreter translated my remarks first into Albanian, then into Serbian. At that unpardonable slight, half the Serbian audience walked out, and the Belgrade press launched a weeklong campaign against this irrefutable evidence of my Serbophobia.

In the nationalist environment of Yugoslavia, many people couldn't understand why the United States wasn't 100 percent for their particular nation. In Croatia it wasn't enough that we supported the democratic process that brought Tudjman to office; we also had to support his myopic policy toward the Serbian minority. In Serbia, nobody seemed to care that we didn't favor the independence of Kosovo; all they saw was our work on behalf of the rights of Albanians there.

The overall U.S. policy of unity and democracy was guaranteed to offend extremists in both camps. So was our even-handed support of the rights of minorities; nationalists don't care about minorities, except their own. One day I was discussing these contradictions at lunch with Sonja Licht, another human rights activist who expended her energy to the point of exhaustion on behalf of victims of nationalist excesses. "You know," Sonja said as she finished her coffee, "I think you must be a good ambassador—everybody hates you."

Josip Broz Tito, the charismatic communist who commanded the
Yugoslav partisans during World War II, used his authoritarian rule
after the war to crush all manifestations of nationalism—thus
ensuring that it would spring up after his death in 1980.

ABOVE: Slobodan Milošević, who gave the most lip service to the preservation of Yugoslavia, was the man who did the most to destroy it. His pursuit of Serbian hegemony made the country uninhabitable for non-Serbs. BELOW: Milošević, president of Serbia, could be personable, engaging, and flexible. He could also be rigid, calculating, and cold, as he appears here at our first meeting, at a reception honoring a Serbian holiday.

LEFT: Borisav Jović, doctrinaire communist and Milošević henchman, used the year of his presidency of Yugoslavia (1990–91) to try to crush the Croats and Slovenes. Jović is now a political enemy and has written a memoir documenting the Serbian leader's masterminding of Serbian aggression in Croatia and Bosnia.

RIGHT: Dobrica Ćosić, nationalist Serbian writer and briefly president of Milošević's rump Yugoslavia, suffered from the disease of many Serbian intellectuals. In their obsession with Serbia's glories and grievances, they opened the way for unspeakable atrocities against other ethnic groups.

ABOVE: Milan Kučan, communist leader and later president of Slovenia, in the late 1980s made his republic the most liberal communist state in history. He wasn't a leader in the Slovenian independence movement but embraced it because of his dislike for Milošević. BELOW: Janez Stanovnik, president of Slovenia from 1986 to 1990, represented the best of the old Yugoslavia. A wise and compassionate man, married to a Serb, he believed that Yugoslavia's peoples had to learn to live together.

LEFT: Janez Drnovšek, president of Yugoslavia from 1989 to 1990 and prime minister of Slovenia beginning in 1992, tried to stave off the violence he knew the breakup of Yugoslavia would provoke. When Slovenia persisted in its independent course, he returned to Ljubljana and helped guide it on the road to democracy.

RIGHT: The ascetic, driven Janez Janša, Slovenian defense minister at the age of thirty-two, outsmarted the Yugoslav army with a successful military and public relations campaign, thus making Slovenia's independence irrevocable.

Franjo Tudjman achieved the presidency of Croatia in the democratic elections of 1990 but quickly moved to establish authoritarian control over the media, the economy, and the police and to build a formidable army.

Tudjman, shown with me at the Zagreb Trade Fair in the prewar days of 1990, was more interested in implanting Croatian nationalism than in trade ties or economic reform.

LEFT: Yugoslav prime minister Ante Marković aspired to
launch the most radical economic reform in Eastern Europe.
But competing nationalist leaders saw reform as a danger
to their aims, and they destroyed it.

RIGHT: Yugoslav foreign minister Budimir Lončar traversed
the well-trod path from Titoist communist to democratic
reformer. When Milošević forced his ministry to spread
nationalist Serbian propaganda abroad, he resigned
with dignity.

LEFT: Defense Minister Veljko Kadijević muttered darkly about the evils of nationalism and sought to crush the emerging armies in Croatia and Slovenia. In the end, he threw his support to Milošević, turning the Yugoslav army into a weapon of Serbian nationalism.

RIGHT: The giant chief of staff Blagoje Adžić, many of whose family were murdered by the Croatian Ustaše during World War II, showed no sympathy for Croats, Slovenes, or Albanians. His inability to accept democratic change contributed to the army's eventual disgrace.

Radovan Karadžić, indicted war criminal, was the leader of the Bosnian Serbs. He developed a joint strategy with Milošević for the conquest of two-thirds of Bosnia. Milošević turned on him when he grew too powerful.

LEFT: Vojislav Šešelj, a self-promoting Serbian racist, was not all bluff—his Nazi-like troopers committed atrocities in both Croatia and Bosnia. Milošević supported him, then dropped him when he became a rival. Šešelj got his revenge by exposing publicly Milošević's direct role in the Croatian and Bosnian wars. RIGHT: The boyish smile of Željko Ražnjatović (nom de guerre: Arkan) disguises one of the most ruthless cutthroats in the Balkans. Arkan's "Tigers" specialized in the murder of civilians in Croatian and Bosnian villages.

ABOVE: The two million Kosovo Albanians were led by Ibrahim Rugova, a soft-spoken poet, who persuaded his people to react to Milošević's assaults on Albanian civil rights with Gandhian, nonviolent civil disobedience. BELOW: Vuk Drašković, a Serbian nationalist of a less virulent sort than Milošević, was the only Serbian opposition leader with the courage to challenge him directly. Drašković and his equally intrepid wife Danica have been beaten and imprisoned by Milošević's police.

Vesna Pešić, a professor at Belgrade University, founded a peace movement to protest the injustice of the Yugoslav army's war in Croatia. A frequent target of death threats, she remains an eloquent figure in the weak anti-Milošević camp.

LEFT: Milovan Djilas, who died in 1995, served nine years in Tito's prisons for the heresy of revealing the essential corruption of communism. Forgotten in Yugoslavia but not in the West, he predicted accurately the horrors of nationalist warfare. RIGHT: The small woman peering through outsize glasses is Gordana Logar, editor in chief of *Borba*, the last independent newspaper in Serbia. When Milošević's minions tried to close it down, Logar defied them and won, taking her staff and founding another paper.

ABOVE: Vasil Tupurkovski, the U.S.-educated Macedonian member of the Yugoslav presidency, knew that the death of Yugoslavia would increase Serbian pressures on Macedonia. He made efforts as gigantic as his 300-pound frame to hold the country together. BELOW: Cyrus Vance (with his deputy Herbert S. Okun to his right) combined integrity, determination, and extraordinary energy to win a cease-fire in Croatia in 1991.

ABOVE: Deputy Secretary of State Lawrence S. Eagleburger had long experience in Yugoslavia and played a critical role in policy making during the Bush administration. BELOW: Secretary of State James Baker, shown describing his meeting with Yugoslav leaders in Belgrade on June 21, 1991, was categorical in predicting war if Croatia and Slovenia proceeded with their plans for independence. By then few leaders were paying much attention even to their own self-interest.

ABOVE: The Yugoslav army's attack on Dubrovnik in the fall of 1991 inflicted little major damage. But it showed the sordid nature of a war in which an unarmed and undefended medieval city could be considered fair game. BELOW: The Yugoslav army shelled the ethnically mixed Croatian city of Vukovar for three months—the first major war crime.

ABOVE: The efficiency with which the Serbs set up detention camps for Muslim and Croatian prisoners in the early months of the Bosnian war—like this one at Manjača—revealed a carefully prepared strategy of ethnic cleansing. BELOW: Alija Izetbegović never seemed to enjoy being president of Bosnia. But he shepherded his country through a war fought against great odds.

ABOVE: My driver Neša Janković, shown with me on a trip to Croatia, was the kind of Serb Milošević should have supported: creative, resourceful, energetic, and companionable. BELOW: My wife Teeny encouraged our young Croatian employee Danijela Hajnal to join us in the United States after her hometown of Vukovar was destroyed. Danijela is making top grades in her senior year at an American university.

POLARIZATION

*"You Americans would become nationalists and
racists too if your media were totally in the
hands of the Ku Klux Klan."*

Milošević and the JNA had failed in their attempt to humiliate
Tudjman, dismantle his novice army, and perhaps blow him away
altogether. But they didn't stop trying. Between the JNA's unsuccessful bid to hijack the federal presidency in mid-March 1991
and the outbreak of war in late June, Yugoslavia was caught between the poles of Serbian and Croatian nationalist extremism,
between Milošević and Tudjman. The struggle between these
self-styled titans compressed and crushed all those in between
who sought reasonable solutions short of war. Tawdry imperson-
ators of Achilles and Hector, heroes of an earlier Balkan conflict,
these strutting paragons of their respective civilizations sought to
sweep the field of lesser men so that they could engage directly in
heroic combat.

For this purpose—and because their vast egos drew them inexorably toward each other—they met privately on several occasions, beginning on March 25. This bizarre polar attraction failed
to settle the primary issues between Serbia and Croatia. But it did
produce agreements to weaken or destroy two of the key advo-

cates of a united Yugoslavia—Yugoslav Prime Minister Ante Marković and Bosnian President Alija Izetbegović.

Tudjman considered Marković a renegade Croat for being pro-Yugoslav and for rejecting the call of Croatian nationalism. He wasn't above disparaging the federal prime minister to his face. Slovenian President Kučan told me the story of a meeting between himself, Tudjman, and Marković in late November 1990 at one of Tito's enormous villas near Zagreb. Kučan was trying to sell Marković on a Slovene plan for the peaceful dissolution of Yugoslavia. Tudjman, always partial to separatist proposals, supported the idea. Marković hesitated a long time before telling Kučan and Tudjman that he couldn't go along: the plan might undermine economic reform, provoke a turndown by Serbia (as later happened), and lead to violence. Tudjman, pointing to the baronial chairs the three were sitting in, said to Marković, "Ante, if you don't go along with us, do you really think this chair will be here for you when you decide someday to come back to Croatia?"

With me, Tudjman never hid his feelings about Marković. "You will see, Mr. Ambassador," he would say, "that Marković represents nothing and counts for nothing." Tudjman ridiculed Marković's poor showing in the elections, claimed that Croatian business was against him, and told me in April 1991, "Maybe he should resign." As for Milošević, he was too smooth to express a personal opinion to me, but his real views were undoubtedly revealed by the vicious campaign against Marković launched by the Serbian press in the spring of 1991. In the same period in a session of the Yugoslav presidency, Milošević's closest ally, Borisav Jović, accused Marković of being an American spy. And the Serbian assembly called on the federal parliament to pass a no-confidence vote against the prime minister.

The Slovenes were no gentler with Marković. Dimitrij Rupel, the Slovenian foreign minister and a strong advocate of independence, complained to me that Marković had rejected two Slovenian offers of negotiation over the republic's status. The more centrist Kučan criticized Marković's obstinacy: "He wants to write all the rules. He doesn't take Slovenia seriously." Even Drnovšek, who was working to keep Slovenia in Yugoslavia, felt rebuffed by Marković's stiff refusals to recognize Slovenia's right to secede. He finally appealed to me to try to get Marković to negotiate with the Slovene leadership, something I was, late in the game, able to do.

Marković could be imperial and abrasive, but there were deeper reasons for the vendetta against him. For the Slovenes and Croats, he was an obstacle to secession; for the Serbs, he was too liberal and Western. As the knives grew sharper, Marković began to lose his popular support. The fiasco of his challenge to the nationalists in the 1990 republican elections hurt him badly. This combination of enemies and setbacks cost the economic reform its momentum. Marković's victory over inflation proved to be temporary. Prices rose, the value of the Yugoslav dinar dropped, and convertibility had to be abandoned. People lost the sense of optimism and rising expectations that the ebullient prime minister had given them.

Marković fought back with characteristic spirit. "They won't find it easy to destroy me," he promised me. But he couldn't resist chastising his enemies. He went public against Milošević's treatment of the Albanians in Kosovo, a subject on which, to win Serbian support for the economic reform, he had preferred to keep silent. He despised both Milošević and Tudjman for their cynical efforts to build a Greater Serbia and a Greater Croatia. In private he told me, "They're both totalitarians, and don't kid yourself that Tudjman is any better than Milošević. Unlike the Slovenes, the Croats know what they think, because only one person decides everything. Tudjman has ended democracy in Croatia, not only for Serbs but for all who disagree with him. Croatian society has been totally militarized, with police and weapons everywhere."

The Milošević-Tudjman cabal against Izetbegović was equally

troubling. If Marković's reforms were the last hope for Yugoslavia's preservation, Bosnia had the most to lose if that hope failed. Bosnia was a Yugoslavia in miniature—a multiethnic state in which Serbs, Croats, and Muslims lived together. It had the highest percentage of ethnically mixed marriages of any Yugoslav republic. From the fifteenth to the nineteenth centuries Bosnia had been under Turkish rule. Many of the Orthodox and Catholic Christians who lived there when the Turks arrived converted to Islam for the understandable reason that they would be better treated. This created the historical oddity of the Bosnian Muslims—all of them Slavs, all of them ethnically indistinguishable from either Serbs or Croats.

Bosnia had a reputation, even in premodern times, as a haven for victims of racial persecution; many Jews fled to Sarajevo after they were expelled from Spain in 1492. During my first trip to Sarajevo as ambassador I was allowed to hold in my hands a fifteenth-century Haggadah, with luminous color illustrations, that had probably been brought on that journey. Bosnia had also suffered its share of ethnic conflict, never worse than during World War II, when it was the bloodiest killing ground of the Yugoslav civil war.

Bosnia's mixed history of ethnic hospitality and ethnic strife would have made the task of its president a daunting one even if Yugoslavia were not breaking apart. When I first met Alija Izetbegović just before the Bosnian elections in 1990, he was already under stress. Though he was the leader of the largest party in Bosnia, the Muslim Party of Democratic Action, he looked like anything but a politician. Mild-mannered to a fault, deferential, and perpetually anxious, he obviously felt more comfortable around his family than around anyone else. He brought his attractive and perceptive daughter Sabina to our first dinner; she later became his main confidante, interpreter, and chief of staff.

Izetbegović emerged from the 1990 elections as the only president of the six ex-Yugoslav republics never to have been a communist. He was a devout Muslim, unlike many Bosnians who chose Muslim nationality when Tito gave them the option. But I never saw any signs of extremism or coercion in his manner. He didn't drink, but he always offered wine to his guests. In 1970 he wrote a book with the title *Islamic Declaration.* Contrary to the Satanization to which it has been subjected, it was an abstract appeal for a return to nonnationalistic Islamic values. It stoked no fire of the Libyan or Iranian sort; in fact, it called for protection of the rights of non-Muslims in countries with Muslim majorities. The book was nevertheless a special plea for a particular religion and way of life, and that was enough to earn Izetbegović a jail sentence in 1983.

Izetbegović wore the mantle of Bosnian president with extreme discomfort. When I went to see him after the election, he told me he bore a double weight on his shoulders. "I have to ensure that Bosnia remains a multiethnic community," he said. "The constitution calls for the executive power to be divided among Serbs, Croats, and Muslims. Our prime minister is Croatian, and the president of our assembly is Serbian. They're being pulled toward extreme positions by the nationalist leaderships in Belgrade and Zagreb—outside forces that we can't control. Nationalism is also very strong here in Bosnia, particularly among Serbs. Still, we have to make this system work, and I'm trying my best to do that."

"There's an even bigger problem," he continued. "It's the preservation of Yugoslavia. Yugoslavia is like a husband and wife who after three months of separation realize they still need each other. Bosnia can't survive the death of Yugoslavia. If Yugoslavia collapses and Croatia goes independent, we will be pulled apart. Milošević and Tudjman already claim the allegiance of Serbs and Croats whose families have lived in Bosnia for centuries. I know the United States wants to keep Yugoslavia together. There can be no greater reason for doing that than the prevention of war in Bosnia."

Izetbegović told me that he had been in touch with Kiro Gligorov, the president of Macedonia, who had parallel reasons for wanting to maintain a unified Yugoslavia. Gligorov, a wise old communist in his mid-70s, had been Yugoslavia's first serious economic reformer. As finance minister in 1965, he had tried to persuade Tito to approve radical economic changes. Tito watered down Gligorov's recommendations, concluding correctly that real reform would weaken the power of the communist party. Gligorov had been Marković's chief economic adviser before returning to Macedonia; now he could apply his years in politics to helping the inexperienced Bosnian president.

The plan the two came up with would preserve Yugoslavia but devolve even more powers to the republics. Izetbegović saw it as creating "a Yugoslavia that consists of sovereign republics in a community recognizable as a state." It was antinationalistic, rejecting Milošević's view that nations (i.e., ethnic groups), rather than republics, are sovereign. Though it had confederal aspects, the plan was dismissed out of hand by the Croatian and Slovenian governments, although Janez Drnovšek, the moderate Slovene in the Yugoslav presidency, supported it. Milošević gave it lip service for undoubtedly tactical reasons. He had no intention of strengthening Yugoslav republics at the behest of two republican leaders so devoid of geopolitical weight.

By the spring of 1991 Tudjman and Milošević were on the same wavelength on Bosnia: keeping it together was less important than dividing it between them. With the artlessness of the true believer, Tudjman was quite open about this. Once, while he was walking me through the presidential palace in Zagreb, resplendent with mementoes of Croatia's thousand-year history, he stopped in front of a huge tapestry of Croatia into which was woven the seal of each constituent part. He pointed out that there was a seal for Bosnia-Herzegovina. "You see, Mr. Ambassador," he said. "History shows that Bosnia-Herzegovina is really ours."

Milošević was much subtler; he didn't tip his hand until much later. But his sidekick Jović was, as always, blunt. He told me in late March, "Bosnia will have to be divided between Serbia and Croatia." Jović added, as if making a big concession, "Of course, the Muslims can choose what part they want to live in." I noticed that, after Milošević and Tudjman started meeting, the Serbian and Croatian press line on Bosnia became nearly identical—the Muslims were trying to establish an Islamic state in the heart of Europe. The ironic reality was just the reverse. It was Milošević and Tudjman, in their desire to divide Bosnia along ethnic lines, who laid the philosophical groundwork for a separate Muslim entity. And it was the besieged Izetbegović who stood alone in advocating the preservation of Bosnia's multiethnic framework.

The new nationalism of Milošević and Tudjman shared one important element in common with the old communism that had formed both leaders. For both communism and nationalism, the press was the primary vehicle for influencing the people. Its purposes were to indoctrinate, manipulate, and intimidate. In nationalist hands, the methods survived but the message changed. For all their sins, the Yugoslav communist leaders rarely incited their captive audience to hate other Yugoslavs; they invoked more abstract evils, such as "class enemies" and "capitalism."

With the nationalist media impresarios of Serbia and Croatia, ethnic hostility became the leitmotiv. News, features, even cartoons drove home the evil nature of the other ethnic group. To give this message a minimal credibility, Milošević and Tudjman actually needed each other. Milošević would fulminate about Tudjman's iniquitous treatment of his Serbian minority, thus giving the Croatian leader new material with which to castigate Serbs for interfering in Croatia's affairs, thus allowing Milošević to escalate the media war to higher levels of defamation. The demands of their respective campaigns of media vilification drove the two leaders into a deadly symbiosis.

Tudjman's use of the Croatian press was considerably coarser than that of his communist predecessors. He put in charge of

Croatian Radio and Television Antun Vrdoljak, a nationalist zealot even by Tudjman's standards. Vrdoljak once told me that Serbs were genetically equipped only for war, not for intellectual activity. He saw his journalistic role in military terms; once the Croatian war began in mid-1991 he described his work as "part of my duty to the homeland in its war for survival. . . . When I ask myself if I have done anything for television, I think I can say: I have achieved my soldierly task." On taking office, Vrdoljak sacked the Serbs, several of them excellent journalists, who dominated Croatian press and television. He then went after publications that took an independent line.

The destruction of *Danas,* a respected independent weekly, was a typical example of press control in the Tudjman style. The Croatian government imposed a new board of management on the magazine, then tried (unsuccessfully) to halt its publication on grounds of bankruptcy. It attacked *Danas* through Tudjman's party press, dried up its sources of advertising, banned it from the kiosks, and finally engineered its sale to a friendly Croatian entrepreneur, who turned it into an outlet for extreme nationalist views. All this was done in the name of privatization.

Milošević's manipulation of mass media was even more insidious. The Serbian president had learned the basic techniques of press control as a communist apparatchik in Belgrade, and he brought them intact to his new nationalist vocation. I was told that after he became president of Serbia, Milošević met with the head of Belgrade Radio-Television every day. To the world Milošević always asserted that the Serbian press was free, and he did tolerate a small opposition press while making sure it didn't reach beyond Belgrade. But his hand was often heavy. A journalist friend of mine once overheard a dispute between an editor and a writer in the studio of Belgrade Radio-TV. The argument ended when the editor said: "Look—this is how the Boss wants it!"

The Serbian leader used his control of the press for several purposes. One was to project infallibility and devotion. In three years

I didn't read or hear a single word against Milošević in media under his influence. Sometimes the adoration reached comic heights. When, for electoral reasons, he changed the name of his party from "communist" to "socialist," the magazine *NIN* ran a cover on which his head was depicted in a celestial firmament containing such socialist luminaries as Willy Brandt, Felipe Gonzalez, and François Mitterrand—instant apotheosis.

For the most part, however, Milošević shunned this kind of self-advertisement; he preferred power to adulation. His exploitation of the press was usually in the service of specific objectives. For example, in 1990 he decided to cultivate a moderate image for himself by secretly contriving to publicize a more rabid nationalist leader on his right. Belgrade television therefore began to give prime time to the psychopathic racist Vojislav Šešelj. When Šešelj became a serious rival to Milošević, however, he suddenly disappeared from the screen.

Milošević also used his tame press to make sure that events turned out as he wanted. In the Serbian elections of 1990 his media treated the politicians running against him as nonpersons. Vuk Drašković, an electrifying speaker, drew tens of thousands of people to rallies in central Serbia, but few knew about him except those who had actually gone to hear him. Finally, under pressure from his own public and from me to make the campaign fair, Milošević made a grand concession. He would give television time to all thirty or so presidential candidates, one after another.

The results were ludicrous. The serious candidates had to compete with the various drunks, religious freaks, rock stars, and stumblebums who had put themselves forward (or had been recruited by the Milošević camp). Milošević himself loftily announced that he wouldn't appear in this rogues' gallery. He told me that, in his devotion to democracy, he "wanted to give all the opposition candidates a fair chance." What he'd really done, of course, was avoid becoming another clown in a television circus. Drašković fumed: "He made fools of us, and there wasn't a thing we could do about it." In such a climate no election in Serbia could be genuinely free.

The pièce de résistance of Milošević's manipulation of the media, as of Tudjman's, was the manufacture of ethnic hatred. The outbreak of sporadic fighting in Croatia during the spring of 1991 aided their efforts. Ever since his election in 1990 Tudjman had tried to oust Serbian police from the Krajina and other Serbian areas and install Croatian police there. The local Serbs, armed by Belgrade, resisted and began to set up autonomous territories barricaded against Croatian authority. It was nearly impossible for diplomats and journalists to sort out who was responsible for each instance of violence. Press reports of the same event in Belgrade and Zagreb were diametrically opposed.

In one sense it didn't matter, since both Milošević and Tudjman wanted violence and did all they could to provoke it. Fresh corpses, laid out graphically on color television, gave their hate campaigns—literally—new blood. The slogans—"Croatia's sovereignty in danger!" "Serbs threatened with genocide!"—bit deep as Serbian and Croatian television viewers were exposed to a nightly fare of defunct compatriots martyred for their nation. At times Belgrade and Zagreb television shared corpses: the same television picture of stiffening bodies was shown in each capital, portrayed in the one case as heroic Serbs, in the other as patriotic Croats. Milošević and Tudjman had a joint interest in polarizing relations between their two peoples, and media control gave them the perfect instrument for doing it.

Those who argue that "ancient Balkan hostilities" account for the violence that overtook and destroyed Yugoslavia ignore the power of television in the service of officially provoked racism. While history, particularly the carnage of World War II, provided plenty of tinder for ethnic hatred in Yugoslavia, it took the institutional nationalism of Milošević and Tudjman to supply the torch. Inherent violence is as much a matter of reputation as of fact. England was considered inherently violent in the seventeenth century because of its savage civil war. Eighteenth-century France became the symbol of violence in Dickens's account of the French Revolution in *A Tale of Two Cities*. Germany has been synonymous with violence since the Franco-Prussian war of 1870. Yugoslavia may have a violent history, but it isn't unique. What we witnessed was violence-provoking nationalism from the top down, inculcated primarily through the medium of television.

Why did so many Serbs, Croats, and (later) Muslims succumb to these racist appeals? One function of democratic government is to protect an open competition of ideas that will, it can be hoped, offset the spread of hatred. When government assumes precisely the opposite role—when it uses its power over the mass media to exhort people to hate—then many citizens look to the press not for information but for emotional reassurance. They can take righteous satisfaction in discharging their anger at their neighbors.

Even more important was the fear factor. The nationalist media sought to terrify by evoking mass murderers of a bygone time. The Croatian press decribed Serbs as "Četniks"—the Serbian nationalists of World War II. For the Serbian press Croatians were "Ustaše" (and later, Muslims became "Turks"). People who think they're under ethnic threat tend to seek refuge in their ethnic group. Thus did the media's terror campaign establish ethnic solidarity on the basis of an enemy to be both hated and feared. Many people in the Balkans may be weak or even bigoted, but in Yugoslavia it's their leaders who have been criminal. Miloš Vašić, one of the best independent journalists in Yugoslavia, has said, "You Americans would become nationalists and racists too if your media were totally in the hands of the Ku Klux Klan."

The virus of television spread ethnic hatred like an epidemic throughout Yugoslavia, becoming even more malignant as sporadic violence turned into full-scale war. Worst of all, the virus had a temporal as well as a geographic effect. An entire generation of Serbs, Croats, and Muslims were aroused by television images to hate their neighbors. Every night for five years nearly everybody in Yugoslavia watched highly manipulated pictures of the maimed and the murdered, the cleansed and the condemned. One can imagine the enduring impression those pictures must have made on the minds of children and young adults, an impression that will last for decades and may even be transmitted by infected parents to children still unborn. It will make a long-term peace even harder to come by. The current nationalist leaders will someday be gone. But the seed they have sown, through their malevolent manipulation of information, will long survive them.

The spring of 1991 was in Croatia a time of growing violence, which was seized on and inflated by the media. The Yugoslav army began to skew its activities toward helping the Serbs, to whom it was supplying arms from military warehouses. Watching the JNA with deep suspicion, the Slovenes pressed on with plans to secede from Yugoslavia on June 26, six months after the referendum that had produced overwhelming Slovenian support for independence. Recklessly, Tudjman announced on April 2 that if Slovenia seceded, so would Croatia. The rhetoric between Belgrade and Zagreb escalated, even as Milošević and Tudjman continued to conspire to divide Bosnia. As usual, Milošević left most of the dirty work to his propagandists, while Tudjman struck patriotic poses in public. "If we have to stand up with arms in our hands and defend the freedom and sovereignty of the Republic of Croatia," he proclaimed, "then we shall do so."

Western leaders began to come to grips with the dangers of a slide to breakup and war. President Bush communicated personally with Prime Minister Marković during the spring of 1991, once by letter, once by phone. His purpose was to show strong U.S. support for Marković but also to lay out clearly the American view. The U.S. government wanted to see the resolution of the nationality disputes within the context of a single state. We believed they could be solved only through democracy, reforms, and peaceful negotiations. I was instructed to reinforce this message with the JNA, whose pro-Serbian bias was beginning to alarm Washington.

On April 11 I informed General Kadijević that the United States was strongly opposed to the use of force. Reading my talking points from the State Department, I said, "Yugoslavia can't be held together at gunpoint. The JNA must not be seen as serving the interests of individual republics." Kadijević, incensed, called the message "insulting": "The army isn't so stupid as to think the country can be held together by force." Dressed in civilian clothes and looking haggard, he brushed aside my assertions that the United States opposed secession and was making this clear in Ljubljana and Zagreb. "The United States has done nothing to preserve unity," he complained. "Now Yugoslavia is on the brink of disintegration."

In early May, as all this flammable material smoldered, Milošević threw a match into it. The issue was the coming selection of the new president of the presidency of Yugoslavia. Every year on May 15 the office rotated among republics by a predetermined order; the vice president traditionally moved up to become president. In March 1989 I had presented my letters of credence as ambassador to then-president Raif Dizdarević, a Muslim from Bosnia. He was succeeded in May 1989 by the Slovene Janez Drnovšek, who had used the office to encourage cooperation among the squabbling republics. Drnovšek was followed a year later by Milošević's crony Borisav Jović, who had run roughshod over the interests of the other republics in his single-minded determination to press the Serbian agenda. Now it was time for Jović to hand over to the vice president, Stipe Mesić, a Croat.

Though a member of Tudjman's party (he later left it), Mesić was no nationalist. In fact, his fierce black beard disguised a friendly personality as well as something unknown among nationalists—a sense of humor. I once played tennis with Mesić against Tudjman and his defense minister Gojko Šušak, a grim-faced, no-nonsense, determined pair. Even in the presence of Tudjman's courtside claque of cheering sycophants, Mesić couldn't resist clowning around and teasing his boss after every missed shot.

Politically, Mesić was a moderate. His family, like many Serbian but few Croatian families, had been wiped out by the Ustaše in World War II. He had a Serbian wife and understood the problems of Serbs in Croatia better than any other major Croatian politician. He might have been considered the best Croat any reasonable Serb could want in the Yugoslav presidency. But Milošević wasn't a reasonable Serb, and he felt particularly threatened by moderates.

As May 15 approached, the Serbian press began to savage Mesić, seizing on an incautious statement he had made that Yugoslavia would not survive. I was concerned that, despite more than a decade of constitutional precedent, Milošević might use his automatic four votes on the eight-member presidency to block Mesić's accession. I asked him about Mesić several days before May 15. "Serbia will always act in the spirit of the highest democratic principles," replied Milošević, who was always at his most mellifluous when expatiating on his devotion to democratic norms. "There will be a democratic vote in the presidency. Jović will not be extended. The regular May 15 rotation will proceed. Serbia will never seek to alter this rotation because it respects the federal constitution."

"But are you going to accept a fair transition from a Serb to a Croat president?" I pursued. "Mr. Zimmermann," he said, "you can tell your government that it has absolutely nothing to worry about." I told Washington that Mesić wasn't a sure thing.

Five days later, Milošević's followers on the presidency blocked Mesić's accession, throwing Yugoslavia into a constitutional crisis. The next day I met Milošević by chance in the presidency building. I asked him what he was going to do about the crisis he had created. He looked at me innocently. "What crisis?" he asked. "I told you Jović wouldn't stay in power and he hasn't."

I said he had also promised a normal rotation. He said, "Everything was normal. Just because there was a vote, that doesn't mean Mesić had to win it. Every country operates according to its constitution, even yours. We Yugoslavs don't need your advice on how our constitution works."

Milošević in the full flush of arrogance was illustrating three important character traits: his cynicism about Yugoslavia's unity and institutions, his natural duplicity, and the pains he always took to avoid direct responsibility for aggressive actions. The third trait was to become particularly relevant to Milošević's hidden hand in the Croatian and Bosnian wars.

On May 20 I outlined in a cable my view of Milošević's motives. He was trying to drive the Slovenes out of Yugoslavia so he could deal with a Croatia shorn of allies. He wanted to cover up Serbia's economic disaster by provoking the Mesić debacle and other political crises. He consistently brushed aside all efforts to preserve Yugoslavia in a loose arrangement that would leave only a few limited functions to the federal government. He now wanted to destroy the country in the interest of a greater Serbia.

His actions against the unity of Yugoslavia told the story: his economic boycott against Slovenia and Croatia, his mega-theft from the National Bank of Yugoslavia, his attempts in March and May 1991 to destroy the Yugoslav presidency, and his smear campaign against Marković. I rated the preservation of Yugoslavia as a declining possibility but urged continued support for Marković since "bloody violence lies behind his failure."

Last-minute attempts multiplied to save Yugoslavia and the possibilities for democracy. Tupurkovski turned into a giant whirling dervish, propelling his bulk into every corner of the country to try to win an end to violence in Croatia and a modus vivendi among republican leaders for a confederal framework. As the representative of Macedonia on the presidency, he had everything to gain from the continued unity of Yugoslavia, since its breakup could throw his republic under the influence of Serbia, of which Macedonia had been a part ("Southern Serbia") in the interwar years. But he also cared deeply about a nonviolent outcome, he believed in the development of a civil society, and he knew democracy would come only through agreement among the republics to hang together. Tupurkovski's efforts to this end were as prodigious as his size. They placed him in the small group of politicians—along with his fellow Macedonian Gligorov, the Albanian Rugova, the Slovene Drnovšek, and Marković—who came through the Yugoslav crisis with honor.

Drnovšek took major personal risks in working for a compromise agreement between Slovenia and Croatia on the one side and Serbia and the JNA on the other. As the representative on the Yugoslav presidency of a republic that had made a decision to secede, Drnovšek risked losing his base at home through his efforts to keep Yugoslavia together. Still, he kept trying because he was convinced—as I was—that breakup meant war.

We formed a close personal relationship during this period. We would often meet to play tennis and talk; tennis provided good cover and was the best way either of us could think of to relax. This shy, introverted economist seemed no match for the puffed-up leaders of Serbia, Croatia, and the JNA, but Drnovšek showed extraordinary political and diplomatic skills. They weren't enough, however, and as Slovenia's deadline of June 26 approached, he threw in his lot with his republic. The polarization was too great even for a courageous Slovene who had been willing to stick his neck out.

American policy is never made in a vacuum, and as Yugoslavia careened toward destruction, the role of the U.S. Congress bulked ever larger. The Yugoslav crisis showed the Congress at its best and at its worst. Its laser-like focus on Kosovo was an inspiration to the unfortunate Albanians there. In dealing with the crisis as a whole, however, the Congress proved incapable of executing consistent and effective foreign policy. Its involvement in Yugoslavia was passionate but sporadic; its efforts often contributed to confusing American policy rather than clarifying it. Even on Kosovo the valuable congressional pressure was finally carried too far, with results opposite to what the lawmakers intended.

Individual members were often driven by ethnic constituents. Representative Joe Dioguardi (Democrat of New York) was himself an Albanian-American who had sounded an early alarm about Milošević's assaults against Albanian rights in Kosovo. Even after he had lost his reelection bid, Dioguardi wielded considerable influence as leader of the Albanian lobby. He worked closely with Representative Tom Lantos (Democrat of California), a Hungarian-American who had made himself a genuine expert on the Balkans. The principal champion of the Kosovo Albanians in the Senate was Senator Robert Dole, whom the Serbs wrongly believed to have Albanian blood. Lantos and Dole peppered the Congress with resolutions condemning Serbian behavior in Kosovo.

The administration opposed the resolutions as the wrong way to deal with an admittedly serious problem. Though I found them marginally useful as a demonstration to the Serbs of how deeply Americans cared about Kosovo, I objected to the Congress using Yugoslavia as a dart board. Accustomed to rubber-stamp parliaments, Serbian nationalists and moderates alike assumed that the administration's strategy had been coordinated with the Congress in a campaign of psychological warfare against Serbia. The resolutions contributed to the rise of anti-Americanism in Serbia, even among those who were uncomfortable with Milošević's aggressive policies in Kosovo.

Senator Dole visited Kosovo in August 1990, in company with Senator Alfonse D'Amato (Republican of New York), who had been vocal on the issue, and other senators. Dole knew there would be strenuous Serbian efforts to manipulate him; he resisted them firmly. In Belgrade Milošević refused to see Dole and fobbed him off on his prime minister, an economist and technocrat named Stanko Radmilović. Radmilović, a high school friend of Croatian presidency member Stipe Mesić and a moderate at least by Serbian standards, clearly didn't relish a confrontation with the American senators. The message he was instructed to deliver was that they shouldn't go to Kosovo—there had been riots there that morning and the Serbian government "could not guarantee their safety."

Dole hit the roof, and Radmilović quickly took cover in his fallback position—they could go, but they would have to be escorted by the Serbian foreign minister, Aleksandar Prlja. This was a bit like inviting the senators to tour a hen-house in the company of a jackal. Prlja was one of the most rabid of the Serb nationalists, and he had an odious personality to boot—a combination of arrogance and condescension toward Westerners, together with obsequiousness and servility toward his Serbian superiors. Dole, who had taken the measure of this courtier, said firmly, "We don't need a chaperon."

The senators were finally allowed to visit Kosovo on their terms, provided they balanced their time between the Albanian dissidents and the Serbian authorities. We were met at the airport in Priština, the capital, by the Serbian gauleiter, Momčilo Trajković, whom foreign journalists had nicknamed "the kid" for his inexperience and ineptitude. As Trajković walked Dole from the tarmac to the car under a canopy of whirring Serbian television cameras, he laid down a barrage of verbiage about the glories of Serbian rule and Albanian freedoms in Kosovo. The game was apparently to get Dole, out of politeness, to voice or nod agreement; even a grunt would probably have sufficed. Dole didn't oblige; he glowered in silence through "the kid's" increasingly frenetic performance.

Dole, D'Amato, and I rode into Priština from the airport in my embassy car. I wondered how Neša, my Serbian driver, felt about driving Serbia's major devil figure into its most sacred precincts; Neša remained typically professional but uncharacteristically subdued. The Serbian police escort sped us into the city at top speed—no dawdling to talk to Albanians. Nevertheless, people ran up to the roadside from the fields and villages to give Dole the Albanian V-sign. News of his visit had spread like wildfire. In the center of the city we found a scene of desolation; the streets were empty except for police in full riot gear. There had indeed been trouble that morning. An Albanian crowd had gathered to greet Dole and had been dispersed violently.

We met Rugova, the Albanian leader, at the oxymoronic Grand Hotel, whose grandeur lay only in its epic seediness. He showed us snapshots of some of the injured; they were badly bloodied but nobody had been killed. Rugova and the heads of other Albanian political parties gave the Dole contingent a sober and impressive account of their tribulations. Dole and company were then ushered next door to be subjected to screaming harangues by a hand-picked group of Serbian extremists. These Balkan harpies began by disputing among themselves over whether they would meet in a room where a picture of Tito was hanging (they wouldn't), then moved into the familiar undocumented catalog of murders, rapes, desecration of graves, and other monstrous acts attributed to Albanians. If their intention was to turn the Americans from hostile adversaries to implacable enemies, they succeeded fully.

As we were leaving, Dole told me he wanted to take a walk to meet some ordinary Albanians. I said I had better check with Rugova. To my surprise, the Albanian was strongly opposed—"The Serbs might use this as a pretext for even worse violence. I think you should go right to the airport." Dole, disappointed, took his advice. I thought of the quality of Rugova's character. A violent incident would surely have been to his political advantage, but he wanted to avoid it because he didn't want people to be hurt.

Members of Congress who followed Yugoslavia greeted the 1990 republican elections with enthusiasm. Their democratic exuberance, however, was innocent of concern about some of the negative consequences of the elections, notably the rise of aggressive nationalism and the weakening of Marković's reform programs. Coming from a populist tradition, the Congress had a tendency to focus on events rather than processes. Democratic elections were good; whether they produced democratic behavior over time was less of a concern. Yugoslavia was too complex to fit into the short attention span of overscheduled politicians. They treated it as if it were Poland, Czechoslovakia, or Hungary: it would merit their support if only communism were swept away, democracy installed, and the brutal dictatorship from the center eliminated.

But the Congress didn't see that Yugoslavia fit none of those stereotypes; that nationalism, not communism, was the problem; and that the first democratic elections, by sweeping nationalists to power, had made the problem worse. Nor did the Congress understand that Yugoslavia, unlike the other communist countries of Eastern Europe, wasn't a dictatorship of the center, that the center was actually too weak for serious reforms.

For the Congress, self-determination was a more important value in Yugoslavia than unity. But in Yugoslavia, a polarized multiethnic country, self-determination for some could only mean no-determination for others. Senator Dole and others came to believe that Kosovo should be independent because the Serbian government was abusing ethnic Albanians who were a majority in Kosovo but a minority in Serbia as a whole. But Kosovo was the heartland of Serbian statehood and culture; the analogy with Israel and Jerusalem was an apt one. The Kosovo issue isn't simple and may have to be settled one day by some form of partition. But members of Congress showed no interest in such complexities when they voted resolution after resolution for Kosovo's independence.

With respect to Croatia, there was a similar lack of attention to the details. A strong and active Croatian lobby in the United States found a willing supporter in Dole, who pressed for Croatia's independence with little regard for the fate of the Serbian minority there or for the war that seemed certain to follow. Even those with good intentions are responsible for the consequences of their actions. In episodic interventions reflecting selective allegiances and antipathies, the Congress made the implementation of a consistent strategy toward Yugoslavia nearly impossible.

The contradictions of trying to conduct a congressional foreign policy by resolutions and amendments culminated in the so-called Nickles Amendment, which was passed in November 1990 and took effect six months later. Don Nickles (Republican of Oklahoma) had been with Dole on the visit to Kosovo in August 1990 and had been understandably appalled by what he had seen. His amendment, which became law over the opposition of the Bush administration, prohibited economic assistance to Yugoslavia unless Serbia ceased its human rights abuses in Kosovo.

The legislation affected only $5 million of assistance; in any case, Secretary Baker invoked his discretionary authority to prevent its taking effect. Nevertheless, the amendment did damage to a rational U.S. policy toward Yugoslavia. As Baker complained, it was aimed at the wrong target. To get at Serbia, it attacked Yugoslavia. Even worse, the only one hurt was Marković, the last hope for a peaceful and democratic solution. Milošević got off scot-free; in fact, he gained, because he could circle his wagons around a brave little Serbia being bullied by the United States.

However well-intentioned, Senator Nickles's foray into foreign policy only complicated the task of seeking a peaceful and democratic outcome to the Yugoslav crisis. To try to head it off, for the first time in my life I telephoned a number of senators, including Dole and Nickles, to explain why it would be counterproductive. A member of Dole's staff told me that, after the senator had gotten off the phone with me, he asked, "Why doesn't that ambassador stop calling senators and do what he's being paid for?"

Several weeks after my heated exchange with Milošević over the Mesić affair, I made another trip to Ljubljana and Zagreb to urge the two republics to pursue their aims through negotiation rather than unilateral action. On June 13 I expressed concern to Tudjman that Croatia's secession would have a "catastrophic" effect. "You could provoke a civil war and even lose Krajina. If you must declare independence, couldn't you at least treat the declaration as the beginning, not the end, of a process of discussions?" Tudjman didn't want to listen. He just wanted to tell me about his recent meeting on the Dalmatian coast with Milošević, where—in Izetbegović's presence!—they had discussed the division of Bosnia between Serbia and Croatia. I did find one sympathetic ear, Stipe Mesić, who said that Croatia and Slovenia may have been moving too fast toward independence.

Mesić was also disturbed by the widening gap between Croatia and its Serbian population. Tudjman wasn't. I told the Croatian president that we recognized Croatian sovereignty over the Krajina but were greatly disturbed by the loyalty oaths, discrimination in employment, and assaults on property that had become features of Croatia's intimidating attitude toward Serbs. I also referred to the now open efforts to build a Croatian army and warned Tudjman that the United States would give no support to the militarization of his republic. Democracy would be the best guarantee of Croatian security, I argued, since it would defuse threats to Croatia from disgruntled Serbs. Tudjman was flushed, irritable, and argumentative. He blamed the Serbs in Croatia for provoking the official reprisals but promised to prosecute those who had violated Serbian rights. He didn't.

With the Slovenian government, which held the key to the breakup of Yugoslavia, I predicted that unilateral acts of secession would lead to violence and instability. I urged Slovenia to seek its future in Yugoslavia; if it decided it must leave, I urged that it do so by negotiation and agreement. I also asked the Slovenes not to withdraw from federal institutions, since this would leave Milošević in full control of them.

President Kučan, the former communist, and Prime Minister Lojže Peterle, a Christian Democrat strongly for separation, made clear that Milošević's efforts to block Mesić and cripple the Yugoslav presidency had killed any hope of reconciliation. How could they take Yugoslavia seriously when Milošević wouldn't even let a Croat assume the presidency by normal rotation? The two Slovenes were adamant that the republic would declare its independence according to its timetable. Otherwise they showed some flexibility. They said that negotiations could continue on a confederal—but not a federal—option for Yugoslavia. Kučan also pledged that Slovenia would take over federal powers gradually and by agreement.

Secretary of State Baker was in Berlin June 19 and 20 for a meeting of the Conference on Security and Cooperation in Europe, an organization comprising the countries of Europe and North America. He decided to throw himself personally into a last-ditch effort to head off the violence that we all expected as an aftermath to the destruction of Yugoslavia. Armed with a statement committing all thirty-six countries to unity, reform, human rights, and a peaceful solution of the crisis, Baker arrived in Belgrade on June 21. During his one-day visit he had nine consecutive meetings with the Albanian leaders from Kosovo, with all six republican leaders, and twice with Yugoslav Prime Minister Marković and Foreign Minister Lončar.

As Margaret Tutwiler, Baker's efficient press spokesperson, hovered protectively to give the secretary space and a few minutes to prepare for each successive encounter, Baker sat by himself and reviewed his briefing material. Listening to him deal with the irascible and complex protagonists of the Yugoslav drama, I felt that I had rarely, if ever, heard a secretary of state make a more skillful or reasonable presentation. Baker's failure was due not to his message but to the fact that the different parts of Yugoslavia were on a collision course.

In an unproductive meeting with Milošević, Baker began by setting a bilateral context: the United States has had friendly relations with Serbia; we don't challenge the unity or integrity of Serbia; there's no economic blockade against Serbia. Then the secretary swung into action. He branded the Serbian leader the main source of the crisis and accused him of propelling his people, his republic, and Yugoslavia toward civil war. The secretary said he had come from Berlin with the proxies of all the European governments. "We reject any claims by Serbia to territory beyond its borders. If you persist, Serbia will be made an outcast, a pariah." Baker also slammed Milošević for stirring up ethnic tensions, repressing Albanian rights in Kosovo, undermining Marković, and blocking Mesić's assumption of the Yugoslav presidency.

Milošević was unyielding and combative. He told Baker, "The Yugoslav crisis didn't begin last week with the Mesić issue. That was only a small detail. The issue is unity. Serbia sees secession as the main threat to Yugoslavia. Mesić was a minor player in Croatia's drive for secession; still, he remains unacceptable to us." Milošević said he liked the Izetbegović-Gligorov plan—"It provides for sovereign republics in a single state"—but he rejected both the name and the substance of a confederal solution for Yugoslavia. He didn't respond to Baker's question on whether he would release his hold on Mesić if Croatia and Slovenia agreed to negotiate seriously about Yugoslavia's future. On Kosovo he reverted to his ridiculous contention that the Albanians there had more rights than any other minority in Europe.

In his meetings with Marković, Baker concentrated on trying to persuade the prime minister to reject military force against Slovenia. Marković's chemistry with the Slovenes had always been bad. The prime minister saw a confederation of the type the Slovenes insisted on as fatal to his economic reform. Nor did he or the Slovenian government show much interest in serious negotiations; each accused the other of bad faith. Marković was therefore in danger of buying in to the JNA's aggressive approach to Slovenia. Baker warned the prime minister that he didn't see the JNA as a stabilizing factor; if it resorted to force, Marković's support in the West would be threatened. "Self-determination cannot be unilateral. It must be pursued by dialogue and peaceful means. But we can only make this argument if there is no use of force."

Marković responded with new flexibility. Softening his previous line, he agreed to accept secession if it were pursued through a democratic process and negotiations between the republics and his government. But he complained bitterly about both Milošević and Tudjman, whom he saw as the primary separatists. He also bemoaned the 1990 elections, which he said had turned democracy on its head: "Democracy has become nothing more than a way to gain power."

With negotiating room from Marković, Baker worked on Tudjman and Kučan. He told them that we saw unity as the best way to preserve human rights and achieve democracy. "If Yugoslavia fragments, who will preserve the rights of minorities? The United States will not recognize unilateral secession, which can only trigger violence and bloodshed. Those who fail to negotiate will be responsible if violence breaks out." The secretary said he realized that the independence declarations would not now be put on hold, but asked if they could be limited to rhetorical statements to allow negotiations to take place. With Tudjman he also made a strong plea for equal rights for the Serbian minority, and he expressed concern about Tudjman's practice of arming members of his political party.

His appeal struck a stone wall. Tudjman said the Croatian decision to leave was already made and would not be changed. He dismissed the Izetbegović-Gligorov plan as a useless hybrid of federal and confederal elements. Tudjman told Baker not to worry about violence. "Fears of civil war are exaggerated by those with no political roots in the Croatian nation, which is one of the oldest nations in Europe. Dogmatic communists and unitarists want to involve the army against Croatia, but the JNA's ideology wouldn't allow it to act against us." As we left the room after the meeting, Baker was shaking his head over Tudjman's extraordinary belief that the JNA wouldn't attack him.

Kučan, who had opposed Slovenian secession as long as he could, was now adamant in support of it. Just to make sure that the supple Slovene president stuck to the script, he was accompanied—and watched, with scowling intensity—by Dimitrij Rupel, the Slovene foreign minister and an ardent secessionist. Baker told the Slovenian president that Yugoslavia was a powder keg; it would take only one match to set it off. "If Slovenia walks away, you will change the balance of forces in favor of Milošević."

Kučan replied that Slovenia wasn't interested in the Izetbegović-Gligorov plan or any other "escapes from real negotiations. The question of secession is not whether, but how." As he had with me the week before, he promised a gradual takeover of Yugoslavia's functions, which included border control and customs collection. Once independence had been declared, Slovenia would be willing to resume negotiations with the rest of Yugoslavia. Kučan said it would be prepared to seek a future community of sovereign Yugoslav nations, along the lines of the European Community. I was struck by this reference to the EC; it showed that by "confederation," a term Kučan had used with me just the week before, the Slovenes were thinking about themselves as a fully independent country rather than as part of a Balkan Switzerland.

The saddest figures in the procession of Baker's interlocutors were Kiro Gligorov and Alija Izetbegović. The presidents of Macedonia and Bosnia-Herzegovina had tried valiantly to bring the Yugoslav republics back together in a confederal framework. Their proposal had only given rise to more bickering. Izetbegović focused on Tudjman's reckless strategy; if Croatia seceded, he told Baker, violence would be unleashed in Bosnia.

Baker was sensitive to the warning. He stressed Bosnia's predicament in his discussions with Milošević and Tudjman, alerting them to the strong U.S. opposition to any conspiracy to carve up Yugoslavia's most ethnically mixed republic. Gligorov also predicted a bloodbath if Croatia and Slovenia seceded. The tragedy of these two sensible men was that they represented weak republics. Like Marković, they lacked the weight to influence events. Only Serbia, Croatia, and Slovenia could determine the fate of Yugoslavia, and each in its own way had set out to destroy it.

Baker neither gave nor implied a green light to Milošević or the army to invade the breakaway republics. But was there a red light? Not as such, because the U.S. government had given no consideration to using force to stop a Serbian-JNA attack on Slovenia or Croatia. Nor at that point had a single member of Congress, as far as I know, advocated the introduction of American military power. Baker did, however, leave a strong political message. Prophetically, he told Prime Minister Marković, "The use of force would be exploited by those who want to break up Yugoslavia and would lose for Yugoslavia the support of most of the international community. I can see no way to prevent Slovenia from taking over the border posts. It might be logical to use the army to prevent this, but it would start an explosion."

Baker told Marković with emphasis, "If you force the United States to choose between unity and democracy, we will always choose democracy." Unfortunately, Milošević and the generals who backed him had lived by force, and they understood it. What they read between the lines of the Baker visit was that the United States had no intention of stopping them by force. It might isolate them and make them pariahs, but that, they concluded, was an acceptable risk.

Baker's message was the right one in the circumstances, but it came too late. If a mistake was made, it was that the secretary of state hadn't come six months earlier, before the action-reaction spiral of nationalist threats had spun out of control. Unfortunately, that was a time that coincided with the massive American preparations for the Gulf War. Even a great power has difficulty in dealing with more than one crisis at a time. By June 1991 Baker was making a last-ditch effort in Belgrade. Even so, it wasn't clear that an earlier visit would have made a difference. The aggressive nationalism emanating like noxious fumes from the leaders of Serbia and Croatia and their extremist advisers, officials, media manipulators, and allies had cast the die for disintegration and violence.

The breakup of Yugoslavia was a classic example of nationalism from the top down. While the peoples of the Balkans have not enjoyed an untroubled history, there is very little to the theory that they have never gotten along and never will. In the Yugoslavia that broke up in 1991, over a fifth of its citizens were members of ethnically mixed families—an unlikely phenomenon if ethnic hatreds were foreordained and immutable. It was primarily the ruthless ambitions of the leaders, manipulating a critical mass of the population through the cynical use of television images, that destroyed the multiethnic experiment of Yugoslavia. During the cold war, when Yugoslavia had been threatened from outside by the Soviet Union, the West had been in a position to help it. The Yugoslavia of 1991 was threatened from inside by its constituent parts, and no outside force could save it.

Shortly before the Slovenian and Croatian independence declarations, the European Community offered the government of Yugoslavia four billion dollars if the country would stay together. The offer was never seriously considered. Nationalist hysteria is not usually susceptible to economic or any other kind of inducements or penalties. If it were, then all the people of the former Yugoslavia, with the possible exception of the Slovenes, would not be worse off today than they were before the misery of war and economic deprivation. American policy had been based on the conviction that, if unity failed, democracy would fail with it. That conviction proved tragically accurate; both unity and democracy were lost.

If it wasn't possible to prevent the breakup of Yugoslavia, was it at least possible to manage that breakup in a way that avoided violence? U.S. efforts to this end proved futile. Our entreaties to

Tudjman to adopt a policy of conciliation rather than militarization and our warnings to Milošević that his aggressive policies
would imperil Serbia's relations with the United States went
equally unheeded. Tudjman, pumped up by Germany and by supporters in the U.S. Congress, dismissed any concerns that the
West might act against him. With Milošević, American threats of
isolation played to the Serbs' historic obsession that the world
had always been against them and they would have to fight alone.
In retrospect, we should have chosen an earlier time to express
our preference for a loosely confederated Yugoslavia; even if we
had, though, I don't think we could have slowed the momentum
toward collapse.

Would more intrusive Western actions have worked? What if
an international conference had been called to bring the extremist
leaders to their senses and get them to compromise on a confederal arrangement mixing unity and sovereignty in acceptable
measures? As it turned out, all the parties were prepared to go to
war to defend their positions; compromise wasn't in their lexicon.
It seems doubtful that a conference, which would have allowed
the leaders to strut their nationalist stuff on a world stage, could
have changed them. Alternatively, what if the West had immediately recognized Croatian and Slovenian independence, as Germany and Austria wanted? There's no evidence that this would
have deterred Milošević and the JNA either—a year later they
moved against Bosnia even as it was being recognized.

Short of a credible threat of force, the United States and its allies lacked decisive leverage. Why, then, wasn't force threatened?
There were two problems. First, in Croatia, where the most se-
vere violence impended, the issues were much less clear-cut than
in Bosnia a year later. In Croatia, unlike Bosnia, Serbs were in
fact being abused. They had a legitimate grievance, even though
the actions they took later to avenge it were abominable. Moreover, the JNA had not yet earned its reputation for brutality. At
the time of Croatia's independence declaration, Tudjman was

complimenting its neutrality and predicting that it wouldn't take him on.

Second—and much more important—there was no consensus for military intervention, either in America or Europe. Herein lies a dilemma that could be called the "paradox of prevention" and that applies to crises everywhere: it's rarely possible to win support for preventive action at a time when the circumstances that unambiguously justify such action have not yet arrived.

Thus the catastrophe waiting to happen did happen. On June 25, 1991, four days after Secretary Baker had left Belgrade, Croatia and Slovenia declared their independence. On June 27 war began in Slovenia, the first of three wars that annihilated Yugoslavia, killed tens of thousands of its citizens, and drove millions more from their homes.

MAELSTROM

The dregs of society . . . rose from the slime to become freedom fighters and national heroes.

The Slovenian and Croatian declarations of independence cast Yugoslavia into a political and constitutional limbo. The country had not yet been destroyed, but it was no longer even minimally capable of functioning as a state. Its presidency, which acted as chief of state and commander in chief, was paralyzed because of Milošević's action to prevent Stipe Mesić from taking his rightful place as president. Ante Marković's government, weak in any case, was further crippled by the defection of some of its Croatian and Slovenian members and staff, including the able Slovenian deputy prime minister Živko Pregl, who returned to their republics.

The JNA, an army without a supreme commander in the country's most serious constitutional crisis ever, was left to make decisions on its own. Its composition was changing in an ominous direction. The chief of staff of the JNA air force, General Antun Tus, an outstanding officer with democratic views, hesitated between the JNA and his native Croatia, finally deciding to return home to become Tudjman's chief of staff. In the lower ranks the

Slovenian and Croatian refusal to supply draftees to the JNA meant that the army was becoming Serbianized from top to bottom, whether it wanted to be or not.

On the other side of the constitutional divide, the Slovenes and Croats, for all the euphoria of independence, failed to secure the recognition of any government. However final they considered their separation, their claims to Yugoslavia's assets would still have to be negotiated with the federal government and the hated Milošević. And, worst of all, their path to genuine independence was challenged by a Yugoslav army that felt tricked, betrayed, and vengeful.

The Slovenes, as usual, had the keenest strategic sense. In order to preempt a JNA reaction, they proclaimed their independence on June 25, a day earlier than expected. While the champagne corks were popping in the Slovenian parliament, Slovenian territorial defense forces and police took over the customs posts on the republic's borders with Italy, Austria, and Hungary; secured the air traffic control towers at Slovenian airports; and raised the newly designed Slovenian flag, with its idyllic symbols of mountains and sea, at the border posts.

At various times in the ten days before June 25, the Slovenes had assured Marković, Baker, and me that the takeover of the sovereign functions performed by the federation would be gradual. They had specifically agreed with Marković just a few days before their secession that federal authority over customs would remain intact. With Baker, Kučan had been ambiguous in his discussion of the crucial issue of the customs; he had omitted the word "gradually" in asserting that Slovenia would take them over. As late as June 24, Drnovšek, who as a pro-Yugoslav Slovene wasn't trusted by the radicals in Ljubljana, told me that he didn't expect any early move on the customs posts. Now in a lightning maneuver the Slovenes had in a few hours moved the borders of Yugoslavia, stable for half a century, a hundred miles to the east. It was the first act of war.

Nobody was surprised at the declarations of independence by Slovenia and Croatia. But everybody was surprised at the audacity with which the Slovenes moved to transform their independence from the rhetorical to the real. Even an army less primitive than the JNA would have reacted to a power play that annexed both the borders of Yugoslavia and its customs revenues—a major source of funding for the army. Ante Marković, feeling double-crossed by the Slovenes and pressured by the JNA, signed a resolution authorizing the JNA to "protect the state border, both at border crossings, as well as in the regions in the border zone." The resolution implicitly condoned force by obliging the JNA to give "assistance" in case of resistance.

Fighting began June 27. The JNA recaptured most of the border posts and, with typical overzealotry, attacked the Ljubljana airport on the grounds that it was a "border." The Yugoslav generals, stuffed with overconfidence and faulty intelligence, thought they could intimidate the Slovene leaders and win over the Slovene people. Their tanks roared through peaceful Slovenian streets, slapping aside compact cars as they lumbered along. They hurled threats of air attacks, expecting the Slovenian government to capitulate.

There was a unique Yugoslav aspect to the war in Slovenia and the war that followed in Croatia. It wasn't accurate to talk about a JNA "invasion," since the JNA was in its own country. Its troops were, quite normally, stationed in camps in every Yugoslav republic. After Slovenia and Croatia declared independence, however, those troops were seen as occupiers, even if they never stirred from their garrisons. The not very heroic Slovenian (and later Croatian) tactic was not to take on the JNA directly, but to lay siege to JNA barracks and try to starve the soldiers out.

This anomalous aspect of the JNA's role—one day a defender, the next day an occupier—had a wrenching psychological effect on ordinary people caught in between. Those in ethnically mixed marriages, those who felt a strong allegiance to Yugoslavia had suddenly lost their country. The sudden onset of human tragedy led almost overnight to the creation of Vesna Pešić's Belgrade peace movement, to mothers demonstrating in front of the Serbian parliament to keep their sons from going to war, to a strikingly high rate of evasion of the JNA's call-ups, and to a mass exodus abroad of draft-age men.

In Slovenia, the local forces, trained by the JNA itself in territorial defense, refused to bend to what the generals thought would be an easy intimidation campaign. The JNA was stalemated, and after ten days of minimal fighting and maximal propaganda on both sides, it began a withdrawal from Slovenia. The republic was effectively independent.

A week later I went to Ljubljana to find the Slovenes bursting to describe their amazing victory. The most revealing talk was with Janez Janša, the ascetic, driven, thirty-two-year-old defense minister. As a journalist three years before, Janša had been imprisoned by the JNA for possessing a classified document. He told me that he had relished every minute of his revenge, including his frequent defiant telephone conversations with JNA commanders during the ten-day war. "It was fantastic," he said. "The JNA had trained our territorial defense forces. Every year they would send their top officers from Belgrade to grade us. They knew exactly what we were capable of. To fall into a trap—not only a trap they knew about but one they had actually helped to create—was the height of arrogance and irresponsibility."

Every Slovene I talked with had the same message: Slovenia was no longer interested in a Yugoslav confederation, no matter how loose. Separation had to be complete. Slovenia's independence had been sealed in blood; there was no turning back. Janša's war had alienated Slovenia permanently from Yugoslavia. The cost to the Slovenes was nine killed; the JNA lost thirty-seven. The meager casualty figures don't bear out the generally held assumption that the Yugoslav army waged an extermination campaign in Slovenia. Nor does the fact that the JNA committed only two thousand soldiers against a Slovene force of thirty-five thousand men whom the army, in its pride and error, didn't expect to stand up to it.

In ten days Janša and his small band of trusted comrades won the support of the world's television viewers and consolidated their entire population behind independence. They made brilliant use of psychological warfare—blowing off air raid sirens even when there was no threat, shooting down an unarmed JNA helicopter carrying only bread and then charging it with aggressive intent, comparing the JNA's limited actions (about which the army had actually informed the Slovenes in advance) with the Soviet Union's 1968 invasion of Czechoslovakia. Unlike the JNA, paranoid about the West, the Slovenes welcomed foreign journalists, to whom they retailed the epic struggle of their tiny republic against the Yugoslav colossus. It was the most brilliant public relations coup in the history of Yugoslavia.

Slovenia's triumph was an extraordinary story. The most extreme faction in a coalition that had itself won only 54 percent of the popular vote had devised a strategy for independence, carried it through against serious initial opposition, provoked a war by stealth without even informing key Slovene leaders, and outwitted one of the largest armies in Europe. To complete their victory, the Slovenes got support from an unusual source—Slobodan Milošević. There's little possibility that they could have prevailed militarily had the JNA counterattacked with major reinforcements. It didn't, because Milošević made a deal with Milan Kučan providing for the JNA's withdrawal from Slovenia.

For Milošević it was the achievement of an objective he had set in 1989 when he first began to hound the Slovenes. He couldn't tolerate their liberal, independent ways, nor their merciless criticism of Serbian policy in Kosovo. "Milošević said to me several times after our elections that Slovenia was free to leave Yugoslavia," Kučan later told me, "but he always added that Croatia, with its Serbian minority, must never leave."

Slovenes and others have argued that Slovenia had the same right of self-determination as the people of the German Democratic Republic, when they chose to join the Federal Republic. This, indeed, may have been the key factor in German Foreign Minister Hans-Dietrich Genscher's tenacious decision to rush the independence of Slovenia and Croatia. But the cases aren't similar. The East Germans were subjected involuntarily to a dictatorship. The Slovenes were an original party to the voluntary compact creating Yugoslavia. Moreover, in choosing their future, the East Germans did no damage to anybody else. The Slovenes knew that their departure would bring a firestorm of violence down on the rest of Yugoslavia.

With Slovenia out of the game, Milošević and the JNA were now free to take on a Croatia no longer buttressed by Slovenia's support. In Croatia the unimaginative Tudjman translated this new polarization into a heightened determination to stand up to the army's pressure. The Slovenian defection had set in motion the dynamics of a Serb-Croat confrontation that was also to lead to war in Bosnia. There was much to admire in democratic Slovenia's single-minded drive for independence from an increasingly inhospitable Yugoslavia. In their self-absorption, however, the Slovenes had left the twenty-two million Yugoslav citizens they had abandoned twisting in the wind of impending war.

The hectic days of late June and early July 1991 marked a turning point in another sense. Until then the crisis in Yugoslavia had moved according to an internal rhythm. Outside forces like the United States and the European Community had tried to arrest the momentum of Yugoslavia's breakup, but their efforts were overwhelmed by the force of the domestic nationalisms. None of the various Yugoslav parties—except Tudjman, who yearned for Western military support—wanted an internationalization of the crisis. Each saw outside influence as a potential impediment to the realization of its goals. Even Prime Minister Marković, for whom international support was a final if flickering hope, wasn't too sure about calling in the world; he expressed his doubts to Secretary Baker on June 21.

After June 25 everything changed. The European Community, sparked by the irrepressible Italian Foreign Minister Gianni De Michelis and by a Dutch government scheduled on July 1 to take over the presidency of the Community for the next six months, launched itself like a rocket into the Yugoslav crisis.

Until then Europe hadn't been famous for its attentiveness to Yugoslavia's problems. American efforts since 1989 to convince the Europeans that trouble was brewing had failed to shake them out of their torpor on the issue. The polarizing events of the spring of 1991 finally brought the Community to see that its interests were indeed engaged. Yugoslavia shared a border with two of its members, Italy and Greece; in fact, its landmass joined Greece to Western Europe. It also formed the overland route between Europe and the Middle East.

The darkening prospect of the first major fighting in Europe since 1945 finally focused Europe's concern. The Community was just beginning to develop a capability for foreign policy coordination—what better place to test it than Yugoslavia? Such arguments met no resistance from the United States. Baker, rebuffed by Slovenia and Croatia, was all too willing to transfer the problem in all its intractability to the Europeans. The dying Yugoslavia thus became the patient of a confident European Community. "The age of Europe has dawned," proclaimed Luxembourg Foreign Minister Jacques Poos in a burst of bravado he was soon to regret.

The European Community leapt into the accelerating maelstrom with a pedagogical rather than a political approach. Without much understanding of the nationalist forces at play, the Europeans lectured the Yugoslavs as if they were all unruly schoolchildren whose naughtiness would deprive them of the sweets only Europe could provide. The dynamic Dutch foreign minister, Hans van den Broek, threw all the resources of his small and overtaxed government into the crisis. His prescription was radical: shock treatment for the bickering Yugoslavs.

On the night of June 30 occurred one of the weirder diplomatic encounters in recent European history. The foreign ministers of the past, present, and future EC presidents—De Michelis of Italy, Poos of Luxembourg, and van den Broek of the Netherlands—assembled in Belgrade and won the permission of the Yugoslav presidency to attend its session. Shaking their collective finger, they demanded that the Croat Stipe Mesić be seated as president—a concession that Milošević, in the process of getting Slovenia out of Yugoslavia, was finally ready to make.

As midnight approached, the EC "troika"—the three foreign ministers—performed the ceremony of transferring EC presidential authority from Luxembourg to the Netherlands. Never before had this solemn biannual act been carried out, or even imagined, at a sitting session of an outside country's highest governmental body. As Poos handed the gavel—he had actually brought one—to van den Broek, the "troika" expounded to the members of the Yugoslav presidency on the goodwill, cooperation, and trust required for a democratic exchange of power.

Counseled, cajoled, and threatened by these European newcomers at a meeting of its highest institution, Yugoslavia had embarked on the final indignities of its demise. As soon as the three ministers had left, Borisav Jović, the Serbian member of the presidency, once again demonstrated his infallible instinct for the petty. He moved for a resolution to condemn Slovenia and Croatia, an act that provoked the Croat Mesić, newly installed as president, to abruptly end the meeting. Yugoslavia's last days were being played as farce.

The European Community's blitzkrieg diplomacy did win some transitory successes. At another Yugoslav presidency meeting on July 7, the Community achieved a three-month moratorium on the implementation of Slovenian and Croatian declarations of independence. In the event, neither Ljubljana nor Zagreb slowed their plans for independence, and fighting broke out in Croatia long before the moratorium expired. Unfortunately, the Community's takeover bid for influence over Yugoslavia's institutions claimed an unintended casualty—Ante Marković. The prime minister, the last vestige of the unity the Community claimed to be trying to preserve, was thoughtlessly left outside the widening perimeter of its attempts to turn Yugoslavia into a political protectorate. Thenceforth he was rarely turned to and rarely included.

As the Community was busy expanding its influence, I ran into Slobodan Milošević on July 12 at a ceremony for the decoration of Serbian veterans of World War I. It was fascinating to see these ancient soldiers, some of them over a hundred years old, in their flowing white mustaches and old-fashioned puttees. This was the sort of diplomatic experience that made it exhilarating to serve in the Balkans. These veterans had done their military service before there had been a Yugoslavia, and they were still around to see it out. But Milošević gave them no more than the minimum time required. He really wanted to talk to Peter Hall, the British ambassador, and me.

Resplendent in a new Palm Beach suit, Milošević was burbling with triumph. The self-styled apostle of a unified Yugoslavia showed zero remorse at its collapse. "Serbia will present no obstacles to Slovenia's departure," he said. Not missing the chance to stick a needle into his nemesis, he added, "Marković behaved stupidly with his halfway measures toward Slovenia. He should have put 100,000 troops into Slovenia or he should have put no troops there. We would have favored no troops. Slovenia isn't worth the life of a single Serbian soldier."

Peter and I asked Milošević about the future of Yugoslavia. "Who cares if it breaks up?" he answered. "Serbia and Montenegro will exist as a federal state and as Yugoslavia's legal heir. We would be happy to consider confederation with others. Serbia has always been an oasis of friendly ethnic feeling. We've had only one aggressive war in our history—against Bulgaria in the nineteenth century." Milošević's mental agility was astonishing. He had consistently worked against Yugoslavia and just a moment before had ridiculed its prime minister. Yet now he had the audacity to claim it as his own.

As the Serbian leader warmed to his subject, a few thorns began to appear in the bouquet he was arranging for Peter's and my benefit. He was contemptuous of feeble Macedonia: "A nonentity, a detail, so insignificant that we don't even need to worry about it. It will disintegrate. The Macedonian nationalists will gravitate toward Bulgaria, Macedonia's Albanians will join Albania, and the rest of the Macedonians can stew in their own juices."

He called President Izetbegović of Bosnia-Herzegovina a "Muslim fanatic" and said Serbia wouldn't mind if the Croats living in Herzegovina joined Croatia. He made no complaint about the treatment of the Serbian minority living in Bosnia, which constituted about a third of the population of the republic, and lodged no claims on its behalf. He reminded me that he had told Baker, "Serbia doesn't covet a single hectare of territory outside Serbia." But he did reject the legality of the current borders: "They're artificial, administrative, illegal, and therefore subject to change."

Turning to Croatia, Milošević dismissed Tudjman, with whom he had recently been in secret talks, as a fascist. "He's arming his own party; nobody has done that since Hitler. You Americans and British totally misunderstand the nature of Tudjman's regime, because you're obsessed with black and white distinctions between 'communists' and 'democrats.' For you Milošević is bad, and Marković and Tudjman are good."

The next day, July 13, I was in General Kadijević's office with an instruction from Washington urging the JNA's neutrality in the war just beginning in Croatia and expressing concern about the increasing Serbianization of the army. In its public statements the State Department had been as critical of the JNA for its aggressive behavior as of the Croats and Slovenes for their unilateral declarations of independence. On June 27 Baker had called on the central government and army to exercise restraint and on June 30 and again on July 2 the State Department had criticized the JNA for its threats against Slovenia. In a meeting with van den Broek on July 3, Baker had again criticized the army. In his memoirs, Janez Drnovšek credits American pressure with diverting a JNA tank column from moving on Slovenia. Thus I was not expecting a particularly friendly reception from Kadijević, whose temper was unimproved by the JNA's recent humiliation in Slovenia. But I wasn't ready for the barrage I got.

His eyebrows bristling, Kadijević accused the United States of a double standard in ignoring the "separatist" military buildup in Croatia. He blamed me personally for misinforming my government about the "true situation in Yugoslavia." He claimed that there were 200,000 new paramilitary troops in Yugoslavia, half of them in Croatia; the Croatian army was bigger than many armies of recognized European states. While Kadijević exaggerated somewhat, Croatia's police and militia probably did add up to an army larger than the armies of Belgium, Canada, the Netherlands, Portugal, Austria, or Sweden, all of which had larger populations than Croatia.

While the "separatists" were gaining troops, he said, the JNA was losing them. It had suffered a shortfall of ninety-five thousand, mainly because Croatia and Slovenia wouldn't send conscripts to a Yugoslav army. "If that's Serbianization," he snarled, "then it's not the JNA that's guilty of it." Kadijević argued—correctly—that the JNA had always sought presidential authority for its actions and—incorrectly—that the army had never threatened Croatia. Cutting short this unpleasant meeting because of his personal attack on me, I left with the growing certainty that all-out war impended in Croatia.

The fighting, sporadic during the spring of 1991, spread and intensified following Tudjman's precipitate declaration of independence. The Croatian leader had done virtually nothing to prepare for separation; in their bilateral talks before June 25, the meticu-

lous Slovenes were flabbergasted at the Croats' lack of organization. Tudjman had made not the least effort, for example, to as-
sure Croatia's Serbian citizens that they would be safe in an
independent Croatia. Given the past year's record of discrimination against Serbs in Croatia, the issue wasn't academic, and
Tudjman's omission wasn't an oversight.

With the increased spilling of blood, the hot-heads among the
Serbs in Krajina and Eastern Slavonia, sites of the greatest Serbian population concentration, were increasingly calling the
shots. They had already held "democratic" referenda to produce
the predetermined result that Serbs in these areas were unwilling
to accept the authority of the Croatian government. Now, with
guidance from Belgrade and military assistance from Serbian
paramilitaries and the JNA itself, they were intent on sealing off
their territory from Tudjman's police and army.

The war in Croatia was a throwback to the ancient bandit traditions of the Balkans. The dregs of society—embezzlers, thugs,
even professional killers—rose from the slime to become freedom fighters and national heroes, exalted by their respective propaganda machines. In the inverted pyramid of war, the last
became first, and villains became heroes. The Serbian side had a
cosmopolitan flavor, with Captain Dragan, a Serbian soldier of
fortune rumored to be an ex-convict from Australia; Vojislav
Šešelj, a Bosnian intellectual with a fascist mentality; and Arkan,
aka Željko Ražnjatović, who, though a home-grown hood,
boasted a police record in several Western European countries.

Arkan's penchant for the indiscriminate murder of non-Serbs
was matched on the Croatian side by the exploits of Branimir
Glavaš, whose specialty was cleaning out Serbian villages and
executing Serbian civilians and Croatian policemen who had
been friendly with them. Glavaš, a philosopher of ethnic cleansing, was quoted as saying that he saw justice in the prospect that
if his city of Osijek fell to the Serbs, all the Croats would be
killed, whereas if it fell to the Croats, all the Serbs would be

killed. These paragons of the martial arts, and others like them, were paid, protected, and sometimes publicly praised by their respective patrons, Milošević and Tudjman.

The Yugoslav army was in a difficult position, in fact was probably split, over the grisly issues of the Croatian war. Even Tudjman and Mesić had admitted that the JNA's record in Croatia since May hadn't been bad. For all his hatred of Tudjman, Kadijević was probably less extreme than Adžić and certainly less extreme than the group of young colonels who were turning the JNA into a Serbian army. Even after the war had been raging for two months, Tudjman told me that "Kadijević is still a communist, but he's somebody I can deal with." In July the JNA proclaimed the evenhanded mission of interposing itself between the combatants. As the summer wore on, this profession of neutrality became increasingly specious. In the guise of pacifying villages, the JNA began to turn them over to Serbs. The war in Croatia was becoming incrementally a war of aggression.

Meanwhile, the Yugoslav political leaders continued their practice of making magical mystery tours around the fractured country, meeting every few weeks in a different republic, one week Bosnia, another Macedonia, a third Serbia. The indefatigable Tupurkovski, who lost seventy pounds to dieting and nerves, shuttled everywhere to find a pinch of agreement. Compromise seemed close on July 22—"fifteen minutes away," Tupurkovski told me—at a summit meeting on Lake Ohrid in Macedonia. But Tudjman got word of an outbreak of fighting in Eastern Slavonia and scurried away. The formal pictures of the six republican presidents, standing together uncomfortably for their photo opportunity on the terrace of some resort hotel or other, portrayed a search for solutions that never really existed. Both Tudjman and Milošević were engaged in a "talk-fight" strategy. The Tweedledum and Tweedledee of destructive nationalism had chosen to pursue their competitive denouements on the field of battle, not at the negotiating table.

The war enabled Tudjman to turn Croatia into what he had all along wanted it to be—a national security state. His cabinet was dominated by people whose inclinations and expertise were in clandestine and military affairs. His prime minister, Josip Manolić, had been chief of the Croatian secret police in the communist days. His defense minister, Gojko Šušak, a pizza millionaire from Canada, came from a family with Ustaše connections and made no secret of his anti-Serbian and anti-Semitic views. Tudjman's chief military adviser, Martin Špegelj, was the former JNA general who in early 1991 had urged war with the JNA. In visiting Tudjman I noticed a new emphasis on military ostentation. There was now a republican guard outside his palace—giant soldiers fitted out in splendid red uniforms designed by the president himself. If the guard was changed while we were meeting, Tudjman would fall silent until the drums and the bugles had ceased.

In late August Tudjman told me of his plans to launch a "war option"—an all-out offensive against the JNA and the "Četnik separatists." I agreed with him that the JNA was not acting in a neutral fashion but asked how he could possibly hope to take it on with his neophyte army. "Oh," he said offhandedly, "your country will come to my rescue with military force." I told him there wasn't a speck of credibility in this assertion and urged him not to base any military calculations on an American bailout. I failed to puncture Tudjman's serenity. "Perhaps I know more about your country than you do, Mr. Ambassador," he said with a smile.

Shaking my head about his informants on American politics, I tried another tack. "Why don't you try to end the Serbian resistance by offering them autonomy within Croatia? In effect they have it anyway, protected by the JNA. A magnanimous gesture on your part might help provide the missing element of trust, and it would be popular in the West." Tudjman showed no interest in the idea. Nor did he want to discuss a proposal that his own ministers had been peddling—an "association of Yugoslav states." The proposal, in which the U.S. government had shown some interest, limited the central government to token powers; defense and foreign policy would be the province of the individual states. Thus the "association" would look more like the twelve-state European Community than Switzerland—not, in other words, a big concession for Croatia to make. Tudjman's only reference to it was his parting shot: "If this war goes on, don't mention any Yugoslav association to me."

The war did go on. In late September the United Nations Security Council slapped an arms embargo on all of Yugoslavia. The motivation for this action was not to put the Bosnian Muslims at a disadvantage, although that became the unintended result after the Bosnian war began half a year later. In fact, one of the sponsors of the Security Council resolution was Austria, a steadfast supporter of the Muslim-led government in Bosnia. The context of the arms embargo was the war in Croatia, which had confirmed the view of most Western governments that there were too many weapons in the Balkans and that something had to be done to stem the flow. The reigning philosophy was disarmament, not competitive arming. While Bosnia's fragility was well understood by September 1991, I don't recall any assertions in Washington or among my diplomatic colleagues that the embargo was an anti-Bosnian act. Bosnia just hadn't come up sharply enough on our radar screens.

During the first week in October 1991 an event happened that was to become a model for the manipulation of war for the purpose of building hatreds and prejudices. A bomb destroyed part of the presidential palace in Zagreb. Tudjman was in the palace at the time, meeting, as it turned out, with Prime Minister Marković. The obvious conclusion was that the palace had been bombed by a JNA plane. Tudjman even told me he knew the name of the pilot. After some hesitation, however, the controlled Serbian press came to a strikingly different conclusion: Tudjman himself had ordered the palace bombed, so that he could blame the army and the Serbs for it. I had my own reasons for knowing this accusation to be false. Tudjman had shown me around the palace several times. He told me he had personally selected every piece of furniture, every curtain, every painting. For him the palace was a symbol of the grandeur of his rule; it was his Versailles. It was absurd to imagine that he would have tried to damage his beloved creation.

Yet, echoing the Serbian press and television, virtually every Serbian official and many ordinary citizens claimed, and even seemed to believe, that Tudjman had committed an act of self-destruction. The tactic worked so well that the Serbs used it over and over again. It reached its apotheosis in the Bosnian war, where, according to the Serbian press, the shelling in May 1992 of a bread line in Sarajevo, killing seventeen Bosnians, was the work of the Bosnians themselves. So was the mortar attack on the Sarajevo market in February 1994, when sixty-eight Bosnian civilians were killed. And so was the second mortaring of the market in August 1995, which killed thirty-eight people. The doctors of demonology in the Serbian high command got a double payback for their grotesque distortions. Not only did they transfer the blame from themselves; they also persuaded their audience that their enemies were so inhumane that they could murder their own people in cold blood.

During the late summer and early autumn of 1991 the JNA made a fateful transition from securing territory for Serbs to targeting civilian populations. It began to shell two Croatian cities, Vukovar and Dubrovnik. The pretty Croatian city of Vukovar, with a mixed population, of which a third was Serbian, came under JNA shelling in August, apparently because of its strategic location on the Danube River between Serbia and Croatia. For three months the army, shrinking from a direct attack that might have cost it casualties, surrounded the city and shelled it to pieces. The civilian population of the city—Serbs and Croats alike—huddled in cellars.

A month into the siege I asked Kadijević what the JNA's military objective was in Vukovar; he brushed off the question as if it weren't worthy of his attention. Hundreds of civilians were killed in the shelling before the JNA finally "liberated" the city. In addition, 261 non-Serbs were removed from the Vukovar hospital and murdered. Three JNA officers were indicted in 1995 by the United Nations war crimes tribunal for those murders.

One of the employees in our embassy residence, a young Croatian woman named Danijela Hajnal, was from Vukovar. Her father was killed in the JNA shelling of Vukovar, and her mother was trapped in a cellar during the siege. During her stay with Teeny and me after Vukovar fell, Danijela's mother described the relations between Serbs and Croats during the attack. "There were a hundred people in that cellar," she said. "Half of us were Croats and half Serbs. We were all friends when we went into the cellar, and three months later when we came out, we were still friends." About the same time I asked Danijela how many Serbs and Croats were in her high school class in Vukovar. She replied that she didn't have the faintest idea. These stories, which could be multiplied thousands of times over, show how natural it was for Yugoslavs to get along with each other, despite the rantings of their leaders.

Notwithstanding solemn guarantees by General Kadijević, the JNA in October shelled Dubrovnik from the hills and sea. This medieval town, which glowed in the Adriatic like a piece of pink marble, had employed its famous diplomatic finesse to deter the threats of Turks, Venetians, and many other would-be predators. Now it was coming under the guns of an army whose constitutional duty was to defend it. Dubrovnik wasn't destroyed, but the damage inflicted by the Yugoslav army exceeded the best efforts of any previous marauder.

Only Milošević pretended that there was any military objective in Dubrovnik. He told me with a straight face that foreign mercenaries were holed up in this city that had known nothing but tourists for decades. General Kadijević didn't even pretend that Dubrovnik was a military target. "I give you my word," he told me, "that the shelling of Dubrovnik was unauthorized. Those who did it will be punished." My repeated requests for the details of their punishment went unanswered.

In this indecent combat, both sides resorted to tactics that breached the rules of war. Both, for example, routinely placed heavy weaponry close to civilian hospitals. But shelling civilian populations is an especially shameful and cowardly act for a professional army. It is also a war crime. The JNA's attacks on Vukovar and Dubrovnik—the first major war crimes in Yugoslavia since World War II—led directly to the merciless aggression against Sarajevo and other Bosnian cities.

No Western government at the time called on NATO's military force to get the JNA to stop shelling Dubrovnik, although NATO's supreme commander, General John Galvin, had prepared contingency plans for doing so. The use of force was simply too big a step to consider in late 1991, and I don't believe Washington did consider it. I didn't recommend it myself; I should have. The JNA's artillery on the hills surrounding Dubrovnik and the small craft on the water would have been easy targets. Not only would damage to the city have been averted, but the Serbs would have been taught a lesson about Western resolve that might have deterred at least some of their aggression against Bosnia. As it was, the Serbs learned a different lesson—that there was no Western resolve, and that they could push about as far as their power could take them.

As the fighting in Croatia grew more bitter, the European Community stepped up its efforts. In late summer it organized and led a team of monitors to keep track of the military situation in Croatia. These unarmed volunteers were often ridiculed because their white uniforms made them look like ice cream vendors. Their record wasn't flawless; they were occasionally guilty of timidity—they were among the first to flee Dubrovnik when it came under attack—and of a pro-Croatian bias. For the most part, however, they behaved bravely and undoubtedly saved lives by their presence. The risks they ran were real: four were eventually killed when their helicopter was shot down by a JNA fighter. They were the first, and not the worst, peacekeeping force on Yugoslav territory.

The European Community also threw into the Croatian war a remarkable Dutch diplomat, Henri Wejnaendts, who exchanged the comforts of Paris, where he was Dutch ambassador, for the risks of shuttling around Croatia trying to set up cease-fire zones. Wejnaendts's helicopter was hit by rifle fire several times, but nothing could keep him on the ground. His courage was exceptional. Wejnaendts and the EC monitors exposed the JNA's pro-Serb aggressiveness, provoking Kadijević, in his mean-spirited memoirs, to charge that the Community was working through Marković to take over control of the JNA.

The Community combined efforts with the United Nations to achieve a cease-fire and an agreement among all the Yugoslav republics. Lord Peter Carrington and Cyrus Vance, old friends and former foreign ministers of the United Kingdom and the United States, respectively, took on the Sisyphean task of achieving a peaceful outcome. Vance's job was to negotiate a cease-fire in Croatia, which could then be followed up by the arrival of UN peacekeepers. His stock-in-trade, other than his incredible energy and determination (at seventy-four he visited Yugoslavia seven times in three months), was winning the trust of all sides.

Vance created some suspicion at the working levels of the State Department when he insisted on treating the JNA with the same degree of respect that he gave the Croatian government. He had a point. Despite its depredations, the Yugoslav army remained a proud institution that the Croats were trying to humiliate. They blockaded JNA troops in their barracks, taunted the officers' wives (many of them Croatian women) on the streets of Croatian cities, and on one occasion sent in dog food when the JNA garrison commander reported that his men were starving. Vance had served in senior positions in the U.S. Department of Defense; he told me he was appalled at this shabby treatment of professional soldiers. Vance's doggedness, his personal stature, and the fact that he represented both the United Nations and (indirectly) the United States made him an effective negotiator in Croatia. But it took a change in the military situation to bring agreement within reach.

The fall of Vukovar persuaded the Croats that they weren't going to duplicate the Slovenes' success with the JNA. When I commiserated with General Tus, the Croatian chief of staff, after that defeat, he lowered his head to his map table and kept it there for several seconds. By late autumn the JNA had secured all areas in Croatia that had significant Serbian populations. The army's last worry was its military hostages blockaded in their garrisons—30,000 officers, men, and family members, according to General Kadijević. Kadijević kept telling me that the JNA was ready to give up its "internal security role" in Croatia if only the Croats would release the hostages and extend self-determination to Croatia's Serbian population. In other words, the army, undoubtedly at Milošević's bidding, was no longer even making a pretense of keeping Croatia in Yugoslavia. Its interest shifted to insulating the Serbs in Croatia from Tudjman's authority. Milošević's policy had now become, on the ground as well as in principle, a policy of "Greater Serbia."

Vance closed the deal on January 2, 1992, with a cease-fire signed by the Croatian government and the JNA. Ironically, Sarajevo was chosen for the signing because it was peaceful and neutral. The JNA, unblockaded, would leave Croatia, as it had left Slovenia. UN peacekeepers would be stationed in the Serbian-held areas. Milošević assured Vance that he would take care of Milan Babić, the rabidly nationalistic Serbian boss in the Krajina, who opposed any UN involvement. The Serbian president was as good as his vindictive word. Babić was reduced, as General Adžić put it to me, to a "sheriff."

Milošević's cold-blooded breaking of Babić's political power advertised the primacy of opportunism over nationalism in the Serbian president's makeup. It also presaged a pattern for Milošević's later treatment of other Serbian politicians, however nationalistic, who had the temerity to challenge the maximum leader. The psychopathic warlord Vojislav Šešelj and the Bosnian Serb leader Radovan Karadžić were later to feel the wrath of a man who tolerated no rivals and who was as adept at discarding as at coopting human material.

Peace in Croatia had been bought but at the price of freezing a status quo in which the Serbs were left holding over a quarter of the republic. The freeze was stabilized by the UN peacekeepers who arrived in March 1992. But the stability was precarious. Tudjman wasn't going to tolerate forever the de facto alienation of a large chunk of his territory. Moreover, in vacating Slovenia and Croatia, the JNA moved many of its troops to Bosnia, including a newly promoted general named Ratko Mladić, who had distinguished himself by his ruthlessness as JNA commander in the Krajina.

Carrington had a more comprehensive job than Vance. He had to get the feuding Yugoslav republics to define the relationship they were prepared to have with one another. His instrument was a semipermanent conference that he convened at The Hague, the Dutch capital. Carrington assumed that independence for all would be the eventual outcome. The agenda he presented at The Hague on October 4, 1991, treated Yugoslavia as no longer existing—a tactical mistake since it played to the Slovenes, who were mentally out of Yugoslavia already and wouldn't have agreed to even the loosest form of association. Carrington's agenda also failed to push the Croats very far. And it may have led the Macedonians and Bosnians, who maintained a strong stake in Yugoslavia, toward the conclusion that independence was the only option the Europeans were going to leave them.

There was no democratic center in Carrington's approach, nothing to bring the republics together. Marković was ignored, and no role was given to the small antinationalist parties in each republic, whose focus on individual rather than collective rights made them the most democratic parties in Yugoslavia. To his credit, Carrington did put great emphasis on the rights of minorities. And he certainly wasn't taken in by Milošević, whose first name he shortened from Slobodan to "Slob" when debriefing allied ambassadors.

Milošević was suspicious of Carrington as a representative of the untrustworthy European Community. He took some persuading to join The Hague conference at all. As he had signaled to the British ambassador and me in July, his aim was to make Serbia the successor and heir of Yugoslavia. His goal at The Hague was to win international recognition for his new "Yugoslavia." The task was difficult. For Croatia and Slovenia, Yugoslavia was already dead; all that was left was to divide its assets. For Carrington, it was in a "state of dissolution" leading to independence for all the republics. Milošević needed to convince the international community that "Yugoslavia" was more than the squalid satrapy of a Serbian dictator.

Milošević's slogan for the times was "Yugoslavia exists." He had his eye on the rest of Yugoslavia's financial assets, having already absconded with as much of them as he could. The embezzled funds usually found their way to Cyprus, which suddenly became home to a thriving community of secretive and wealthy Serbs. Milošević also wanted to maintain Yugoslavia as a sovereign entity. He had hopes of persuading Bosnia and Macedonia to remain under the shrinking Yugoslav tent, along with Serbia and docile Montenegro. Failing that, he wanted to preserve a legal framework for those Serbs in Croatia, Bosnia, and perhaps even Macedonia who "chose to remain in Yugoslavia."

Seizing on his now total control of the Yugoslav presidency, Milošević installed as "president" one of the more obtuse leaders of the Montenegrin communist party, Branko Kostić. Milošević, with his aversion to potential rivals, had a habit of slotting the least, rather than the most, qualified people into senior positions. Kostić fit this pattern perfectly—he parroted the Serbian line in international meetings in bull-headed fashion. He once publicly warned that Serbs would never succumb to U.S. pressure but would rather "eat roots"—a nutriment that Kostić's ample dimensions suggested he had not yet tried. Lord Carrington finally got so sick of Kostić that he kicked him out of The Hague conference.

I had my last extended conversation with Ante Marković on October 12, 1991. It was sad. He was sitting by himself in his vast office, with a lone secretary outside—no aides bustling about, no phones ringing, no sense of energy or dynamism. The man who had worked so hard to make things happen now seemed out of touch. A few weeks before, he had lost a showdown with the JNA, unsuccessfully demanding Kadijević's and Adžić's resignations for their blatant partiality toward the Serbian side in Croatia. He was desperately trying to secure a role for himself at The Hague conference, from which he'd been excluded.

The bravado of Marković's early days in power had turned to bluster. He told me that only he could broker an agreement at The Hague meeting and that he had a plan for keeping the Slovenes in Yugoslavia. He claimed that the JNA bomb exploded on the Croatian presidential palace was intended for him, not Tudjman. I thought of King Lear, his achievements behind him, weaving deathbed fantasies and prattling of "gilded butterflies." Marković's butterflies, now dipping and soaring out of reach, were economic reform, the rule of law, and ethnic tolerance.

Marković's government was falling apart. Most of the Slovenian and Croatian ministers had returned home. The defense minister, General Kadijević, and the interior minister, a Serb, were openly working against the prime minister. His loyal foreign minister, Budimir Lončar, who had been subjected to a scathing vilification campaign by Milošević for refusing to sell the Serbian line abroad, resigned with an eloquent statement on the qualities that had made Yugoslavia worth preserving. Marković himself resigned on December 20, 1991, unmarked and unmourned.

Although defeated by an ad hoc cabal of nationalists, from the liberal Slovenes to the neocommunist Serbs, he still departed as a symbol of what his country needed. A semiheroic, semitragic figure, he had aspired to be Yugoslavia's savior rather than the Yugoslav Kerensky. Marković had treated Yugoslavia like a patient with a serious cancer—nationalism. While others fed the cancer or, assuming its triumph, adjusted to it, he did his best to arrest it, because he knew what would happen if the patient died. The war in Croatia, the impending war in Bosnia, and a future that promised years of violence in the Balkans were the direct result of his failure and Yugoslavia's death.

James Baker's inability to head off the Slovenian and Croatian declarations of independence cooled whatever ardor the secretary of state may have had for propelling the United States into the deepening crisis. During the summer and fall of 1991, it had been fair enough to give the European Community a chance to deal with what it called a "European problem." While no longer in the lead, the United States hadn't been idle during this period. We had laid down a clear public line that the Yugoslav army bore the primary responsibility for the fighting in Croatia. We had pressed both the JNA and Tudjman to settle their differences. We had given Vance full support in his efforts for a cease-fire in Croatia. And we had helped Carrington by urging the Slovenes to participate in discussions over the future of Yugoslavia. Baker used his UN address on September 25 to castigate Serbia and the JNA. Eagleburger continued to knock the heads of high-level republican visitors to Washington in an effort to promote reconciliation.

In the field the State Department encouraged my proddings of republican leaders to find a formula for living together. My shuttles began to assume a flying Dutchman aspect. For one thing, I could no longer get to Zagreb from Belgrade by road; the "Brotherhood and Unity Highway" had been closed by the war between Serbs and Croats. A trip that used to take four hours now took all day and involved crossing four borders: plane from Belgrade to Zurich, Switzerland; plane from Zurich to Graz, Austria; car from Graz through the Slovenian and Croatian borders to Zagreb. As the ambassador to a Yugoslavia no longer recognized by Slovenia or Croatia, I wondered if my access to officials in Ljubljana and Zagreb would be limited or cut off altogether. It wasn't; I was received cordially by Kučan, Tudjman, and their ministers as if nothing had happened.

On the other hand, in Belgrade, where I was formally accredited to the presidency of Yugoslavia, I could have nothing to do with Milošević's rump version of that body. Under his front-man Kostić, it had become a wholly owned subsidiary of Serbia. To do business with it would be to recognize Milošević as the rightful heir to Yugoslavia. So I systematically boycotted Kostić's many efforts to get me to meet with him or attend presidency functions. There were no bars to my seeing the president of Serbia, however, and somewhat to my surprise Milošević continued to receive me. During our meetings he never once mentioned my principled snubbing of Kostić. I doubt if any American embassy has ever found itself in a more bizarre position—carrying out the full range of diplomatic business while being officially accredited to nobody.

The unique situation of our diplomatic missions in a country that was crumbling under our feet requires a digression. Diplomatic memoirs rarely describe how embassies and consulates function normally, still less how they operate under stress, as we were forced to do during Yugoslavia's permanent crisis. Ambassadors are flatteringly described as moving decisively here and there, making skillful demarches, convincing visiting senators, cabling trenchant recommendations. The truth is that no ambassador can be at all effective without the talented professional diplomats whom the U.S. Foreign Service routinely sends to American posts abroad. Unlike the American military, they have no moneyed constituency at home. Thus they labor in obscurity or, worse, in the opprobrium heaped on them by political yahoos like Senator Jesse Helms.

Often it's only when foreign service officers are killed—like Bob Frasure, a brilliant strategist and negotiator, who died with two colleagues when his armored personnel carrier plunged off a mountain road in Bosnia in August 1995—that people realize the risks they run. In fact, more foreign service officers have been killed on duty in the last twenty years than FBI agents have been killed in the entire seventy-year history of the bureau.

Most stereotypes about American diplomats are wildly inaccurate. The foreign service isn't a refuge for effete Ivy Leaguers; as an Ivy League graduate myself, I'm sensitive to the charge. Our senior officers in Belgrade and Zagreb were graduates of Western Michigan, Johns Hopkins, Franklin and Marshall, Miami, Yale, Ursinus, City College of New York, Wheaton, Princeton, Loyola (Baltimore), Virginia, Wheelock, and University of California at Los Angeles. What I got in Yugoslavia—what every ambassador gets anywhere—is a dedicated group of men and women from all over America, ready to undergo the difficulties of modest pay and frequent disruptions to their lives.

Teeny and I moved nineteen times in thirty-three years in the foreign service, a typical rate. Every foreign move is to a house or apartment not one's own, usually with furniture chosen by someone else. Spouses, when they're not in the foreign service themselves, are typically uprooted from jobs at home and moved to countries where foreigners often can't work and where employment in the embassy, if available, is below their qualifications. The frequent moves are even harder on children. American or international schools abroad are often good, but they're usually small, there's no choice among them, and a child is almost sure to leave after three years. Communicators, secretaries, and other support staff don't get full language training, so it's more difficult for them to adjust to a foreign environment.

Working conditions, I suspect, are more than usually arduous. Officers don't get paid for overtime, yet very few in my experience work less than ten to twelve hours a day. The diplomatic receptions celebrated in song and story are simply extensions of the workday. Their sole purpose is to provide a location for the giving and receiving of information. I've never met a foreign service officer who wouldn't abolish them all forever. Weekends are often regarded as just the final two days of the workweek. To get away from this syndrome, so damaging to morale and family, I ostentatiously avoided the office Saturdays, sneaking in a few hours of work at home, if necessary. But that didn't stop many embassy employees from working a large part of the weekend.

Nor was it easy operating in the dangerous environment of Croatia at war or the increasingly anti-American atmosphere of Serbia. In Zagreb one of our consulate drivers had his leg blown off by a landmine that Tudjman's overzealous security detail had planted too close to a parking area. In Belgrade one of our marine guards was stabbed in a bar for being an American (he was given outstanding treatment at the JNA hospital). At one point during the Serb-Croatian war, our consul general in Zagreb, Mike Einik, had to organize an evacuation of dependents—a major disruption for spouses and children, who couldn't return for a year.

Of course, there were large compensations for these various kinds of stress. It was a rare challenge to deal with one of the most important foreign policy problems facing the United States. It was fascinating living in a part of the world that had been the birthplace of Alexander the Great and three major Roman emperors (Constantine, Trajan, and Justinian); that had felt the military weight of Caesar's legions, of Eugene of Savoy, and of Napoleon, not to mention Hitler and Mussolini; that had formed a fault-line between Christianity and Islam, West and East, Europe and Asia;

and that had been the inspiration for Rebecca West's beautifully written classic *Black Lamb and Grey Falcon.*

Nearly all our officers had studied Serbo-Croatian and could thus operate with full professionalism. Their production was of the highest standard, from early warning on Yugoslavia's breakup, to the pluses and minuses of Prime Minister Marković's economic reform, to stringent prediction and analysis of the effects of nationalism. Assisted by one-person U.S. Information Service posts in all the republican capitals, they knew virtually everybody who counted, and they could take frequent and accurate readings of the local pulses. Jim Swigert, who had succeeded Louie Sell as political counselor, encouraged his energetic staff to get out on the road and learn things firsthand. Jim himself produced brilliant cables based on insights he had picked up all over the country. I never sent Washington an analysis or recommendation without seeking the advice and comment of the officers closest to the problem; their judgment was uniformly reliable.

Being the U.S. ambassador in Belgrade, a middle-sized post in global terms, was a bit like being the mayor of a small town. Every small town needs a city hall to care for its citizens. In our embassy, the deputy chief of mission, Bob Rackmales, and the administrative counselor, John O'Keefe, showed an exceptional concern for human problems. Their success in dealing with them earned the embassy an inspection report rating it one of the best-managed American missions in the world. Teeny's outgoing nature was an important factor in the post's high morale. She made it clear that she was available for people in trouble or pain and dispensed sensible, no-nonsense advice.

In addition to 110 Americans, the embassy in Belgrade and the consulate in Zagreb had 260 Yugoslav employees: drivers, budget specialists, maintenance people, cleaners, and so on. As virulent nationalism grew in Serbia and Croatia, they felt acutely their divided loyalties. I urged the American staff to continue to treat them like the professionals they were. Our own household employees came from all over Yugoslavia; they were a multinational mirror of the country. Teeny called them a "collective," a communist word meant partly as a joke and partly as a way to encourage them to take cooperative decisions on household affairs. Her periodic meetings with them helped create a strong spirit of cooperation and responsibility. Nobody was approved as a new hire unless the "collective" had interviewed her or him and passed judgment.

As for Neša, with whom I spent more time than with practically anybody else, I often thought that if Milošević had taken the route of reform instead of nationalism, Serbs like this enterprising driver—with his energy, friendliness, attention to detail, and entrepreneurial talent—would have turned Serbia into a Balkan success story instead of the economic sinkhole it has become. Neša's perpetual good humor was occasionally marred by concern about my safety. He asked if I would seek Washington's approval for him to carry a gun. I tried but was turned down on the grounds that Neša, though a young and athletic ex-soldier, didn't have the proper training. Neša hounded me about the gun for a few months more, then suddenly stopped talking about it. I soon learned why. One day, while Neša was putting our luggage in the trunk of the car, I saw a familiar bulge in his hip pocket under his jacket. I never said anything, and neither did he. But I did feel safer.

One near-tragedy to an American family illustrated the different issues an embassy must be prepared to deal with. In early 1991 I was visited by a distraught young American woman, Shayna Lazarevich. Shayna told me that in her home state of California, she had met and married a handsome Yugoslav, Dragiša Lazarevich, by whom she had two children. It turned out that Dragiša had a criminal record for illegal possession of firearms and unauthorized entry. Shayna divorced him and won custody of the children. Then disaster struck—in September 1989 Dragiša kidnaped the children, Sasha (aged seven) and Andre (aged four), and fled to Yugoslavia. Shayna pursued, won custody in a Serbian court, but couldn't get the Serbian authorities to return the children, give her visiting rights, or even help her find them.

With a determination that was moving, Shayna told me that she was prepared to turn over every stone in Serbia to find and reclaim her children. I told her we would do all we could to help her but worried privately that with U.S.-Serbian relations on a downturn, it would be pretty hard to build incentives for Serbian behavior. Our consul general, Bob Tynes, made Shayna's case his top priority; he importuned and harassed the Serbian courts and police. I went directly to Milošević several times; he promised to help, but didn't. I also asked Secretary Baker to raise the issue with Milošević; he did, with the same lack of result.

Shayna went through months, then years, of anguish, drawing on her savings to spend as much time as she could in Belgrade. The Serbian authorities occasionally allowed her glimpses of her children, but only for a total of sixteen hours in the nearly six years of separation. Her tenacity and persistent pressure by the embassy over all that time finally paid off. With the help of Milošević, who apparently decided after years of delay to clear his bilateral slate with the United States, the children were released to Shayna by the Serbian police in June 1995. They're now back in California with her.

As 1991 dragged through autumn, it became increasingly clear that Lord Carrington's Hague conference was going nowhere. The Slovenes and Croats saw it primarily as a means for disassembling Yugoslavia. The sole Serbian objective was recognition as Yugoslavia; the rest was pure damage-limitation. Threats to the integrity of Bosnia were growing, and the European Community, under German cajoling, was stumbling toward recognition of the breakaway republics. Still, there was resistance in Washington to getting the United States further involved. At a U.S. ambassadors' meeting in Berlin in November, a friend from the State Department's European Bureau told me that Yugoslavia had become a tar baby in Washington. Nobody wanted to touch it. With the American presidential election just a year away, it was seen as a loser.

Near the year's end, I had a meeting with Vuk Drašković, the mercurial firebrand of the Serbian opposition. Drašković had a reputation as a Serbian nationalist and did little to enhance the cohesion of the small parties opposing Milošević. But most of the time I found his ideas a perceptive and interesting antidote to the dominant Milošević line. Milošević was aware of our periodic meetings and found ways to let me know he didn't like them. "How's your friend Drašković?" he would ask sarcastically when I called on him. This time Drašković gave me a thumbnail sketch of the major players in the Yugoslav drama. Carrington in his view was on the right track with his plan for a negotiated outcome, despite its faults. Izetbegović was "moderate and wise," and understood that Serbs and Muslims must learn to live together. Tudjman was the "Croatian Hitler." Milošević was the "Serbian Stalin."

PURGATORY

"Our vision of Sarajevo is like Berlin when the
wall was still standing."

Bosnia's President Alija Izetbegović was a worried man singing a worried song. Ever since Croatia had opted for independence in mid-1991 he saw the writing on the wall for his republic. He scurried throughout Europe and the United States looking for ways to head off disaster. He tried, without success, to fan the embers of the dying Izetbegović-Gligorov plan for a loosely connected Yugoslavia. He asked for, and got, European Community monitors in Bosnia. He asked for, but didn't get, UN peacekeepers there. Cyrus Vance, concentrating on the urgent need for a peacekeeping force in Croatia, took the traditional, if puzzling, line with me that peacekeepers are used after a conflict, not before. Neither the U.S. government nor the UN supported Izetbegović's request for peacekeepers. In a cable to Washington I urged this innovative step but didn't press for it as hard as I should have.

I visited Sarajevo in late October 1991 to find Izetbegović nervous and on edge. Unlike Milošević and Tudjman, this republican president clearly didn't love his job. He seemed diminished, rather than inflated, by the opulence of the presidential palace. As usual, the only other Bosnian at our lunch together was his daughter Sabina—apparently the only person he fully trusted. The Bosnian parliament, which had a Muslim plurality though not a majority, had just passed a vote declaring Bosnia a "sovereign" republic. The Serbian deputies, accusing Izetbegović of secession, had walked out.

Izetbegović was anxious to explain the vote. He assured me that its purpose was simply to give Bosnia equal status with the other five republics in the negotiations on the new Yugoslavia. He pointed out that Milošević had accepted that concept in expressing approval of the Izetbegović-Gligorov plan, which referred to "sovereign republics in a sovereign state." The vote was emphatically *not* a vote for independence, Izetbegović stressed. "Independence is not our goal, though it's an option."

The Bosnian president told me that the West must not recognize Croatia. Negotiations had to be given a chance. He believed that Tudjman wanted to find a political solution. He criticized Lord Carrington's latest draft because it neglected the concerns of the Serbs. He professed the desire for normal relations with the JNA, even though the army supported the Serbian agenda. He even believed a JNA presence to be necessary in Bosnia—"there are too many armed civilians around here."

Izetbegović categorically denied the charge that Bosnian Muslims wanted an Islamic republic. "What we want is a civil state based on the right of individual citizens with constitutional protections for the rights of minorities." He was, however, willing to consider the theoretical possibility of a three-way partition of Bosnia among Muslims, Serbs, and Croats. "It might be a good idea if it were possible, but it's not possible because the populations are too mixed." Little did he or I imagine that the ruthless Serbian (and Croatian) policies of mass expulsions of Muslims would create in four years the very conditions whose absence he believed prevented the partition of Bosnia. I noted during the conversation the moderate nature of Izetbegović's views and his charity to people—Tudjman, the JNA leadership, the Bosnian Serbs—who were reviling him in the most scabrous way.

Though charitable, Izetbegović wasn't naive. He voiced great suspicion about the motives of Bosnian Serb leader Radovan Karadžić. Karadžić's record had aroused suspicion ever since he had catapulted onto the scene when his Bosnian Serb Party won 30 percent of the assembly seats in the republic's first election in December 1990. Copying the Serbian strategy in Croatia, the Bosnian Serbs, beginning in May 1991, declared three "Serbian autonomous regions" on Bosnian territory. The JNA secretly armed them, then in September infiltrated troops to "protect" them—in effect defining their borders and putting them beyond the reach of the Bosnian government's authority. The Bosnian Serbs, with JNA help, seized TV-Sarajevo repeaters around Bosnia and reprogrammed them to carry TV-Belgrade, a key factor in the incitement of ethnic hatred. Then came the walkout of the Bosnian Serb deputies that had gotten Izetbegović so upset.

The Bosnian president was disturbed at what seemed an attempt to partition Bosnia incrementally. He complained to me that in their "autonomous areas" the Serbs refused to share power with Muslims or Croats. He was convinced that Milošević and Karadžić were "building a rump Yugoslavia and acting as if Bosnia is one of its provinces." As an example of their methods, Izetbegović said that Bogić Bogičević, the courageous Bosnian Serb who, as Bosnia's member of the Yugoslav presidency, had blocked the efforts of Milošević and the JNA in March 1991 to crush the Croatian and Slovenian armies, was now receiving "hundreds" of death threats. Izetbegović was convinced they were part of a campaign orchestrated by Karadžić.

Karadžić, whom I had first met during the Bosnian election campaign, was the polar opposite to Izetbegović. Where the Muslim preached conciliation, the Serb habitually used the language of confrontation. "Boycott," "war," "violence," "demand," "unacceptable," "genocide," "hell," and "annihilation" peppered his vocabulary. He was a large man with flamboyant gray hair, an outwardly friendly manner, and the unlikely profession of psychiatry. In the great tradition of nationalists who don't come from their nation (Hitler, Napoleon, Stalin), Karadžić was from Montenegro, not Bosnia. There was also a Yugoslav precedent for this. Ante Pavelić, the head of the Nazi puppet state of Croatia during World War II, was from Bosnia, not Croatia. Karadžić's single-mindedness in pursuit of the most radical Serbian agenda was matched by his deep-seated hostility, amounting to racism, toward Muslims, Croats, and any other non-Serbian ethnic group in his neighborhood.

During our meetings Karadžić repeatedly startled me with his extravagant claims on behalf of Serbs. He told me that "Serbs have a right to territory not only where they're now living but also where they're buried, since the earth they lie in was taken unjustly from them." When I asked whether he would accept parallel claims on behalf of Croats or Muslims, he reacted with shock. "Of course not," he said, "because Croats are fascists and Muslims are Islamic fanatics." His disdain for facts was supreme; he insisted that "Sarajevo is a Serbian city," which it has never been. His apartheid philosophy was more extreme than anything concocted in South Africa.

In days to come Karadžić became the architect of the massacres in the Muslim villages, the ethnic cleansing, and the attacks on civilian populations. In his fanaticism, ruthlessness, and contempt for human values, he invites comparison with a monster from another generation, Heinrich Himmler.

In our meeting in October 1991 Karadžić displayed many of the elements that made him hateful to the Muslims. He complained that Bosnia's borders were arbitrary, that they "don't reflect history." He said, "The chronic dishonesty of the leaders of Izetbegović's party is due to their Muslim religion. They're prone to oriental despotism. They're always cheating us. We can't stand it anymore." He called Izetbegović a "secessionist," ignoring his own responsibility for creation of the Serbian "autonomous regions" and for his party's walkout from the Bosnian parliament. Four days later he was to take another secessionist step in proclaiming an independent Bosnian Serb parliament.

I asked Karadžić why he seemed uncomfortable with participation in democratic institutions. A year before he had threatened to boycott Bosnia's first elections; now his party was boycotting the Bosnian parliament. Were the rights of Serbs really being violated in Bosnia? Karadžić could think of only one instance—the alleged firing of Serbian municipal employees in a Muslim area of Sarajevo. He fell back on the broader accusation that the "self-determination" of Serbs was being denied. I told him: "It seems to me you're just angry that Serbs are a minority. But that's how the elections came out; that's democracy. Your creation of autonomous regions is provocative, and your unilateral changes of Bosnia's borders are destabilizing." It was growing increasingly obvious that Karadžić had no intention of playing by the rules.

During that autumn of 1991 German Foreign Minister Genscher was pressing the European Community for early recognition of Croatia and Slovenia—just what Izetbegović most feared. Izetbegović visited Genscher in Bonn in late November. He had been carefully prepared by my friend and colleague, Hansjorg Eiff, the German ambassador to Yugoslavia, who told him which arguments would be most effective in convincing Genscher that EC recognition of Croatia would bring violence to Bosnia. Unaccountably, Izetbegović failed to raise the issue. The omission can only have led Genscher to assume that he had a green light from Izetbegović for recognition.

I was urging Washington to try to persuade the Community to defer recognition. All the EC ambassadors in Belgrade were also lobbying their governments against premature recognition. Even Eiff, with great courage, put his career on the line by urging Genscher to reconsider. Washington shared these concerns but didn't do enough about them. President Bush had made a personal intervention with German Chancellor Helmut Kohl at a NATO summit in Rome in early November, but it had been pro forma.

Just before the EC summit the State Department sent a perfunctory cable to U.S. embassies in EC capitals instructing them to urge postponement of recognition. It was enough to show we had done something, but not enough to produce results. Both Cyrus Vance and Lord Carrington took the strong view that there should be no Western recognition of the independence of any Yugoslav republic until all had agreed on their mutual relationships. Vance told me on December 5, "My friend Genscher is out of control on this. What he's doing is madness."

None of these appeals prevailed. Bowing to German pressure, the EC leaders on December 17, 1991, decided to recognize Croatia and Slovenia and to offer recognition to Bosnia and Macedonia. The State Department's statement following the action was weak and nuanced, mainly to avoid ruffling the Croatian community in the United States. Both Carrington and Vance had urged Genscher not to go ahead with recognition. Carrington, now undercut by his own organization, complained loudly and publicly. So did Vance. The prospect of war in Bosnia accelerated.

A few days after the Community's decision, I had lunch in Belgrade with Ejup Ganić, Izetbegović's deputy and a Muslim who had studied at the Massachusetts Institute of Technology. I asked him, "Is Bosnia really going to go for independence in the face of all the dangers Izetbegović has repeatedly warned about? Wouldn't it be better to tell the European Community that you need more time to work out the political issues involved?" Ganić looked at me as if I had just dropped out of the sky. He said, "Of course we're going to move ahead on independence. With Croatia and Slovenia now gone, Bosnia can't survive in a 'Yugoslavia' controlled by Serbia. We've had plenty of time to see how Milošević deals with minorities in Serbia: the Hungarians, the Muslims, and the Albanians. We'd be crazy to make ourselves vulnerable to that kind of oppression."

I agreed with Ganić's argument but concluded from his abrupt change of tack that Izetbegović was playing a double game. With the European Community supporting Bosnia's independence, he seemed to think he could get away with it under the guns of the Serbs. Perhaps he counted on Western military support, though nobody had promised him that. Whatever his motives, his premature push for independence was a disastrous political mistake. Serbia, Bosnia's vastly more powerful neighbor, now had the pretext it needed to strike—the claim that 1.3 million Serbs were being taken out of "Yugoslavia" against their will. I have no doubt that Milošević and Karadžić had already decided to annex the majority of Bosnian territory by force. But the Community's irresponsibility, the United States' passivity, and Izetbegović's miscalculation made their job easier.

I drafted a discouraged cable to Washington on December 20. It noted that the EC decision had shifted the entire political terrain; the U.S. policy of nonrecognition, now isolated, would soon lose effectiveness. I said that war in Bosnia now seemed certain. "Let nobody believe that the ten thousand or so who have died so far [in Croatia] mean that violence has reached its peak. A war in Bosnia could increase that number tenfold."

In mid-January 1992, a few weeks after the European Community's decision, I had long talks with Milošević and Tudjman. The two had met several times during 1991 to discuss dividing Bosnia between Serbia and Croatia. Once they even had the arrogance to debate such a carve-up in the presence of Alija Izetbegović. As a place where Serbs, Croats, and Muslims had coexisted more or less peacefully for centuries, Bosnia was an affront to these two ethnic supremacists. Now that the Community was pushing it toward independence, it became a challenge to them.

Milošević, more cunning than Tudjman, carefully projected the image of a Serbian leader without territorial designs. He had assured Baker in June 1991 that Serbia didn't covet "a single hectare" of land outside Serbia. After the European Community's decision on Bosnia he remained seemingly unconcerned. On January 10, 1992, one day after the Bosnian Serbs had taken their latest secessionist action by declaring a "Serbian Republic of Bosnia-Herzegovina," he told me that Serbia wouldn't recognize it. A month later, contradicting his thesis that all Serbs should be able to live in one state, he said to me that Serbia would accept the independence of all four of the republics requesting it, including Bosnia.

Milošević's rhetoric about the situation of Serbs in Bosnia was much more subdued than his fulminations about the deprivation of Serbian rights in Croatia by Tudjman's "fascist" regime. In fact, Milošević would draw the distinction himself. "You see, Mr. Zimmermann," he said on February 11, as if he were explaining elementary history to an eight-year-old, "Serbs in Bosnia are not threatened. How could they be threatened when they occupy 64 percent of Bosnian territory with only 35 percent (the real percentage was 31) of the population? Repression against the Serbs in Bosnia is an impossibility."

There were usually worms in Milošević's apples. After careful examination of his Bosnian apple, we in the embassy found several, all of them inching toward a more ominous Bosnia policy than the Serbian leader wanted to reveal. The first worm was his persistent denigration of Izetbegović as a dangerous Islamic fundamentalist, which didn't square with his benign remarks on Serbian intentions. The second was his failure to respect the integrity of Bosnia. He had told me during the past summer that Croatia could seize part of Bosnia. If Croatia could do this, we wondered, then why not Serbia?

The third worm was the condition he put on Bosnia's independence—that there had to be agreement among all three of Bosnia's constituent nations (the Serbs, the Muslims, and the Croats) on new constitutional arrangements. While this was not an outrageous demand from the Serbian point of view, it would give Karadžić and the Bosnian Serbs a veto power over independence. And since Karadžić was implacably opposed to Bosnia's independence—he wanted the republic to remain part of Serbia-dominated "Yugoslavia"—there was no doubt that the veto would be used.

The fourth worm in Milošević's apple was the slimiest. It was his assertion that Serbs in Bosnia lived on and therefore possessed 64 percent of the territory of the republic. I have no idea where he got that figure; neither then nor later did he or Karadžić ever produce a shred of evidence to support it. Milošević explained that Muslims were urban and Serbs rural, so naturally Serbs occupied—and deserved—much more land. With so much territorial control, "they would not have to respect any illegal acts." The thought left hanging, but not expressed, was that Serbs "living on" 64 percent of Bosnia's land had the right to control it by force and to deny it to others.

Milošević usually made an elaborate pretense to me of not knowing Karadžić very well and having few operational contacts with him. This fiction suited his habitual "clean-hands" strategy, employed first in Croatia and now in Bosnia. He always reacted with injured innocence when I accosted him over Bosnia. "But why do you come to me, Mr. Zimmermann? Serbia has nothing to do with Bosnia. It's not our problem." Karadžić's approach was slightly different. He would say that he had to work closely with Milošević but often disagreed with the Serbian leader. "He wants us to work out our own problems, but we push him to protect us. We think he's too close to Izetbegović; he believes what this lying Muslim says."

Although Milošević and Karadžić later split, there's no doubt that in this period they were cooperating closely on a common strategy for Bosnia. The fiction of distance or discord suited both leaders—Milošević to escape responsibility for aggression, Karadžić to avoid the charge that he was a henchman of Milošević rather than a Serbian folk hero in his own right. But Karadžić's actions to partition the republic, beginning in the spring of 1991 and continuing right through the Bosnian war, would have been impossible without the JNA. And the JNA depended on Milošević.

During the early weeks of 1992 we warned Washington that Karadžić and the Bosnian Serbs, sitting behind the JNA's guns, might set up their own government (following the pattern in Croatia) and press to annex most of Bosnia-Herzegovina to the "New Yugoslavia." As it turned out, the territory seized by the Serbs during the Bosnian war corresponded almost exactly to the 64 percent figure that I had first heard from Milošević.

Tudjman as usual was more bluff in his approach to Bosnia. Among his closest advisers was his defense minister Gojko Šušak, a Darth Vader–like individual with black eyebrows and a permanent scowl, whose Canadian fortune had gone into supporting Tudjman's party and, it was believed, buying arms for Croatia. Šušak was originally from Herzegovina, and his foremost objective was to wrest the Croatian part of Herzegovina from Bosnia and join it to Croatia. Šušak and his ilk relentlessly pressed this agenda on Tudjman, but the Croatian leader didn't need a lot of encouragement. In a long meeting with me on January 14, 1992, just a few weeks after his German protectors had bullied the European Community into supporting Bosnia's independence, Tudjman spent over an hour trying to convince me that Bosnia should be split up between Croatia and Serbia. It was the most astonishing single discussion of my years in Yugoslavia.

Tudjman began with a fifteen-minute monologue. He had just met with a delegation of Croats from Bosnia, who told him they felt threatened by Izetbegović's policies. Tudjman's description of those policies was breathtaking. "The Muslims," he said, "want to establish an Islamic fundamentalist state. They plan to do this by flooding Bosnia with 500,000 Turks. Izetbegović has also launched a demographic threat. He has a secret policy to reward large families so that in a few years the Muslims will be a majority in Bosnia [at the time they were 44 percent]. The influence of an Islamic Bosnia will then spread through the Sandžak and Kosovo [Muslim areas of Serbia] to Turkey and to Libya. Izetbegović is just a fundamentalist front man for Turkey; together they're conspiring to create a Greater Bosnia. Catholics and Orthodox alike will be eradicated. I tell you, Mr. Ambassador, that if we in Croatia abandon the Croats in Bosnia to such a fate, they will turn on us. Some will become terrorists, and they won't spare Zagreb in their acts of revenge."

Tudjman admitted that he had discussed these fantasies with Milošević, the Yugoslav army leadership, and the Bosnian Serbs, and "they agree that the only solution is to divide up Bosnia between Serbia and Croatia." Magnanimously, Tudjman said he didn't insist on a 50–50 division. "Let Milošević take the larger part; he controls it anyway. We can do with less than 50 percent. We're willing to leave the Muslims a small area around Sarajevo. They may not like it, but a stable Balkans is possible only if there's a change in Bosnia's borders, no matter what the Muslims think. There's nothing sacred about those borders. Bosnia isn't an old state, like Croatia, which once extended all the way to Zemun [a western suburb of Belgrade]."

Listening to Tudjman, I realized I had to abandon diplomatic niceties. With considerable emotion I reminded him, recalling the Iran hostage crisis, that the United States had a lot more experience with Islamic fundamentalism than he did. In our view Izetbegović was neither a radical fundamentalist nor a threat to anybody. The United States would strongly oppose the breakup of Bosnia. "Nobody who wants to do this can count on any assistance from us. The threat in Bosnia comes from the Serbs and the JNA, not from the Muslims. There will be war in Bosnia if you try to divide it. Don't you think the Muslims will react? What you propose ignores the rights of a large share of Bosnia's population."

Tudjman was unrepentant. He accused the United States of short-sightedness for not seeing the Muslim danger: "A greater Muslim state is not only a threat to Serbia and Croatia. It's also a threat to Europe and the United States." He then began, astoundingly, to defend the Serbian position on Bosnia. "The reason there's no peace there is that the Bosnian Serbs haven't been properly dealt with. New borders will solve their problems and reduce tensions." I asked, "Mr. President, how can you expect the West to help you get back the large part of Croatia taken by the Serbs when you yourself are advancing naked and unsupported claims against a neighboring republic?"

Tudjman replied that Bosnia "doesn't really exist—it was created by colonial powers and reaffirmed by communists." I told him Bosnia was as real as Croatia. Tudjman retreated to a might-makes-right argument: "If the two major groups agree, the Muslims will be compelled go along." I asked, "How can you expect Milošević to respect a deal with you to divide Bosnia when he's trying to annex part of Croatia?" Amazingly, Tudjman said about his sworn enemy, "Because I can trust Milošević."

During this surreal discussion I could see that Tudjman's aides in the room were as flabbergasted as I was at the Croatian president's tirade against Izetbegović and the Muslims. Several times Tudjman's chief of staff, Hrvoje Šarinić, a moderate technocrat skilled at taking the sharp edges off his boss's diatribes, tried to divert Tudjman from his multiple self-incriminations. Šarinić explained that the proposal to divide Bosnia had been Milošević's, that he had raised it with Tudjman the week before in Brussels, and that he had claimed that Greece and France also favored the idea. Tudjman brushed off this and other efforts to rescue him from his cynical assertions. He was determined to tell me that, even as his own Croatian people were suffering the effects of a terrible war, he was ready to collude with their aggressor to carry out a similar aggression against another people.

Just before I left, I told Tudjman heatedly that, if he was trying to seek compensation in Bosnia for Serbia's incursions in Croatia, he could expect zero support from the United States. As Šarinić accompanied me down the stairs, I asked him if I had gotten too emotional in defending the integrity of Bosnia. "Oh no," he replied, "You were just fine."

This extraordinary meeting crystallized Tudjman's complicity in the violent death of Yugoslavia and the wars in Croatia and Bosnia. His toleration, even encouragement, of racist attitudes toward Serbs in Croatia made his republic undemocratic and explosive. The Krajina Serbs were militant and provocative, but Tudjman's insensitive policies only locked them into their intransigence. More than half the Serbs in Croatia didn't live in the border areas; many had Croatian spouses and were integrated into Croatian life. They too were insulted at the second-class status they were assigned.

Tudjman showed contempt for Yugoslavia and its Croatian prime minister. That was his prerogative, But when he connived with Milošević, his implacable adversary, to divide Bosnia against the will of the Muslims and most of the Croats there, he transgressed the most basic of democratic norms. It was one thing to seek to leave Yugoslavia, quite another to take a piece out of a republic that merited the same sovereign rights as Tudjman's Croatia.

If Bosnia was to be partitioned, the support of the Yugoslav army was crucial. I spent a lot of time over the next few months jawboning with the generals. The JNA's role in the Croatian war wasn't an auspicious harbinger for Bosnia. The army had taken an increasingly pro-Serbian position, culminating in its attacks on Vukovar and Dubrovnik, its sealing off of territory for the Croatian Serbs, and its complicity in the mass expulsions of Croats. By January 2, 1992, when Cyrus Vance finalized a cease-fire in Croatia and an agreement to bring in UN peacekeepers, over a quarter of the territory of Croatia was in Serbian hands, thanks mainly to the JNA. When the army withdrew from Croatia in the succeeding months, it left a well-armed civilian Serbian militia in its wake. And it assured the Krajina Serbs that it would be just over the border in Bosnia, ready to return if necessary.

In a meeting on January 6, 1992, I found General Kadijević singing Vance's praises. "There are two roads," he said. "You can follow the road of Germany with its early recognition policy; that road leads to bloodshed. Or you can follow Vance's road in search of a comprehensive political solution; that road leads to peace." I tried to prepare Kadijević for Europe's recognition of Bosnia's independence, which, following the European Community's decision, was virtually inevitable. "If war breaks out," I said, "it won't be the Muslims or Croats who start it. The Serbs can wage war only with the help of the JNA. The army has a huge responsibility." I urged Kadijević to try to understand Izetbegović's situation: "He can apply for recognition, or he can resign himself to a Bosnia dominated by Milošević." Kadijević wasn't buying; he said that Western recognition of Bosnia would lead to war.

A day later Kadijević was out of office, forcibly retired, the rumor went, because he hadn't been firm enough in pursuit of Serbian objectives. This was a chilling thought, since Kadijević had been the general in command throughout the Croatian war. General Adžić, more clearly a nationalist, became acting defense minister. While Kadijević had been born in Croatia of mixed Serbian-Croatian parentage, Adžić was a Bosnian Serb from Herzegovina—an ominous background as the threat of war in Bosnia increased. When I met with Adžić four days after his promotion, he assured me that the JNA would not use force to keep Bosnia in Yugoslavia. But he was not reassuring in his other comments. Bosnia was a "special case"; its remaining in Yugoslavia would "simplify matters"; the Croatian and Muslim parties had established "illegal paramilitary forces." Like Kadijević, Adžić said "there would be war" if Bosnia was recognized as an independent state.

It became clear only later that, despite its professions of innocence, the JNA was engaged in a secret strategy that depended critically on force. We knew that in addition to its direct support for the Bosnian Serbs since the spring of 1991, the JNA leaders had infiltrated fresh troops into Bosnia from Slovenia and Croatia, as the wars in those republics ended. What we didn't know was that in early 1992 they began to transfer out of Bosnia all soldiers who were not Bosnian Serbs and bring in Bosnian Serb troops from other parts of Yugoslavia. The result, by the time fighting began in Bosnia in the spring of 1992, was a formidable Bosnian Serb army, soon to grow to a strength of eighty to ninety thousand. This cynical masterstroke, the joint conception of Milošević and the JNA, gave the Bosnian Serbs the immense military advantage over the Croats and Muslims that sustained their victories and their atrocities for over three years.

The Yugoslav army, constitutional protector of Yugoslavia, betrayed its history and its mission in Yugoslavia's final agonies. I had myself been ambivalent about the JNA, perhaps giving it the benefit of the doubt for too long. I had been impressed by its partisan tradition and its firm opposition to nationalism over the decades. But as the last institutional defender of communism, it lost its bearings with the 1990 elections and with the rise of Slovenian and Croatian nationalism and separatism. It resolved its hesitations by throwing in its lot with Milošević and becoming the military arm of Serbian nationalism.

I suspect there was considerable inner turmoil within the officer corps, perhaps reflected by General Kadijević himself, before the JNA made its infamous choice. Kadijević, a complex man, spoke strongly to me against nationalism and in defence of constitutional procedures, and he impressed—at least for a time— such different men as Tudjman and Marković. Yet it was the army he commanded that destroyed Vukovar, attacked Dubrovnik, and laid plans with Milošević and Karadžić for the decimation of Bosnia. The JNA never abandoned its supply and command-and-control relationship with the Bosnian Serb army, and its soldiers were to commit atrocities in Bosnia unheard of since the time of Hitler. Kadijević complains in his book that the JNA was "an army without a state." Its own actions helped to make it so.

Izetbegović had agreed with the European Community to schedule a referendum on Bosnia's independence. While the Bush administration had seriously questioned the Community's rush to recognition, a referendum was at least a way to probe the views of the three Bosnian peoples. In Sarajevo in mid-January I had a heated debate with Karadžić, whose increasingly bellicose actions now included the declaration on January 9 of a Serbian republic— an act of rebellion against the legitimate Bosnian government.

At our meeting Karadžić, as always, was accompanied by Nikola Koljević, the number two in the Bosnian Serb Party. Koljević looked like, and was, an intellectual—a scholar and translator of Shakespeare. Despite his unlikely vocation, the quality of Koljević's mercy toward the Muslims was very strained. He habitually called Izetbegović a liar, accused him of pursuing a secret population policy to create a Muslim majority, and insisted on the building of fences to separate Bosnia's three communities.

I decided to try a tougher tack with these two Bosnian nationalists in an effort to underline their lack of support in the West. I said to Karadžić, "It's time to start dealing with reality. Since Europe has decided to recognize the Yugoslav republics, American recognition is inevitable, just a matter of time. Why don't you participate in the referendum on independence and come to terms with the fact that with 30 percent of the population Serbs can't expect to dictate the outcome? By participating you can at least affect the timing and content of independence. Your branding of Izetbegović as a dangerous fundamentalist is seen in my country as racism. And your proclamation on January 9 of a Republika Srpska can only be a threat to your neighbors."

Looking at Koljević, who had just been conferring with Tudjman about dividing Bosnia between Serbia and Croatia, I asked if he really wanted to be remembered by history as the coauthor of a new Molotov-Ribbentrop pact. I encouraged the two to lead their Serbian community rather than being the most radical elements in it. "A reasonable approach would win Western support, but if you resort to threats and the search for outside help, then you'll be isolated and marginalized."

Not surprisingly, Karadžić took this in bad spirit. His porcine eyes narrowed, and the affability that he usually feigned left him. He predicted that the independence of Bosnia would lead to "catastrophe"; Serbs would never accept it. Bosnian Serbs, he said, want to remain in "Yugoslavia." I said that Yugoslav institutions now amounted to nothing more than a second Serbian government by another name. Karadžić said, "If Bosnia declares its independence, then I might have to resign the leadership of the Bosnian Serb Party." I knew his threat wasn't serious but have often thought how differently things might have turned out if he'd followed through on it.

After this confrontational meeting, Koljević came to see me privately. He told me that not everyone in the Bosnian Serb Party was as radical as Karadžić. He himself represented a more moderate current. Koljević recommended that I continue the tough approach I had used on Karadžić. "Be strong with my friend. Press for Serbian participation in the referendum on independence." I had difficulty knowing what to make of this professor with the horn-rimmed glasses and the nervous smiles. Was he taking a genuine, perhaps even dangerous, initiative? Or was it a trap? If Radovan Karadžić was the Heinrich Himmler of Bosnia, was Nikola Koljević the Albert Speer? I still don't know.

Whatever uncertainties or dissensions there may have been in the Serbian camp, they had disappeared by my next trip to Sarajevo a few days before the referendum on independence scheduled for February 29. The Serb, Muslim, and Croat leaders of Bosnia had just returned from Lisbon, where they had been engaged in intensive negotiations over Bosnia's future with José Cutileiro, a Portuguese diplomat whose country had succeeded the Netherlands to the presidency of the European Community. The Bush administration strongly supported these talks. In Washington just a week before, Eagleburger had told Izetbegović that the United States would back a negotiated outcome under EC auspices. (The war, once under way, changed American attitudes. In August 1992 Eagleburger began to criticize the EC's efforts as dividing Bosnia.)

At our meeting on February 25 Karadžić was ecstatic over developments in Lisbon, where Cutileiro had won the preliminary approval of the three parties to ethnically based cantons within a unitary republic. "Bosnia," he said, "will consist of three constituent units or states, based on three constituent nations and joined by a common government and assembly." Koljević, not sounding like the moderate he had secretly claimed to be, exulted, "Now we Bosnian Serbs can have dual citizenship—of Bosnia and of Serbia. Each of Bosnia's three republics can have its own foreign minister." I said I doubted that this was exactly what Cutileiro had in mind. "He's trying to preserve the territorial integrity of Bosnia," I said. "What you're describing is partition."

On the independence referendum, just four days away, Karadžić was savage. "This referendum is not based on consensus, therefore it's illegal. The outcome will not be valid for the Serbian territories. If some Europeans recognize the independence of Bosnia, anything can happen. Serbs will close off the regions they dominate and there could be violence. The Europeans should wait until the EC talks yield a final compromise." It was clear that Karadžić was embarked on a classic talk-fight strategy. The "talk" part was to play out the EC negotiations so as to give the Bosnian Serbs a veto over independence. Even better, the negotiations might yield the division of Bosnia that Karadžić craved; that's why he was so bullish about Lisbon.

The "fight" element lay in the threat of war if independence were carried through. Both Karadžić and Milošević were adept at playing both sides of this strategy. They had a common bottom line: a division of Bosnia leaving the Serbs in control of two-thirds of it. As if to confirm the cynicism of Karadžić's approach, the Bosnian Serb leader met a day later with one of Tudjman's closest aides to discuss the details of the division of Bosnia—a direct rebuff to the EC negotiations that Karadžić had just been praising.

That same day I saw Izetbegović, who had heard about Karadžić's collusion with the Croats and was furious. The Bosnian president had other concerns as well. He wrung his hands about the provisional agreement at Lisbon. "We can accept regions within Bosnia based primarily on economic and geographic principles, with account taken of ethnic and cultural factors. But I was astonished by the EC proposal for the creation of ethnically based regions. This could create three states within Bosnia and amount to partition from within." Izetbegović contended that any such attempt at ethnic division would fail because there would be no agreement on how to draw the boundaries. Bosnia was too ethnically mixed.

I asked Izetbegović why he had agreed at Lisbon to compromises that he was now criticizing. He said he had been put under pressure by the other parties, including Cutileiro, and felt he had to give in. When he got back to Sarajevo, his Muslim colleagues upbraided him for weakness. Now he didn't know what to do. Drawing on my instructions to support whatever could be worked out between the European Community and the three Bosnian parties, I encouraged Izetbegović to stick by what he'd agreed to. It wasn't a final agreement, I said, and there would be future opportunities for him to argue his views.

According to Cutileiro, writing much later, Izetbegović didn't renege on the Lisbon approach, but agreed with the other two sides on March 18 to accept the EC principles as the basis for future negotiations. In the hindsight of history, Cutileiro's plan, although it introduced for the first time the concept of Bosnia's division, would probably have worked out better for the Muslims than any subsequent plan, including the Dayton formula, since the divisions would have closely followed the actual ethnic percentages of the populations. But the Bosnian Serbs never accepted Cutileiro's map and, given Karadžić's track record, there's little chance they would have. Thus, the plan was never really viable.

In the same conversation Izetbegović commented sharply on Karadžić's tactics: "He claims territories where Serbs are the majority, or where there are some Serbs, or where Serbs used to live, or where they need land to fill out their territories. He's continuing to flout Bosnia's laws and to pursue his goals through intimidation. He promised to suspend the creation of new Serbian autonomous units during the negotiation with the European Community, but he's just created two more in Sarajevo and Banja Luka."

With all his suspicions, Izetbegović still seemed willing to rely on the Yugoslav army. He said the regular army, though not the reservists whom he saw as undisciplined, would be welcome to stay in Bosnia as long as it recognized civilian authority. He and I both knew that the JNA was unlikely to accept his civilian authority since it didn't accept Bosnia's independence. Still, I detected no inkling on his part of the massive aggression that the JNA, together with Milošević and Karadžić, was mounting against him.

When I got back to Belgrade, I cabled home my view that the time had come to move on recognition of Bosnia's independence. Heretofore I had used the specter of recognition tactically with the Serbs. Now I believed it was time to take action. I recognized that this would be a major change in the U.S. position. I had backed, in fact had helped to create, the U.S. policy of nonrecognition of Croatia and Slovenia before the EC decision of December 17, 1991. But the Community's action had changed the whole political landscape. Now the Europeans had recognized Croatia and Slovenia, and Izetbegović's Bosnia was threatened with isolation in a Milošević-dominated "Serbo-slavia." To keep Bosnia in international limbo would increase that isolation and assist Serbian designs. Cutileiro's negotiations, though worth continuing, held out little hope. Either they would go in Karadžić's direction, as he had boasted to me, or he would simply string them out while illegally establishing more Serbian autonomous areas throughout Bosnia.

I believed that early Western recognition, right after the expected referendum majority for independence, might present Milošević and Karadžić with a fait accompli difficult for them to overturn. Milošević wanted to avoid economic sanctions and to win recognition for Serbia and Montenegro as the successor to Yugoslavia; we could offer him that recognition in exchange for his recognition of the territorial integrity of the four other republics, including Bosnia. I conceded drawbacks to my proposal. In the understatement of the year, I said, "I don't deny that there is some chance of violence if Bosnia wins recognition," but added my belief that "there is a much greater chance of violence if the Serbian game plan proceeds unimpeded."

My ideas coalesced with the thinking in the National Security Council and the State Department, which were more focused on the importance of recognizing a government that had met all the democratic tests put before it by the European Community. The result was an active American push for recognition. The decision has been controversial in light of the Serbian aggression that followed it. It needn't have been. Milošević and Karadžić had been embarked for nearly a year on a comprehensive strategy to tear away two-thirds of Bosnia and incorporate it into Serbia ("Yugoslavia"). Western recognition didn't provoke that aggressive strategy, nor would the lack of Western recognition have deterred it, as Serbian propagandists charge.

Unfortunately, international recognition didn't prevent the long-prepared Serbian onslaught. But recognition, followed by Bosnia's admission to the United Nations, did give the West a necessary platform for the support of Bosnia. How well that platform was used is another story. But its absence would certainly have facilitated the swallowing of most of Bosnia by Milošević and Karadžić.

The Bosnian referendum produced the expected result—a 64 percent vote (almost entirely Muslims and Croats) for independence with almost all of the Serbs boycotting. Just after the vote Karadžić turned Serbian demonstrators onto the streets of Sarajevo, ostensibly to avenge the murder of a guest at a Serbian wedding, more likely to destabilize and if possible overturn the Izetbegović government. The attempt failed, but emotions were getting out of control. On March 4 I took a personal message from Baker to Milošević. It minced no words in implicating the Serbian leader in Karadžić's efforts to annul the referendum results through force and intimidation. Baker warned that Milošević's actions would have a long-term effect on how the United States dealt with Serbia.

For the first and last time I saw Milošević rattled. His clean-hands policy wasn't fooling the Americans. He was ready to reap the profits from Karadžić's mad actions, but he certainly hadn't expected to be blamed for them. He bobbed and weaved, arguing that Serbia was for peace, dialogue, and the EC negotiations; that Serbs in Bosnia, unlike Serbs in Croatia, weren't threatened; and that the U.S. embassy had been misinforming Washington. He admitted to good relations with Karadžić, but only in the interest of calming him down. "I've used every bit of my influence over Karadžić to work for peace." Why, in any case, should he be blamed for Karadžić's actions? "Should I be blamed if Serbs are responsible for violence in Chicago?" He recalled that he hadn't even taken a position on the Bosnian referendum, although his tame press certainly had.

Milošević then changed tack—he really didn't have much to do with Karadžić at all. "Karadžić is independent," he said, "Nobody is his master. Washington is misinformed about this." I asked Milošević for his reaction to a recent speech by Karadžić in which the Bosnian Serb leader had threatened to close off 60 percent of Bosnia's territory "so tight that not even a bird could fly into it." "Why the hell do I have to be associated with somebody else's speech?" Milošević raged. "My own speeches are for peace." I asked Milošević why he hadn't publicly criticized

Karadžić; he claimed erroneously that he had. "Bloodshed in Bosnia would be terrible," he said. "Only a criminal would be crazy enough to support that." Noting my silence, he added, "Surely Washington doesn't consider me a criminal. Please tell Secretary Baker that I'm a man of peace." He repeated the plea as he showed me out.

However much Milošević may have craved American respect, he pressed forward with his plans for aggression in Bosnia. EC recognition of Bosnia's independence came on April 6. In deference to Serbian sensitivities—April 6 was the anniversary of Hitler's bombing of Belgrade in 1941—the United States delayed its recognition by one day. At the same time Serbian irregulars were pouring across the Drina River, the boundary between Serbia and Bosnia. With the help of the JNA, now partly disguised as the Bosnian Serb army, they captured Bosnian towns, most of them with Muslim majorities, along the river. There's little doubt that these paramilitaries, many of them common criminals, were under the direct control of Milošević's secret police, which encouraged their black market operations and may even have paid their salaries.

The pattern of Serbian atrocities that continued throughout the war was set in these first few days. Typically, the Serbian paramilitaries would storm a town, killing civilians in the assault; would expel the Muslim population; and would turn the town over to Serbs, who, protected by the JNA, could destroy mosques and other Muslim symbols at leisure. Military-age Muslims were sent to concentration camps or executed.

Not all of this barbarism was visible when I saw Milošević on April 6, but some of it was. I had with me another message from the State Department, this one charging Serbia with working to destabilize Bosnia with the object of eventual partition. Mike Einik in Zagreb delivered a similar message to Tudjman in response to Croatian attacks into Bosnia for the purpose of securing areas populated by Croatian majorities.

This time Milošević was ready for me. His eyes widening in disbelief, he pled innocence of any wrongdoing. He said that the Serbs in Bosnia were beyond his influence and that "not a single Serb from Serbia" had been involved. I countered that gangsters from Serbia proper, including the notorious Arkan who had left a trail of pillage and murder during the Croatian war, were displayed on Belgrade television, swaggering on the debris of Muslim towns.

I told Milošević that the presence in Bosnia of irregulars from Serbia drained all credibility from his assertions that Serbia had nothing to do with what was going on there. "Our television is free to broadcast whatever it wants," said Milošević. "You shouldn't take it so seriously. I have instructed the Serbian minister of interior to prevent any armed Serbs from crossing into Bosnia. Arkan's presence in Bosnia isn't confirmed. As I understand it, he's no more than a simple sweetshop owner." Arkan, who did own an ice cream parlor in Belgrade, was a sweetshop owner in the same sense that Dion O'Banion, the Chicago gangster and Al Capone's rival, was a florist.

This Teflon dictator was prepared to go to ridiculous lengths to avoid being drawn into any admission of involvement in Bosnia. At the end of our meeting I urged him to speak to Karadžić. He said that the phone lines to Sarajevo were down so he couldn't. I told him that we at the embassy had spoken to Sarajevo several times that morning. He had no reaction. He was in denial—denial that he bore primary responsibility for the growing violence in Bosnia; denial that his contempt for frontiers ("administrative borders") had given paramilitaries from Serbia a license to invade both Croatia and Bosnia; denial that his pernicious doctrine of "all Serbs in one state" was an incitement to aggression; denial that his creation of the Bosnian Serb army had given Karadžić a crushing military advantage in Bosnia; denial that his press and television, through distortion and lies, had goaded the Serbian people toward support of the most rapacious nationalism.

Serbs in Bosnia had an understandable grievance, though not a legitimate one. Most of them didn't want to live in what they saw as a Muslim-dominated state cut off by international borders from Serbs in Serbia and other republics. Their preferred objective— apartheid—was hardly the most civilized of solutions. But it was not their political objectives but their methods for achieving them that turned them into aggressors, outlaws, or criminals. Milošević's repeated assertions that Serbs weren't being abused in Bosnia reduced the Serbian argument for naked aggression to the assumption that Serbs had a right to murder, torture, and expel simply because they didn't want to live under an independent multiethnic government that wasn't abusing them.

In mid-April Ralph Johnson, the deputy assistant secretary in charge of the Yugoslavia account in the State Department, flew out with messages from Baker for each of the republican leaders. The secretary's aim was to try to calm things down and to warn the aggressors of a worsening relationship with the United States if they persisted. I met Ralph at a U.S. military base near Pisa, Italy, and we prepared to fly into Sarajevo on the first U.S. Air Force relief flight of the many hundreds that followed. Our cargo was blankets and food for Sarajevans, who were already being shelled by Serbian gunners from the hills above the city. I had been flying into Sarajevo uneventfully for over twenty-five years. Now, strapped into a mammoth C-130, I was having trouble understanding why the air force considered this a combat mission or why the young pilot from the Mississippi National Guard seemed so nervous as he began his approach to the Sarajevo airport.

I realized during that short and, as it turned out, safe flight that Sarajevo was for me a symbol as well as a city. Since its fifteenth-century occupation by the Ottoman Turks, it had been a haven for diverse ethnic groups and a model—though not always a consistent one—of racial tolerance. It stood for precisely the values that Karadžić's policy of apartheid was intended to stamp out. There was a special spirit about Sarajevo that Rebecca West caught in

Black Lamb and Grey Falcon: "The air of luxury in Sarajevo has less to do with material goods than with the people. They greet delight here with unreluctant and sturdy appreciation, they are even prudent about it, they will let no drop of pleasure run to waste."

Sarajevo was a city of chestnut trees and minarets, streetcars trundling along the Miljačka River, and the swarming fifteenth-century Turkish market where you could buy tiny spicy hamburgers, called *ćevapčići* from an Arabic root. I recall the words of Teeny's hairdresser, a large friendly Serbian woman named Vera, who was married to a Muslim from Sarajevo: "I'm so glad we have the Muslim and Sarajevo connection, because it means we'll avoid all the nationalist craziness that's ruining the rest of Yugoslavia."

The Sarajevo where Ralph and I landed had already changed. As we drove through the old part of the city, we could hear sporadic rifle fire and could see the damage to the facade of the parliament building, hit the night before by Serbian artillery rounds. We found Izetbegović stunned and angry. He had finally abandoned his tolerance of the Yugoslav army; he claimed that it was now 90 percent Serbian and bent on joining Bosnia to Serbia. He said it should transform itself or leave.

Izetbegović charged that the Serbs were trying to change the demographic situation in Bosnia by forcing Muslims and Croats to leave their homes. I remembered Koljević's self-righteousness in blaming Izetbegović for population tactics to create a Muslim majority. In fact it was Karadžić and Koljević who were using such tactics in pursuit of what later came to be called ethnic cleansing. Izetbegović told us that he continued to support Cutileiro and his negotiating efforts, but that it was impossible to negotiate while the Serbs were shelling Muslim towns. "They're creating a new situation by force; then they're trying to negotiate on the basis of that situation." The Bosnian president pleaded for preventive air strikes by NATO. Ralph's instructions compelled him to say that no military resolution from outside was possible.

In Belgrade on the evening of April 19 we had a long meeting with Milošević. It was my last encounter with the Serbian leader, and it surpassed the others in its surreal nature. Ralph Johnson began by outlining a firm message from Washington. The United States was prepared to consider the "potential" international acceptance of Serbia and Montenegro as a common Yugoslav state but only if Serbia stopped condoning the brutal use of force and intimidation. We were looking for actions, not words, to reverse and prevent armed incursions by Serbs into Bosnia, to withdraw the JNA, and to oppose Karadžić's aggressive actions.

If Serbia didn't respond, the United States would work for its political and economic isolation. Ralph made clear that the evidence of Serbian complicity, through irregulars and through the JNA, was overwhelming. "We see a Croatian pattern emerging. Serbian irregulars move in to force people out of their villages. The JNA intervenes ostensibly to prevent further violence. The villages are then secured for the Serbs."

Milošević as always listened carefully to the list of charges, then proceeded to deny them all. "No armed Serbian irregulars have crossed into Bosnia," he asserted. When I reminded him of the evidence I had given him two weeks before of the presence of the criminal Arkan, he said, "I've checked, and I've discovered that Arkan was in Bosnia only as a bodyguard for one of the Bosnian Serb politicians." As for Karadžić and company, Milošević complained, "It's unfair to make Serbia responsible for the actions of a million and a half Bosnian Serbs. I have no influence over Karadžić. I haven't even talked to him for fifteen days."

"The Serbian policy is peace," Milošević continued. "That's proven by the fact that thousands of refugees have fled to Serbia and are well cared for here. They don't flee anywhere else (this was before over a million Muslim and Croatian refugees fled Bosnia for Croatia and Western Europe). Violence in Bosnia is not in Serbia's interest; we have no territorial pretensions in Bosnia. We favor the EC negotiations. Those shelling Sarajevo—

if the shelling is really happening—are criminals. As for population changes, they're only temporary; refugees will be allowed to return once the EC talks resume. It's ridiculous to think that Serbia is encouraging the creation of ethnically pure areas in Bosnia. This is impossible in a mixed region such as Bosnia and is in any case contrary to my own principles." Milošević defended the JNA's actions in Bosnia, claiming that the army still reflected the republic's ethnic mix of Serbs, Muslims, and Croats—so obvious a lie that even his closest aides had stopped spreading it.

All this was vintage Milošević—a lie on every point of fact, but told with the utmost apparent conviction. He even brushed away the assertion of his foreign minister, Vladislav Jovanović, that Serbian violence had been triggered by premature Western recognition of Bosnia. Milošević wasn't even prepared to admit that there had been any Serbian violence. The word he kept using was "misinformed." Nor did he want to confront the threat of isolation by the United States. He grimaced when he heard it, but he never referred to it. At 11 P.M., after three-and-a-half hours of strained discussion, he looked at his watch, apologized for being a bad host, and ushered us in to a dinner of glutinous lamb that had been congealing in the next room for several hours.

The dinner conversation bore no connection to the confrontational exchanges that had been going on next door. Milošević was a genial and expansive host, acting as if the future contained nothing but sunshine. He seemed totally oblivious to the damage that his policies were about to wreak on his neighbors and on the Serbian people. His chosen topics were the strong basis for Serbian-American relations and the bright prospects for Serbia as a Balkan power.

He waxed eloquent on the economic potential of the new Yugoslav state formed from Serbia and Montenegro. "With its efficient agriculture, energy resources, and key location for transportation—plus a free-market system—it will be in a strong position to attract foreign investment. Why, only this week we were approached by French businessmen about a project for building a high-speed train. Our state is bigger than Greece and Hungary; it will be the major Balkan power. But it will have no territorial pretensions. It will be open to ties to the republics of former Yugoslavia, perhaps in the form of a confederation, perhaps something even closer."

It was astounding to us Americans at the dinner that Milošević seemed to see no contradiction between the vistas of economic affluence he was projecting and the savage war he was masterminding—a war that would turn Serbia into an economic disaster area. Yet he was oblivious to—perhaps he had even forgotten—the strong message from Secretary Baker. Instead, Milošević spent a large part of this Daliesque dinner expatiating on Serbia's historic ties with America. "Serbs can never imagine that Americans could think badly of them. After all, we fought side by side in two world wars. We share a distinguished military tradition. We have sent you a million immigrants."

He then reverted to the need for validation that I had noticed at our last meeting. "I'm not so bad, am I?" he asked, looking at Ralph and me. "Am I such a black sheep?" Then, turning squarely to me, he said, "You know, Mr. Zimmermann, we've had some differences. But I've always felt we had a mutual understanding. In fact, I predict that, before the next six months have gone by, we'll be good friends." For the first time since I'd known him, I was speechless.

Beginning with the first crossings of the Drina in early April, the Serbian and Bosnian Serb offensives in Bosnia accomplished most of their territorial gains in the first few months of the war. Izetbegović, unlike Tudjman, had done almost nothing to build a Bosnian military force. The Bosnian Serbs, on the contrary, enjoyed the full resources of the JNA, which "withdrew" from Bosnia during this period, leaving a fully trained and fully equipped Bosnian Serb army under a new commander—General Ratko Mladić, who had earned a reputation for savagery in the Krajina in Croatia.

In early May, as this pattern was unfolding, I received a mysterious phone call from a man who muffled his voice and refused to give his name over the phone. He said he needed to see me urgently. The next day, a Saturday, the guard at my residence told me there was somebody at the front gate. I went out to see. It was Nikola Koljević, the number two Bosnian Serb.

I invited Koljević in and gave him a glass of wine. After some aimless conversation, he came to the point. He had been talking to Dobrica Ćosić, the Serbian nationalist novelist, and the two of them agreed that Milošević had become a liability for Serbia. It was time to replace him. Koljević told me that Ćosić would be a much better president of Serbia. He said that such a change would eliminate a major problem for the United States and the West.

I replied that it was no secret that the U.S. government saw Milošević as a major problem. But Koljević should understand that we also saw *him*—as well as his ally Karadžić—as major problems. If Koljević was looking for support, he never asked for it, and I gave him no encouragement. Even if this wasn't some kind of provocation, it was a squabble between two odious elements of Serbian nationalism. A line from *Macbeth* summed up this duplicitous thespian: "False face must hide what the false heart doth know."

Koljević was in my office a few days later, May 14, this time with Karadžić. Perhaps it was fitting that I should have one of my last meetings in doomed Yugoslavia with this macabre pair, the professor of English literature and the psychiatrist. At least Shakespeare and Freud would have understood the power of the irrational that provoked these and other madmen to destroy the human fabric of Yugoslavia. They would have understood the purgatory—that place where the innocent suffer and are cleansed—to which Karadžić and his ally Milošević were prepared to condemn the non-Serbian people of Bosnia.

Karadžić said he wanted to see me to clear up any misunderstandings I might have about events in Bosnia. I said it would help if he would answer some questions. Was he ready for a real cease-fire? Would he lift the siege of Sarajevo? Would he allow humanitarian aid to the city? Would he withdraw Serbian paramilitaries from the Sarajevo airports and the hills around? Would he stop the aggression along the Drina? Would he remove heavy weapons from Bosnia? Would he participate in good faith in the talks with Cutileiro? And would he stop making dirty deals with the Croats?

As I expected, Karadžić was not prepared to make any commitments on these questions, just to blame Izetbegović for the war and the lack of progress in negotiations. He took a fatalistic approach. "Bosnia," he said, "has never really known peace. It has lived peacefully only under the dictatorship of foreign occupation. It can be compared to Nagorno-Karabakh (the luckless Armenian enclave in Azerbaijan where war had already been raging several years), and to Cyprus, and to Lebanon." Unbelievably, Karadžić intended me to take these horrendous examples of human suffering as models of what he wanted to create in Bosnia.

Like a punch-drunk fighter, Karadžić flailed about him with flurries of distortions and lies. "American views are based on hopeless misunderstandings and disinformation. You think I'm close to Milošević; in fact, he has nothing to do with our Bosnian Serb Party. War was imposed on us by the Croats and Muslims. Serbs are making maps not to divide Bosnia, but only to protect themselves. Serbian forces have no intention of holding onto non-Serbian cities like Višegrad (Višegrad remained under Serbian control throughout the Bosnian war). There are no Serbs from Serbia in Bosnia, just a few criminals. Only we Serbs are really interested in negotiations, which must of course end in the partition of Bosnia."

Koljević chimed in to say that if I hadn't overlooked the "sequence of events," I would have seen that the Bosnian Serbs were consistently for negotiation. I replied, "The Bosnian Serb strategy is clear to all: create new 'facts' by establishing the borders of a 'Serbian republic' by force, then get those facts ratified by negotiation. Even Hitler preferred to win without fighting. Don't you see that the world considers you barbarians? If you continue, your isolation is likely to continue and increase."

This set Karadžić off on a stream-of-consciousness justification for everything he was doing. "You have to understand Serbs, Mr. Zimmermann. They've been betrayed for centuries. Today they can't live with other nations. They must have their own separate existence. They're a warrior race and they can trust only themselves to take by force what is their due. But this doesn't mean that Serbs can hate. Serbs are incapable of hatred." I sought to pin him down. "What sort of Bosnian Serb republic do you have in mind," I asked. "Will it be a part of Serbia?"

"That will be for the Bosnian Serb people to decide," he said. "But our first goal is independence, so we can live separately from others." "Where will your capital be?" I asked. "Why, Sarajevo, of course." "But how can a city that is nearly 50 percent Muslim and only 30 percent Serb be the capital for the Serbs alone?" Karadžić had a ready answer. "Sarajevo was built with Serbian money. So we have a right to divide the city into Muslim, Serbian, and Croatian sections, so that no ethnic groups will have to live or work together."

"Just how do you plan to divide it?" I asked. "By walls," he said matter-of-factly. "Of course people will be able to pass from one part of the city to another, as long as they have permission and go through the checkpoints." I thought of Sarajevo with its tradition of civility and openness to all ethnic groups. Then I thought of Berlin, where the wall that had symbolized all the hatreds and divisions of the cold war had been torn down just a few years before. "Do you mean," I asked, "that Sarajevo will be like Berlin before the wall was destroyed?" "Yes," he answered, "our vision of Sarajevo is like Berlin when the wall was still standing."

DEPARTURES

*The conflagrations didn't break out through
spontaneous combustion. Pyromaniacs
were required.*

On May 12, 1992, the State Department announced that I was being recalled to Washington in protest against the Serbian aggression in Bosnia. Nothing was said about the duration of my absence, but it was pretty clear that it would be permanent. EC and other European ambassadors received similar instructions. Most of us would depart in a matter of days. Nobody believed that this diplomatic move would have much effect on the strategy worked out jointly by Milošević, Karadžić, and the Yugoslav army for seizing most of Bosnia against a nearly nonexistent Bosnian force. The objective was a different one—to signal that there would no longer be even the pretense of normal relations with Serbia. The action was modest, but it was the right thing to do.

Teeny and I set about drawing down our intense three-year stay in Belgrade. Teeny's closest connection had been to a volunteer program that in many ways represented in miniature the hopes and frustrations of Yugoslavia. She and two friends, Mary Rackmales from the embassy and Talat Delhavi, the wife of the Pakistani ambassador, had decided at the beginning of our second year to create a volunteer program that would involve diplomatic wives in local children's institutions. Teeny knew that Mary and Talat were warm-hearted women with die-hard perseverance and a talent for management.

Hands-on volunteer work was virtually unheard of in Yugoslavia, as in many European countries. At first the three got nowhere. One reason was a suspicion about Teeny's motives— why did the wife of the American ambassador want to involve herself in Belgrade social services? More important, nobody could understand what they wanted to do. The breakthrough came when a young Yugoslav psychologist, Julia Klaić, got them accepted at the Children's Psychiatric Hospital. Most treatment there took place only in the morning, leaving the children to run wild or lapse into depressed boredom in the afternoon. So a small group of nervous but determined foreign women set out to provide some entertainment and diversion.

Talat's coming from a nonaligned country was a useful ideological asset. She had enough clout finally to get permission from suspicious Belgrade authorities for the group to work both in the main children's hospital and in an orphanage. Ultimately, the volunteers grew to about fifty, representing about a dozen foreign countries. Mary soon began to recruit Yugoslav women, giving the program a character that would survive the transience of the diplomats.

It took time for the hospital staffs not to feel threatened and for the volunteers themselves to get used to hospitals with shabby medical practices and overt ethnic discrimination. A doctor might call his five-year-old patient to his face a "shitty little Shiptar" (an abusive word for Albanian) or a "horrible stupid Muslim." The nurses struck, shook, and screamed at the children. And the director of the children's hospital once invited the volunteers in for a drink, saying as he poured a liberal dose of brandy for himself, "I can't stay long. I have an emergency appendectomy to perform in ten minutes."

The children were suffering from serious neglect. The volunteers brought toys and games, keeping them in a cupboard that was opened with great fanfare when visiting hours arrived. There was little language communication; but the communication by smiles, body language, and warm attention was extraordinary. The children began to brighten and to get involved, even those with serious and sometimes fatal illnesses. After a rocky start, even the nurses began to see the value of these simple human contacts, sometimes seeking out the volunteers for their patients with special problems.

Now Teeny was paying a final visit to say goodbye to the children and the staff at the children's hospital. The reasons for our departure had been published in the Serbian press, with the most venomous accusations of iniquity against the United States and me personally. A nurse who had always been friendly spat on the floor as Teeny approached her. The formerly bibulous and friendly director turned away from the door of his office and refused to look at her or even speak. The children were mystified by what was going on and disturbed by the tension. Two of the older ones followed Teeny out to tell her in tears how much they would miss her. Fortunately, Mary Rackmales kept the program going after Teeny's departure and got it back to reasonable normalcy.

Before we knew of our recall, Teeny and I had invited a few friends for dinner; it was scheduled for the evening before we were to leave. We decided to go ahead with the dinner and to expand it into a farewell party for the people who had meant the most to us. At short notice we invited opposition politicians, human rights activists, independent journalists, university professors, novelists, painters and sculptors, business people, musicians, diplomats, actors, and doctors, plus colleagues in the diplomatic corps and other foreigners working in Belgrade.

The guest list of over a hundred turned out to be a Who's Who of independent Yugoslavia—people who rejected the nationalist tide that was sweeping all before it, who were not afraid to embrace Western values, and who admired the United States and what it stood for. For the first time in our experience, every single person who was in town accepted our invitation, even though I had become the most visible foreign symbol of opposition to a regime that wielded near-absolute power over their careers and futures. If we needed any assurance that the nationalists didn't speak for everybody in Yugoslavia, we got it that night.

It was a warm May evening. We set up trestle tables on the terrace and ransacked freezers, cupboards, and bar to lay out every scrap of food and drop of drink in the house. In this gigantic smorgasbord, šlivovica jostled with scotch and bourbon, fresh Serbian lamb with hastily defrosted Montenegrin shellfish, Diet Coke with Bosnian mineral water, Croatian chocolates with Hershey bars. There wasn't a Yugoslav there who didn't know that his or her life was about to go into a free fall to cataclysm. Yet, amazingly, the atmosphere was festive as well as elegiac. Perhaps the best parties are given on the brink of disaster.

During the dinner people would come up to us with personal messages. Janja Lončar, the attractive and gentle wife of the now-resigned foreign minister, told Teeny and me of her worries for her mother, a Croatian woman living in war-ravaged Bosnia. Vuk Drašković wanted me to know that his turn against nationalism and toward Western values was permanent. Vesna Pešić, the founder of the peace movement, told us that she was going to run for the Serbian parliament as a way of expanding her antiwar, antinationalist platform. Gordana Logar, perpetually anxious and perpetually brave, mourned for the future of her beloved Yugoslavia and her beloved *Borba*. And Sonja Licht, who had once joked with me about my unpopularity, said she was proud to be in an American house, because the United States was the only country that had consistently stood for genuine democratic values in Yugoslavia.

As people were getting their dessert, Neša, my driver, came up to me in uncharacteristic haste. He said that a gang of men had just driven up in a truck and had started spraying insecticide into the garden. Teeny knew the insecticide; it was called malathion and was occasionally and imprudently sprayed by crop-dusting airplanes over the Belgrade hills to kill mosquitoes. At close quarters it was obviously dangerous. I asked Neša if there could be some mistake. He said no; in fact, he had seen nearby a jeep belonging to Arkan, the notorious mass killer of Croatians and Muslims. I remembered having received that morning an anonymous telephone call threatening unspecified punishment if I went through with the party. I hadn't taken it too seriously; now I wondered.

Neša, backed by the timorous embassy guards, went out on the street to tell the interlopers to get out. He returned victorious, though dripping with the chemical they had sprayed at his eyes as a parting shot. The guests stayed on. Those who knew the score were defiant. The others congratulated us on finding a much better way than crop-dusters for dealing with mosquitoes.

The next day, May 16, I delivered my last demarche about Bosnia to Milošević's foreign minister; the Serbian leader was not disposed to receive my farewell call personally. That afternoon Teeny and I left for Washington on Pan American, a doomed airline leaving a doomed country. Milošević's press celebrated my departure with headlines reflecting its habitual glee with my German last name: "Auf Wiedersehen, Herr Zimmermann."

The days before our departure and the weeks after gave us time for introspection about a country where we had lived six years and that had affected us deeply. How was it possible that such attractive people, on whom the gods of nature and fortune had smiled, could have plowed their way straight to hell? Shortly before we left Belgrade, I tried to answer that question in a cable entitled "Who Killed Yugoslavia?" It was intended as an analysis of the fatal elements in Yugoslavia's distant and recent past, laced with some nostalgia for what had been lost. I used as a framework the old English folk song "Who Killed Cock Robin?" a tale of murder complete with witnesses, grave-diggers, and mourners, but nobody to save the victim or bring him back to life. The cable is reproduced in an appendix.

With the perspective of years, of the Bosnian war, and of many gross misrepresentations of Yugoslavia's collapse, it's important to eliminate some of the reasons often cited. First, Yugoslavia was not destroyed by ancient Balkan hatreds. This doesn't mean that the Balkans don't seethe with violence. The First World War was touched off by the assassination in Sarajevo of an Austrian archduke by a Bosnian Serb; the Second was for Yugoslavia not only a liberation war but a civil war with over half a million Yugoslav deaths.

But is Yugoslavia so unique? Europe, taken as a whole, has endured two civil wars in this century, involving sixty million deaths, including the genocidal annihilation of six million European Jews. Placid England suffered in the fifteenth century the Wars of the Roses, which moved Charles Dickens to remark: "When men continually fight against their own countrymen, they are always observed to be more unnaturally cruel and filled with rage than they are against any other enemy." The English lived through an even bloodier period in the seventeenth century: a king was executed and many of the people of Ireland massacred by Cromwell's forces. France had its wars of religion in the sixteenth century and its blood-drenched revolution in the eighteenth. Nor has the United States been immune from domestic conflict. More Americans died in our civil war than in any foreign war we have ever fought.

Balkan genes aren't abnormally savage. Bosnia enjoyed long periods of tranquility as a multiethnic community. Serbs and Croats, the most antagonistic of adversaries today, had never fought each other before the twentieth century. The millennium they spent as neighbors was marked more by mutual indifference than by mutual hostility. Serbs, though demonized by many as incorrigibly xenophobic, don't fit that stereotype. Milovan Djilas's son Aleksa, author of a brilliant history of nationalism in Yugoslavia, points out that, with all the manipulative tools at Milošević's disposal, it still took him four years to arouse the Serbian population and that, even then, thousands of Serbs fled the country to avoid fighting in Croatia.

The Yugoslav wars can't be explained by theories of inevitable ethnic hatreds, even when such explanations conveniently excuse outsiders from the responsibilities of intervening. There was plenty of racial and historical tinder available in Yugoslavia. But the conflagrations didn't break out through spontaneous combustion. Pyromaniacs were required.

Second, religion wasn't at the heart of Yugoslavia's demise. The Yugoslav wars were primarily ethnic, not religious, wars. The major proponents of destructive nationalism weren't driven by religious faith. Franjo Tudjman had been a communist most of his life; he converted to Catholicism when he turned to nationalist activities. Milošević, a lifelong communist, never, as far as I know, entered a Serbian Orthodox church except for blatant political purposes. I recall a visit he made for electoral reasons to a Serbian monastery on Mt. Athos in northern Greece. Not even the official photographs could disguise the disconcerted and uncomfortable look on his face. Even Bosnia was largely a secular society; a 1985 survey found that only 17 percent of its people considered themselves believers.

None of this absolves the Serbian and Croatian churches. There were many religious people in Yugoslavia, particularly among rural folk. The Serbian Orthodox Church and the Catholic Church in Croatia were willing accomplices of the political leaders in coopting their parishioners for racist designs. These two churches were national churches, in effect arms of their respective states when it came to ethnic matters. They played a disgraceful role by exacerbating racial tensions when they could have urged their faithful toward Christian healing.

With regard to Bosnia, both the Serbian and Croatian regimes felt the need to impute fanatic religiosity to the Muslims in order to satanize them. But the portrayal was false. The Bosnia I knew was probably the most secular Muslim society in the world. The growing number of Muslim adherents today is a consequence of the war, not one of its root causes.

Third, Yugoslavia was not a victim of communism or even of its demise. Yugoslavs didn't live under the Soviet yoke, unlike their neighbors in the Warsaw Pact, for whom communism was an alien and evil implant. Gorbachev's withdrawal from Eastern Europe liberated whole countries but had little direct effect on Yugoslavia, whose communism, whatever its defects, was home-grown. In Eastern Europe the fault line was between communism and Western-style democracy; in Yugoslavia it was between ethnic groups. Tito's relative liberalism within the European communist world coopted many people for the Yugoslav party who would have been Western-oriented dissidents in Czechoslovakia or Poland.

In Yugoslavia the dissidents were for the most part nationalists, not liberals, and they marched to domestic drummers beating out racist, not Western, themes. Communists in Yugoslavia wore black hats or white hats, depending on whether they were nationalists or not. The most rabid nationalists, like Milošević or Tudjman, were or had been communists. So had many antinationalist, democratic figures, like Drnovšek, Gligorov, Tupurkovski, and many courageous journalists and human rights activists. In most of Eastern Europe, the word "communist" explained a good deal about a person; in Yugoslavia it explained next to nothing.

Fourth, Yugoslavia wasn't destroyed by foreign intervention or the lack of it. General Kadijević, in his paranoid account of the end of Yugoslavia, blames the United States, Germany, and the European Community, acting in collusion with traitors in Slovenia, Croatia, and Kosovo. Foreign countries did make serious mistakes in Yugoslavia, but they didn't destroy it. The failure to do more to support Prime Minister Marković, the lack of a forceful Western reaction to the shelling of Dubrovnik, and the European Community's premature decision to recognize the independence of Yugoslavia's republics were all mistakes, but not fatal ones. Whatever inducements or penalties the West might have devised, they wouldn't have been enough to suppress the nationalistic rage that was overwhelming the country. The war in Bosnia was another matter; there the West could have saved the situation and didn't. But the murder of Yugoslavia was a crime of domestic violence.

The victim itself had congenital defects. Yugoslavia was a state, but not a nation. Few felt much loyalty to Yugoslavia itself. Tito sought to encourage fealty by guaranteeing ethnic autonomy rather than by trying to create an ethnic melting pot. Political energy was directed more toward gaining a better position in Yugoslavia for one's ethnic group than toward preserving the viability of the state. Nobody wanted to be a member of a minority; nobody expected minorities automatically to be protected. Vladimir Gligorov, son of the wise president of Macedonia and a perceptive scholar, captured this feeling when he asked ironically, "Why should I be a minority in your state when you can be a minority in mine?"

These character traits damaged, but didn't doom, Yugoslavia. The country didn't commit suicide. As the court of history pursues its investigation of the death of Yugoslavia, I can imagine the following indictments: Slovenia for selfishness toward its fellow Yugoslavs; Tudjman's Croatia for insensitivity toward its Serbian population and greed toward its Bosnian neighbors; the Yugoslav army for ideological rigidity and arrogance, culminating in war crimes; Radovan Karadžić for attacking the principle of tolerance in Yugoslavia's most ethnically mixed republic; and—most of all—Slobodan Milošević for devising and pursuing a strategy that led directly to the breakup of the country and to the deaths of over a hundred thousand of its citizens. Nationalism was the arrow that killed Yugoslavia. Milošević was the principal bowman.

The Serbian leader made Yugoslavia intolerable for anybody who wasn't a Serb. He is hated among Albanians, Slovenes, Croats, Muslims, Macedonians, and Hungarians. And he has brought his own people into poverty and despair. The potentially prosperous and influential Serbia on which he expatiated in our last meeting in April 1992 is now an economic and civil shambles. Much of its youth and middle class—the foundation of democratic construction—has fled to the west. Milošević's dream of "all Serbs in one state" is a nightmare today; Serbs are now scattered among four states—"Yugoslavia" (Serbia and Montenegro), Bosnia, Croatia, and Macedonia. In seeking to dominate Yugoslavia, Milošević destroyed it. In seeking to tear out the pieces where Serbs lived, he wrecked, for a generation or more, the future of all Serbs.

When I got back to Washington, I found Baker preoccupied with the Bosnian war. The secretary understood clearly the collusion among Milošević, Karadžić, and the JNA. Baker wanted to do something fast to punish Milošević; his preferred action was an economic embargo on Serbia and Montenegro. I had mixed feelings about economic sanctions. Those at whom they're directed can often avoid the direct effects while wrapping themselves in the mantle of martyrs. Sanctions often bite hardest on the middle class and other innocent people—usually the ones we have most interest in encouraging.

On the other hand, sanctions could humiliate a dictator, making clear that he wasn't fit to deal with the civilized world. I felt it would be repugnant to continue a normal relationship with Serbia after its aggressions in Bosnia. More concretely, Milošević's desire to get the sanctions lifted would give us a bargaining chip; three years later that chip was to play an important role in Milošević's decision to end the Bosnian war. And as a longer shot, we could also hope that in time the sanctions would help push the Serbian people to turn on their leader. When Baker asked me for my view, I recommended going ahead with the sanctions and trying to "Saddamize" Milošević. The members of the UN Security Council supported the U.S. initiative; sanctions were voted on May 30, 1992.

I worried that we didn't have a more comprehensive strategy for dealing with the overt Serbian aggression. By mid-July 1992 I had decided that nothing short of Western force could repel the Serbian plan; we ought to begin a campaign of air strikes. My view was that the Serbs were acting in the belief that NATO wouldn't react. Indeed, no other conclusion could be drawn from the West's past actions. I didn't have much respect for Serbian military capabilities, despite their overwhelming advantages in numbers and JNA-supplied equipment. In addition to regular forces, they were relying on untrained and often drunk irregulars. Moreover, all but the extremists knew they had no real right to the territory they were seizing. This was an adventure for them, a land grab, not a Serbian vital interest. Finally, I knew that the Serbs had great respect for American military power when used resolutely. I believed they would continue to push, but only until NATO pushed back.

There was no debate in the U.S. government about the causes of the Bosnian war; everybody knew that Milošević and Karadžić were the guilty parties. The issue was whether U.S. interests and the military difficulties in Bosnia warranted our intervention. I tried out my thinking on Eagleburger. As usual he was open to discussion. He said his own views were heavily influenced by Vietnam, where a modest American involvement had escalated into a debacle, and Lebanon, where the imprudent stationing of U.S. Marines in 1983 had led to a terror bombing that killed 241 Americans.

Eagleburger also believed that the victory in the Gulf War vindicated the view of Colin Powell, chairman of the Joint Chiefs of Staff. Writing in *Foreign Affairs* in late 1992, Powell listed the necessary criteria for military intervention, including a clearly defined political objective, probability of achieving it by military force, exhaustion of nonviolent approaches, and a knowledge of the consequences of intervention. It was doubtful that the complex Bosnian crisis could meet such criteria; in fact, Powell consistently opposed military intervention there.

I also pressed my views on General Brent Scowcroft, President Bush's national security adviser and, like Eagleburger, an expert on Yugoslavia. Scowcroft seemed extremely interested in the possibilities of the limited use of NATO air power. He asked detailed questions about what we could and should do. I concentrated on Sarajevo, saying that we ought to knock out the threat to civilians represented by the artillery on the hills above the city. Such NATO attacks would carry a potent message to the Serbian leadership. I also suggested that consideration be given to other air attacks on Serbian military installations and supply routes in Bosnia. The aim would be to drive the Serbs toward a negotiated settlement that could deliver a fair deal to the Muslims and Croats.

Scowcroft thanked me warmly for coming to talk to him. He told me later that he had been personally sympathetic to military action in the summer and fall of 1992. But he had been dubious that air strikes would be effective. And if they weren't, what would we then be prepared to do? The prevailing view in the Bush administration was that, for the sake of credibility, we would have to do what was necessary to prevail, even to the point of using ground troops. Since no senior official was prepared to wage a ground war, the line had to be drawn short of the use of force in general.

In the end, nothing happened, even after the American press discovered Serbian concentration camps in Bosnia in July. The Vietnam syndrome and the Powell doctrine proved to be powerful dampers on action by the Bush administration, particularly in an election year.

I believed that the arguments against the use of American force in 1992 were outdated and wrong, mired as they were in the inappropriate examples of Vietnam and the Gulf. The U.S. military was far more capable of waging limited war than it professed. There were intermediate options between total involvement and no involvement. There was no Vietnam-like inevitability of escalation, since the disposition of American forces always requires specific decisions by the president. Nor did the not-so-intrepid Bosnian Serbs resemble the fanatical North Vietnamese, who had been far more determined and disciplined. Modern precision air power, even without ground forces, could prove a potent weapon against the Serbs, who were not to be bombed back to the Stone Age, just to the negotiating table. Finally, a doctrine precluding virtually any military engagement except an absolute sure thing would keep American power on the sidelines of almost every imaginable future crisis. Bosnia was a clear case of aggression; we had a moral, perhaps even a legal, obligation to deal with it.

Late in the game, the Clinton administration came to most of these conclusions. The refusal of the Bush administration to commit American power early in the Bosnian war—even though that refusal was based on an honest perception of the U.S. national interest—was our greatest mistake of the entire Yugoslav crisis. It made an unjust outcome inevitable and wasted the opportunity to prevent over a hundred thousand deaths.

Shortly after my return to Washington, Baker decided to leave Belgrade without an American ambassador. The embassy would continue its active but limbolike status under the able direction of Bob Rackmales as chargé d'affaires. I became director of the State Department's Bureau for Refugee Programs, a challenge different from anything I'd ever done before. In refugee work I learned a lot about personal commitment from the dedicated people in the refugee bureau and from the young volunteers from far-flung countries who make refugee camps places of hope rather than despair.

I also learned the obvious fact that Bosnia wasn't the only, or even the worst, refugee disaster in the world. Rwanda, a catastrophe that came later, was a killing ground for perhaps nine hundred thousand people—about six times more than have died in Bosnia. This factor didn't make me less convinced that the United States had to act in Bosnia; we had interests and a history of engagement in the Balkans that didn't apply in many other areas. But it did convince me that, acting with others, we had to do our fair share globally to help reduce the suffering of those trying to escape civil war, ethnic abuse, and other man-made calamities.

In September 1992 Eagleburger asked me to set aside my refugee work for two months to serve as the U.S. coordinator for decisions taken at the just-concluded London conference on Bosnia. One of my main tasks—monitoring compliance with the London agreement—was infernally simple. Bosnian Serb shelling of Sarajevo and other population centers continued without interruption in violation of commitments made in London. It was clear that nothing would change without a credible threat of NATO force. But the U.S. government had no intention of leading a Western coalition to put military pressure on the Serbs. The Europeans, led in retreat by the British, were equally adamant against a force option. Cyrus Vance was also hesitant to recommend the use of force, although his new negotiating partner, former British Foreign Secretary David Owen, saw the usefulness of air strikes.

My own convictions on the need for force were strengthened by hearing former Secretary of State George Shultz speak on Bosnia at a fund-raiser for the International Rescue Committee, an important American refugee organization. Without the use of a note, Shultz argued passionately for nearly an hour that America's most basic interests required the use of force on behalf of the Bosnians. This moving appeal by a man frequently and erroneously described as cold and passionless inspired me to collect my own thoughts on the U.S. stake in Bosnia.

It seemed to me that the United States had three major interests. None of them was vital but, taken together, they clearly justified military intervention. The first was geopolitical. Bosnia lies across a traditional fault line of instability stretching from Poland to Albania. A Bosnia left to seethe could affect the stability of three U.S. allies—Greece, Turkey, and Italy—as well as of Croatia, Hungary, Macedonia, and Albania. A Bosnia relegated to the Serbian sphere of influence could demoralize democratic dissidents and minorities in Serbia, including the Albanians of Kosovo, and invite a Milošević power play against them.

Second, there was a global aspect. Long U.S. engagement in Yugoslavia had made Bosnia a test of American leadership and resolve in the eyes of other governments, including assertive dictatorships. If we stumbled in Bosnia, we could be challenged elsewhere. Our third interest was moral. The Bosnians were fighting for the preservation of a multiethnic tradition, for a state where different ethnic groups could live together. The United States was the world's most successful multiethnic society, the inspiration for what they wanted to build themselves. I believed it would just be wrong for us to turn away from their anguish and their hopes.

Unfortunately, through the waning months of the Bush administration there was no inclination toward greater activism. In my role as coordinator I often accompanied Eagleburger or Arnold Kanter, the undersecretary of state for political affairs, to Deputies' Committee meetings at the White House, where the second- or third-ranking official of each foreign affairs agency met to discuss leading issues. The Bosnia meetings were chaired by Jonathan Howe, a deputy national security adviser and a hardworking admiral with considerable State Department experience. Howe, no doubt reflecting guidance from above, ran the meetings like academic seminars rather than mechanisms for forcing decisions. In fact, decisions for engaging the United States were rarely taken or even proposed. Instead, there was a lot of carping at European governments and at the UN High Commissioner for Refugees (UNHCR) for not doing enough.

The representatives of the Department of Defense and the Joint

Chiefs of Staff took the consistent position that no U.S. military personnel were to be put in harm's way. They even had a rule that no member of the U.S. armed forces could travel to the former Yugoslavia for any purpose without the personal approval of Secretary of Defense Cheney. They sought successively to block a "no-fly zone" to interdict military flights (mostly Serbian) over Bosnia, the initiation of a supply airlift to Sarajevo, the protection of land routes to Sarajevo and Mostar for the supply of humanitarian relief, and (later, during the Clinton administration) the institution of air drops to towns beyond the reach of aid convoys.

The Pentagon's tactic was never to say no—that would undercut its "can-do" approach—but simply to raise objections that would make the proposals unworkable. The military argued that it would take fifty thousand ground troops to protect the relief routes from Split to Sarajevo. When its opposition to a Sarajevo airlift was overridden, it tried to limit the amount of goods to be flown in. It ridiculed air drops as infeasible in view of Bosnia's mountainous terrain and uncertain weather. It opposed putting U.S. military observers on the ground in Bosnia to support a no-fly zone, recommending instead foreign service officers or retired military personnel.

At the heart of the military's visceral opposition to involvement was an understandable aversion to casualties. This was taken to ludicrous lengths, given U.S. interests in Bosnia and the fact that we had an army of volunteers who had enlisted in the knowledge that they would run some risks. In the event, the American military participated actively and with distinction in the no-fly zone, the Sarajevo airlift, and the air drops, with negligible casualties.

If no Western government was prepared to take military action to stem the Serbian offensive, at least an international humanitarian effort could be mounted to protect its Muslim victims. The humanitarian campaign in Bosnia was a major, and largely unrecognized, success. In the fall of 1992 the CIA was predicting up to a hundred thousand non-war-related deaths during the coming Bosnian winter. The winter of 1992–93 turned out to be providentially mild, but it was primarily the work of the relief agencies, convoyed by the much-maligned UN Protection Force (UNPROFOR), that turned the threatening situation around. During the Bosnian war, very few people died of hunger or exposure—a tribute to the professional relief workers who trundled food, plastic sheeting, and small stoves past the hostile and venal guards at the Serbian checkpoints.

This humanitarian triumph was a collective achievement of people from many organizations and countries. But three individuals also stand out in my memory. The first refugee official I met was Roy Williams, a wiry black American with a craggy face that could have been cut out of Mount Rushmore. A logistical genius who directed the International Rescue Committee's (IRC's) worldwide operations, Roy decided months before the Bosnian war began to activate the IRC in Bosnia. Starting with one man in Sarajevo, the IRC became the largest and most effective American voluntary organization in Bosnia.

Perhaps the most imposing individual on the refugee scene was Fred Cuny, a tall Texan with a toothy smile and the look—which he cultivated—of a lone cowboy. With the backing of the financier George Soros, Fred worked during the Serbian artillery barrage to give the people of Sarajevo an entire water system. On one of his infrequent trips out of Bosnia, he regaled me over a drink at Zagreb's Esplanade Hotel with stories of the inefficiencies of the UN bureaucracies in Bosnia. Fred Cuny hated red tape; he traveled fast and light, and he performed life-saving miracles. He was later lost in Chechnya, a hero of humanitarian work on several continents.

Sadako Ogata, the UN high commissioner for refugees, combined an American education, flawless English, and impressive academic and diplomatic experience with a dedication and determination rare even in the refugee business. UNHCR is the largest refugee organization in the world; it has over 5,000 employees and operates in 120 countries. Mrs. Ogata, a small Japanese woman, is a firm, well-organized, and effective manager who husbands her power and uses it skillfully. But she wasn't thinking of this when I first met her in her modest and comfortable office in Geneva. She was thinking of getting the flower arrangement on the coffee table just right. It was only when she had taken a minute to do so that she was ready to settle back and talk with conviction about her plans for Bosnia.

Sadako Ogata took UNHCR over a watershed in Bosnia. The organization's traditional mission was to care for people who had fled their country because of persecution or fear of persecution. Technically, a person wasn't even a refugee if he hadn't left his country; he was a displaced person. Except for the special circumstance of ministering to the Kurds after the Gulf War, UNHCR had never dealt with displaced persons inside their own country; nor had it operated at the center of a shooting war. Under the leadership of this courageous woman, in Bosnia it did both. Mrs. Ogata shrugs this off. "What was I supposed to do?" she would ask me. "The problem was there. We had only two choices. We could walk away from it, or we could try to solve it." A large and sometimes cumbersome organization, UNHCR has absorbed a lot of criticism in the Balkans, as elsewhere. But as the lead relief agency in Bosnia, coordinating all the others, it's a large part of the reason why more people didn't die.

When Bill Clinton succeeded George Bush, it looked as if the United States would adopt a more militant policy on Bosnia. As a candidate Clinton had criticized the Bush administration for "turning its back on violations of basic human rights" and had called for air strikes against the Serbs for blocking relief operations. In the third week of his presidency he said that a failure to act in Bosnia "would be to give up American leadership." In the week after inauguration I sent an informal memo to Peter Tarnoff, the newly appointed undersecretary for political affairs and a former foreign service colleague. I wrote that only force would impress Milošević and Karadžić and argued that we mustn't abandon Bosnia. A few days later Secretary Warren Christopher invited me to participate in an informal discussion of Bosnian policy.

Christopher asked our small group for views on the Vance-Owen plan, which provided for a primarily ethnic division of Bosnia but contained some benefits for the Muslims. It held the Serbs to 43 percent of the territory of Bosnia, divided the country into ten provinces rather than the three envisaged by Cutileiro, provided for multiethnic provinces, and preserved at least nominally the sovereignty of Bosnia. The secretary had not yet discussed the plan with Vance, whose deputy he had been in the Carter administration. I said I thought it was an acceptable compromise in the circumstances, since the Serbs had by then consolidated their hold on more than two-thirds of Bosnia.

Christopher said he was concerned that the Muslims would reject the plan. I told him I had a piece of accidental inside knowledge on that. I had been in Vance's office in Geneva a few weeks before, when Vance and Owen received the Bosnian government's reaction to the plan. It was not only positive, but enthusiastic; the Muslims said they were ready to announce support immediately. Vance urged them to delay; he was afraid a quick Muslim acceptance would cause the Serbs to raise the price. With that background, I gave Christopher my view that any current Muslim objections were likely to be tactical and that in the end they would probably accept the plan. Unfortunately, the administration delayed in its support for the plan, thus missing a chance to get it launched.

The conversation turned to policy options. Bob Galluci, then in charge of political-military affairs, and I argued that air strikes had to be a serious option; we both felt they would be necessary. Others in the room were more cautious. Tarnoff drew up an inventory of possible steps that could be taken short of force. They included such things as breaking diplomatic relations with Milošević's rump Yugoslavia and tightening the economic embargo. Perhaps unwisely, I said that nothing on that list would deter Milošević; the language of force was the only language he understood. Christopher said with a smile that this was a pretty gloomy way to end a meeting. He added that he would convene the same group often for further discussions. But we were never called again.

Hopes didn't survive long that Clinton would pursue a tougher policy toward the Serbs. The Bush administration had clear reasons for what I believed was a mistaken policy: Vietnam, the Powell doctrine, possibly the 1992 election. With Clinton there were also reasons, for example, Powell's continuing influence in the first months of the administration, Clinton's difficult relations with the military over his avoidance of the Vietnam war and his effort to press the issue of gays, and the president's priority concern with domestic policy. Beyond this I sensed a discomfort, not discernible among the Bush people, about using force at all. A State Department colleague, who had tried to persuade both administrations to use force in Bosnia, vented his frustrations to me one day. "First I tried with the Bush people and failed," he said. "Then I tried with the Clinton people and failed. But I'll tell you one thing. If the Bush people had decided to use force, they'd have known how."

During the first year of the Clinton administration, policy toward Bosnia revealed little resolve, determination, or consistency. The highly publicized debates among senior officials led to failures to pursue any single approach for very long. Fluctuations in the way administration officials described the problem reflected this inner tension. Depending on the degree of American activism desired at the time, Bosnia was variously described as a U.S. strategic concern and a test for the post–cold war world and for American leadership, or else as a civil war, the result of ancient hatreds, and an issue for the Europeans. Everybody, however, could agree with Secretary Christopher's characterization of it as a "problem from hell."

The Clinton administration had inherited a mess not of its making. The Serbs' pursuit of ethnic cleansing made the creation of refugees an objective of the war, not a by-product. Over three million Bosnians were displaced: a million to Croatia, Germany, and other Western European countries; the rest to other parts of Bosnia and to Serbia. Discoveries of mass graves have made it clear that murders were carried out on a scale unheard of since Nazi times.

We were watching a cultural genocide, an attempt to wipe out an entire culture—its civil institutions, its mosques, its libraries and schools, its future leaders. What wasn't eradicated had to be moved far away, and all incentives for return had to be destroyed. These war crimes weren't accidental. They were the direct result of the policies of Slobodan Milošević and Radovan Karadžić. They are guilty as surely as if they had primed the explosive charges, pulled the triggers, or driven the bulldozers over the grave sites.

UNPROFOR, a multinational force with French and British but no American troops, was out of its depth. Its primarily humanitarian mission, the small size of its force, the restrictions on its combat role, the weakness of its combat capabilities ("You don't go into battle in a white jeep," one UNPROFOR commander, Sir Michael Rose, told me), and its strong emphasis on "neutrality" all combined to render it next to useless in shortening the war or encouraging a political settlement. I still find it perplexing why most UNPROFOR commanders, especially General Rose and Canadian General Lewis MacKenzie, found the Bosnian Serb army so compatible and its contention that "everybody commits atrocities" so convincing. Was it Serbian military spit and polish when contrasted with the ragtag Bosnians in tennis shoes? Or was it simply a failure to learn how this war had begun and what it was really about?

The fate of Clinton's major initiative of 1993, "lift and strike," reflected the administration's crippling ambiguity of purpose. The idea, a good one, was to "lift" the arms embargo on Bosnia while using NATO air power to "strike" at any Serbian effort to prevent the Bosnians from receiving the new arms and training on them. Christopher's unsuccessful effort in the spring to sell the plan to the Europeans allowed the president thereafter to talk tough without doing much. He could take credit for a muscular policy on behalf of the Bosnians while blaming the Europeans for preventing its enactment. The administration argued that since the United States didn't have peacekeeping troops in Bosnia, it was in a difficult position to urge toughness on the Europeans, who did. This "alibi diplomacy" reappeared in multilateral guise in the UN Security Council's establishment of six "safe areas" in Bosnia without any military provisions for making them safe.

Besides European objections, there were other obstacles to the use of American force. They included the genuine risk to UN peacekeepers, the strong opposition of Secretary General Boutros Boutros-Ghali and the UN bureaucracy, the lack of consensus in NATO, the Russian support of the Serbs, and a U.S. Congress that was prepared to micromanage without a discernible strategy. The reigning issue for the Congress was whether to lift the arms embargo, a move strongly backed by Senator Dole. Those in favor wanted to help the Bosnian government even the military balance, which had been skewed by the fact that the Serbs could draw on JNA stocks and therefore didn't need to import arms.

The lawmakers were right in the justice of lifting the embargo but wrong in failing to measure its probable consequences, which would probably have left the Bosnians worse off. If the embargo were lifted, it seemed likely that, to prevent a change in the balance of forces, the Serbs would hit the Bosnians with everything they had, including the strategic reserve of JNA forces stationed across the border in Serbia. At that point the Bosnians would plead for American intervention. But most of the Congress didn't want direct U.S. military involvement. They wanted a "free lunch": to help the Muslims militarily and to keep the United

States out. Neither the Congress nor the administration was prepared to draw the only conclusion that would make a difference, that the United States had to exert leadership to persuade its allies that NATO air strikes were necessary to bring the Serbs into a serious negotiation.

As 1993 wore on, it became increasingly difficult for me to justify my personal participation in a policy whose tentative nature was being exploited by the Serbian aggressors. We were dealing fairly successfully with the humanitarian symptoms of the Bosnian war, the refugees and the displaced, but we weren't treating the causes. There was a tendency among administration officials to give public emphasis to the humanitarian issues as a way of disguising the lack of a consistent political approach. I sent several back-channel memos to Christopher suggesting variants of forceful responses but received no acknowledgment that they'd even been read.

In December Teeny and I took a week's vacation in the Caribbean. She could see I was troubled and suggested that I try to define exactly what was bothering me and what could be done about it. It was remarkable how helpful it was to face the problem. My frustrations with Bosnia and with an unrelated personnel issue pointed inexorably to leaving. Resignation for cause is rare among foreign service officers. Few, if any, had resigned over Vietnam; four midlevel officers had resigned in 1992 over Bosnia. The strongest argument against resignation rang in my memory; I had heard it made by Justice Felix Frankfurter at a dinner party thirty-five years before. "People who resign," he said, "are no longer there to try to influence the policy with which they disagree." I worried simultaneously that I was not pressing my support of air strikes hard enough but that, if I was to stay in the government, I had to be a team player. In my case, I concluded that I was having no influence; perhaps I would have more as a commentator on the outside.

When I got back to Washington, I told my boss Tim Wirth, the activist undersecretary for global affairs and an old friend, that I had decided to leave. He understood right away and gave me his full support. I wrote Christopher a letter, explaining that I was retiring over Bosnia and personnel issues and asking for a farewell meeting. He graciously got right back to me with a date. We met on January 20, 1994, in gloomy circumstances. Because of a heavy snowstorm, the government had been closed; the usual bustle outside the secretary of state's office was absent. One lone receptionist nodded me in. I found the secretary in his shirt-sleeves in a dimly lit office working on a speech. As we sat down, just the two of us, he raised Bosnia right away and invited my views.

I made as strong a case as I could for NATO air strikes to take out the artillery around Sarajevo. I contended that Karadžić and Milošević would be impressed with nothing less. The arguments, both military and political, against our use of force seemed to me grossly distorted. If we tried force, it would work. Not only would it give Sarajevo a respite, but it would have a strong effect on overall Serbian behavior. I recognized that the Joint Chiefs of Staff were opposed, but a firm presidential decision would change everything. If we made it clear we were prepared to move unilaterally, I thought the allies would come along.

The secretary listened carefully, thanked me, but made no substantive comment. He didn't tell me that the administration was finally beginning to doubt its own approach. On February 5, two and a half weeks after our meeting, a mortar fired into the Sarajevo market killed sixty-eight people. On February 9 NATO threatened force if the Bosnian Serbs didn't withdraw their artillery; they complied. Sarajevo, after nearly two years of shelling, was now free of it. Tragically, no lessons were learned from this Serbian capitulation to American toughness, and for a year more our Bosnia policy lapsed back into weakness and hesitancy.

In our meeting I also asked the secretary if I could say a few words about the foreign service, in which I had spent thirty-three years. I expressed the conviction that a country like the United States needs a professional service with the most qualified men and women who can be found. A professional service can't be turned on and off; people have to know what they can aspire to. If they can compete for the most important ambassadorships and the highest positions in the State Department, then first-rate young people will apply at the bottom of the personnel ladder. If they can't, then the applications will come from potential colonels instead of potential generals.

Unfortunately, I continued, recent administrations weren't acting as if they shared these beliefs. There had always been a problem with ambassadorships going to campaign contributors; it hadn't gotten any better under President Clinton. Now the top jobs in Washington were being politicized as well. I told Christopher that, for the first time in my career, no foreign service officer held a position of undersecretary of state; before the Clinton administration there had always been at least one. The politicization had also penetrated down to lower levels than ever before.

I made clear that I wasn't against nonprofessionals, if they were qualified. I had myself served twice under one of the very best, Max Kampelman, and I had been greatly heartened by the nomination of Strobe Talbott, a clear-headed former journalist, to be Christopher's deputy. I also strongly supported diversity and was proud that my bureau was 65 percent women. But no White House personnel office was going to understand that the foreign service is a vital institution whose quality can be easily degraded. It would take the secretary of state, going to the president if necessary, to drive home that point. Again the secretary listened carefully and without comment, except to say that he hadn't heard the issue put in those terms before.

My retirement date was March 4. As this landmark in my own personal history approached, one of the thoughts that crowded in on me was how much perceptions of the past had influenced people in countries I had lived in. This was particularly true in the

Slavic world, where Teeny and I had spent eleven years. In Yugoslavia we had witnessed the attempts of extreme nationalists to re-create their nations' pasts in the distorted images of their current ambitions.

Those images were highly selective. Slobodan Milošević chose to recall the Serbia that had once been a leader in the Balkans, but not the Serbia whose aggressive behavior had from time to time infringed the rights of its neighbors. Franjo Tudjman remembered the Croatia that had once extended to West Belgrade but conveniently forgot the Croatia that had been a Nazi puppet state. The two dictators played on and manipulated their national myths for racial ends, not caring that those myths could be overlapping, contradictory, or explosive. In the process they killed the fragile concepts of civility and tolerance that multiethnic Yugoslavia, at its best, was trying to create.

We in America have our own myths, but they're based on values rather than race. Of course we've had violent or criminal episodes, like our civil war, the Indian wars, and the injustices done to black Americans. Still, the universalism of the Declaration of Independence and the Bill of Rights is supplemented in our history by a tradition of accommodation to the views of others. In the absolutist Balkans I often tried an eloquent line from Arthur Schlesinger Jr.: "Compromise is the strategy of democracy." The reception it got can be imagined.

Another contrast comes to mind. Americans can study their past, draw lessons from it, and gain inspiration from it. But they aren't prisoners of it. We are a future-oriented people. Problems are to be solved, not used as ways to distort the past, lay blame, or take revenge. At a farewell reception with State Department colleagues given by Tim Wirth, I summed this up with a quotation from Herman Melville: "The past is the textbook of tyrants, the future the bible of the free."

EPILOGUE

As evening fell the day's oppression lifted;
Far peaks came into focus; it had rained:
Across wide lawns and cultured flowers drifted
The conversation of the highly trained.

Two gardeners watched them pass and priced
  their shoes:
A chauffeur waited, reading in the drive,
For them to finish their exchange of views;
It seemed a picture of the private life.

Far off, no matter what good they intended,
The armies waited for a verbal error
With all the instruments for causing pain:

And on the issue of their charm depended
A land laid waste, with all its young men slain,
Its women weeping and its towns in terror.

—W. H. Auden, "Embassy"

Those who practice diplomacy need constantly to be reminded of the human damage their efforts, or lack of them, can cause. For three years of the Bosnian war, the Western countries had attempted to rebuff the Serbian aggressors, bloated by their use of force, without making them fear that force would in turn be used against them. Western diplomacy was reduced to a kind of cynical theater, a pretence of useful activity, a way of disguising a lack of will. Diplomacy without force became an unloaded weapon, impotent and ridiculous.

During 1994 diplomacy yielded two results, whose significance would emerge only if Western power were applied to consolidate them. The first was the March agreement between the Bosnians and Croats to form a federation. The agreement implicitly recorded the recognition of the two parties, at war with each other for a year over parts of western Bosnia, that all they were doing was helping the Serbs. This geopolitical breakthrough was due primarily to the dogged negotiating work of Charles Redman, a foreign service officer who had become Warren Christopher's representative in Bosnia. The federation weakened the Bosnian Serbs' position by reducing their ability to exploit division in the enemy. But it also represented the first partition of Bosnia.

The second achievement was the plan worked out in mid-1994 by the "contact group" (the United States, the United Kingdom, France, Germany, and Russia), which provided for the Serbs to retain 49 percent of Bosnia (down from the 70 percent they actually held but up from the aborted Vance-Owen plan) and for the federation to get the rest. Not only did the plan set the parameters for a possible future settlement, it also had the effect of splitting the Serbian leadership. Milošević, in order to get the economic sanctions lifted from Serbia, strongly backed the plan, although with characteristic guile he assured the Bosnian Serbs that it would never be implemented. Karadžić and General Mladić vehemently opposed it, and the Bosnian Serb "parliament" rejected it. The war continued.

In 1995 the Clinton administration began to find its moral footing, and to act from the conviction that Serbian force could only be stopped by NATO counterforce. Two events in the summer finally galvanized the president to action. In August Tudjman's Croatian army struck—illegally, ruthlessly, but victoriously—at the Serbian-held Krajina, routing virtually the entire Serbian population, some of whose ancestors had lived there since before the time of the Habsburg Empress Maria Theresa. The Croatian blitzkrieg won back most of the territory Tudjman had lost to the Serbs in 1991. It also transformed the balance of forces in Bosnia. General Mladić had relied on the Krajina for both supplies and men. Now the Bosnian and Croatian forces in western Bosnia began to take back territory they had surrendered to the Serbs. Then, on August 28, another mortar hit the Sarajevo market, killing thirty-eight people.

The near-achievement of military equilibrium, combined with another atrocious war crime, gave Clinton an unprecedented opportunity. To his credit, he seized it. At the urging of the United States, NATO carried out a pinpoint bombing campaign from August 30 to September 14 against Serbian military targets. All the American objections to the use of air power, objections that had helped prolong the war for three years, miraculously melted away. After failing in their normal tactic of appealing to the faint-hearted UN leadership, the Serbs agreed after two weeks of bombing to negotiate an end to the war. The result was the Dayton agreement, which was inspired and carried through by the brilliant diplomacy of the American negotiator, Richard Holbrooke.

I heard Haris Silajdžić, the Muslim prime minister of Bosnia, describe the Dayton agreement several days after it had been initialed. "It's not a just agreement," he said, "but it's probably the best we could get." The territorial settlement gave the Serbs 49 percent of Bosnia—a bonus since their prewar population had been less than a third of the republic's, and following a mass wartime exodus into Serbia, their postwar population may have become even less than that. Moreover, the Bosnian Serbs achieved at Dayton their primary political aim—their own republic within Bosnia, "Republika Srpska." None of the earlier Western proposals had offered them such a giant concession. Moreover, the actions of the Bosnian Serbs in the wake of Dayton made clear that they had no intention of honoring the right of non-Serbian refugees to return to "Republika Srpska." Ethnic cleansing thus continued, and few refugees returned. Finally, the Serbs got to keep their army intact, leaving Bosnia with three armies: Serbian, Muslim, and Croatian.

Still, as Silajdžić implied, the Bosnian Muslims did better at Dayton than might have been expected in view of their military reverses during the three years of Western procrastination. The Bosnian-Croat Federation gained 51 percent of the territory of the republic and Sarajevo became again a unified city, thus foiling Karadžić's grandiose dream of controlling 64 percent of Bosnia and dividing its capital. The Bosnians achieved at least the framework of a unified and sovereign state of Bosnia: a single government with a constitution, a multiethnic presidency, a bicameral parliament, a court, and a central bank. They also got a NATO force to guarantee the cease-fire and a European Union "high representative" to monitor civilian implementation of the peace settlement. Nobody, however, expected the new Bosnian government to function effectively, since it depended on consensus, a principle that had broken down disastrously in 1991–92 in the ethnic disputes preceding the war. Tudjman was probably the big winner in the Dayton settlement. While the Croatian entity in Bosnia was officially merged into the Bosnian-Croat Federation, it continued to operate without hindrance as an integral part of Croatia.

The presence of NATO, and particularly American, troops in Bosnia has remained the strongest insurance against a new outbreak of violence. The most dangerous period will be after the troops leave. How stable will Bosnia be then? The agreement contains no self-enforcing provisions. If important interest groups in Bosnia want to renew the violence, they will be able to do it. The thousands of internecine killings, the smoldering lust for revenge, the years of hate propaganda, the criminal inculcation of children and young adults in racial hostility—all these factors suggest that the most optimistic hope would be for low-level tensions, perhaps stopping short of war, for a generation or more.

With such a gloomy prognosis, some have urged that Bosnia simply be partitioned among its three ethnic groups, since none of them seems intent on implementing the multiethnic elements of the Dayton accord. In fact, partition would be disastrous for the people of Bosnia. It would almost certainly re-ignite the war, since there would be disputes over the partition lines. It would give the ethnic supremacists a signal victory—a constitutional outcome based on the principle of apartheid. And it would deprive the Bosnian Muslims of almost everything they won at Dayton, making the main victims in the war the main losers in its aftermath. The Muslims would be shrunk into an enclave which—as their grievances festered and their enmities grew—could even become a European base for Islamic terrorism.

What will it take to win the gamble on a multiethnic Bosnia? First, it will take a discrediting in Bosnia of radical nationalism and its leaders. The UN war crimes tribunal is essential to this objective. It has performed better than expected, but it must demonstrate that it can bring to justice leaders and not just underlings. Second, Serbia and Croatia must stop meddling in Bosnia. Without the malign influences of Belgrade and Zagreb, Bosnia's ethnic tensions would never have exploded into war. Third and most important, Bosnia will survive only if its own people decide that they've had enough of war. Much of the nationalism in Bosnia was generated by the polarizing effects of the war itself. In the beginning, nationalism was a top-down process—the ideology of vicious leaders manipulating the fears of people haunted by a turbulent past. Many Bosnians can still remember the violence of World War II, but even more can remember the reconciliation and relative prosperity of the postwar decades. Both options are available in Bosnia. The question is whether the momentum toward peace generated by a prolonged cease-fire can overcome the baser human instincts which, in the grip of tyrants, have exploded into war and can explode again.

The war in Bosnia was a vaccination against violence in Kosovo. Milošević was not keen to deal with enemies on two fronts, and Rugova understood that any move on his part would bring swift and bloody Serbian retribution, unopposed by a West distracted by Bosnia. The issues of Kosovo were thus set aside but not solved. Milošević had a whole decade after his 1989 assault on Albanian rights to work out a modus vivendi with Rugova, whose nonviolent approach represented no military threat to Serbia. The Serbian dictator spurned the opportunity, preferring to treat Kosovo like a colony. With the lifting of the restraints imposed by the Bosnian war, Kosovo, like colonies of earlier times, produced a national liberation movement dedicated to the ejection of the colonial power.

The rise of the Kosovo Liberation Army in 1998 had a decisive effect on Milošević's strategy. No longer was he dealing with the Gandhiesque intellectuals, however determined they may have been. Now he was challenged by an armed group of militants, whose ranks were swelled by Europe-based emigrants and by Kosovo's numberless unemployed young men, whose political program was total independence, and whose tactics included the assassination of Serbian police. It was probably in mid-1998 that Milošević made the jump to a breathtaking new strategy—a final solution. It was necessary to destroy the KLA. That in turn meant destroying the significant element of the Albanian population which protected the KLA. But even that wasn't enough, since the KLA was the consequence of the conditions Milošević had imposed on Kosovo; as long as those conditions continued, new guerrillas would reappear like the heads of a hydra. So Milošević resolved to get rid of the entire Albanian population of Kosovo by expulsion and—where advisable or instructive—by murder. Serbs would then have Kosovo all to themselves, a situation they had never enjoyed in their thousand-year association with the region. Milošević's scheme, amounting to the largest forcible displacement of people since World War II, seems to have been too ruthless even for elements in the army and secret police; both were purged at high levels in the fall of 1998.

The enormity of Milošević's final solution was not as clear in late 1998 as it became later. But there were enough signs of a Serbian crackdown to reactivate American and NATO diplomacy. Richard Holbrooke's negotiation with Milošević in October produced no more than a handshake agreement calling for an outside monitoring presence, which proved useful, and a partial Serbian troop withdrawal, which was not implemented. Had NATO bombed in October, as it had threatened, it might have caught the Serbs before their preparations for Milošević's gigantic cleansing operation were in place. That opportunity squandered, Western efforts focused on a negotiation to make Kosovo autonomous within Yugoslavia under the guarantee of a large NATO troop contingent. Neither the Albanians, whose negotiators included KLA members, nor the Serbs liked the arrangement presented at Rambouillet, France, in February 1999. Western arm-twisting brought the Albanians around, but Milošević refused to accept NATO troops in Kosovo. This time NATO's threat of force wasn't a bluff; bombing of Serbia began March 24. Milošević responded with an expulsion campaign which surpassed the ethnic cleansing of Bosnia in both rapidity and scale.

Bosnia and Kosovo are both metaphors and symbols for issues that transcend the Yugoslav crisis and the Balkan peninsula. Ethnic conflicts are as old as history, but today's world has suffered a surfeit of them, from Sri Lanka, Kashmir, and Rwanda to Sudan, Chechnya, and Nagorno-Karabakh. Even America's two neighbors, Mexico and Canada, are feeling ethnic tensions. The veneer of civilization lies thin over racial relations, especially where democratic institutions don't exist to thicken it. The problem is made more difficult by the fact that people inspired by ethnic furies are rarely able to draw rational judgments about their own best interests.

Not all ethnic challenges sufficiently affect the primary interests of the international community, or at least of its strongest members, to warrant intervention. Nor are all susceptible to international influence, even when major interests are involved. For the rest, however, more effective strategies are needed. In the broadest sense, the realization must take hold that we live in a world of multiethnic, not national, states. Less than one-half of one percent of all the people in the world live in monoethnic states ("nation-states" in the pure sense of the word). The rest of us have to learn to live with members of different ethnic groups. This condition, where it exists, has proven no bar to freedom or prosperity, as the examples of multiethnic North America and Western Europe show.

As a rule, nation-states have nothing to unify them but their nationalism. Power within them will tend to gravitate to the most strident nationalists. This is a powerful reason why a partitioned Bosnia would be neither democratic nor stable. Multinational states can be deeply conflicted. But they can also be schools of tolerance, since the need to take account of minority interests moderates behavior. Yugoslavia had its democrats as well as its demagogues. The challenge to the world community is not to break up multiethnic states, but to make them more civil. It's the borders in the mind—the borders of prejudice, supremacy, and hate—rather than the borders on the map that are most in need of changing.

There's nothing to be gained, therefore, by accepting claims of self-determination at face value, even when referenda have been held to determine the wishes of a particular ethnic group. The question of viability arises immediately. If each ethnic group were given its own nation-state, there would be thousands of new countries, and old countries like Spain and India would disappear. Beyond this, changing borders almost always affects more people than those who want to make the change. The dream of the Kurdish people for self-determination is compelling. But it doesn't serve either justice or stability to dismantle the four states where Kurds live in order to make that dream come true. Instead of giving pious lip service to self-determination, as the UN Charter does, the international community should require those seeking independence to show that their objectives don't adversely affect the interests of other states or peoples.

Against this standard Kosovo is a hard case. Serbs and Albanians have never coexisted there with as much tolerance as the people of Bosnia. They are different races with different languages; all three ethnic groups in Bosnia are Slavs, with the same language. Ethnic intermarriage was frequent in Bosnia; in Kosovo it was almost nonexistent. Serbs and Albanians both make persuasive, and contradictory, claims to Kosovo. Serbs claim a Kosovo that is their historical, religious, and cultural heartland and where they have enjoyed sovereignty. Albanians claim a Kosovo that they inhabited first and where they have a majority population. The Rambouillet formula was an attempt to reconcile these claims—Serbian sovereignty, Albanian autonomy—in a multiethnic framework similar to Bosnia's. The proposal also had the virtue of promising less disruption to Kosovo's neighbors, since no borders would be changed. But the Rambouillet approach was based on the already tenuous assumption that Serbs and Albanians could continue to live together peacefully. That assumption has now been threatened by the savagery of the Serbian assault on the Kosovo Albanians.

Yet alternatives to Rambouillet all have major defects. Independence for Kosovo could penalize future Serbian leaders who might be more moderate than Milošević and would in any case fuel Serbian revanchism. Independence could also destabilize the borders of contiguous Albania and Macedonia, with their Albanian populations, and even disrupt the entire Balkan region. At the other extreme, Western acceptance of continued Serbian hegemony in Kosovo would destroy NATO's reputation and make the West complicit in massive human rights violations. Between these extreme options the partition of Kosovo between Serbs and Albanians might appear a viable compromise solution. If the two groups could agree on a dividing line—a daunting challenge—their mutual hostilities could at least be fenced off. But partition carries its own baggage. Not only would it be subject to the same defects as a partition of Bosnia; it might even be exploited as a precedent for dividing Bosnia and wrecking Dayton. A partitioned Kosovo would produce an Albanian state or entity that would have the same attraction for Albanians in Albania and Macedonia as a wholly independent Kosovo, leading to a disruptive drive for union.

If the world is to support the idea of multiethnicity as an organizing principle for states, as I believe it should, then it will have to do more to ensure the protection of minorities within multiethnic states. Since the birth of the United Nations, chiefs of state, mostly repressive ones, have complained about international interference in their internal affairs. Claims of "sovereignty" have become the last refuge of dictators. Yet human rights pressures over the past two decades have severely eroded those claims. The way a government treats its people is now seen as an international, not just an internal, concern. International human rights policy, which helped to overthrow apartheid in South Africa, can and should be used more intrusively elsewhere. NATO was right to hold Milošević to account for his treatment of Albanian citizens of Yugoslavia, and to attack Serbia when he dismissed its concerns.

The promotion of democracy, a political system consistently sensitive to the will of the people, is also indispensable. Elections are a necessary, though not a sufficient, condition for democratic life. This is true even though, in the short run, they can be counterproductive. In Yugoslavia in 1990 elections strengthened destructive nationalism. Democratic choice wasn't followed by democratic conduct. People voted their past grievances instead of their future hopes. Perhaps Yugoslavia wasn't "ready" for democracy, although it's not clear how a country gets ready for democracy without having a chance to practice it. Elections didn't make

Yugoslavia a democratic country, since democracy is a process rather than an event. It's always a gamble to give a demagogue a certain legitimacy through elections. But it seems to me a bigger gamble not to have elections, though their timing can be critical, as in Bosnia. If a country can be encouraged on the path of greater civil liberties and freedom of choice, then in time frequent elections should begin to flush away the waste of an undemocratic past.

The case of Spain shows the critical difference democracy can make to prosperity. In the 1960s Yugoslavia and Spain, despite the ideological gulf between them and the higher development of Spanish culture, were quite similar—two countries on the fringes of Europe, belonging to no major European blocs or organizations, in early stages of economic development (Spain was a shade ahead), living in the aftermath of bloody civil wars, plagued by serious ethnic problems, and run by powerful dictators. Spain prospered; Yugoslavia collapsed. The reason was that Spain made itself a democracy and Yugoslavia didn't. For whatever motives, General Francisco Franco set his country on the right course.

The various forms of democracy in multiethnic states deserve more attention than they have so far received. The ideal is to treat people as individual citizens rather than as members of groups. But that won't soon be attainable in states where ethnic groups feel a strong sense of identity and nurse real or imagined grievances. Alternative forms of power sharing seem called for, so that an ethnic majority can't abuse an ethnic minority, as happened so often in Yugoslavia and its successor states. Switzerland, Belgium, the Netherlands, Austria, and Malaysia have all worked out successful power-sharing arrangements, using coalition governments, proportional representation, local ethnic autonomy, or limited minority vetoes. The U.S. Constitution, with its checks and balances, is a power-sharing device, though not an ethnic one. Yugoslavia was a failed experiment in power sharing. Post-

Dayton Bosnia is the latest fragile Balkan candidate to submit to the test.

To preserve democratic ideals in a multiethnic environment, there must be some form of international enforcer. It was the power of NATO, led by the United States, that achieved the breakthrough toward peace in Bosnia and contested Milošević's criminal activities in Kosovo. The alliance's stumbling performance before August 1995 was a textbook warning of what not to do—not to speak with many voices, not to show weakness, not to threaten without being prepared to follow through. Unfortunately, some of those defects also plagued NATO's Kosovo campaign. In Bosnia, once NATO acted with resoluteness and power, the Serbian challenge collapsed. This doesn't mean that NATO should become an all-purpose global enforcer. It does suggest a potential post–cold war mission for the alliance in certain ethnic conflicts not always limited to NATO's traditional area. NATO had no treaty commitment to defend Bosnia or the Kosovo Albanians, yet only NATO could have produced a decisive result.

Bosnia and Kosovo teach us something about preventive strategies. Prevention is inherently difficult, since it must be undertaken before the circumstances that require it have arisen. On Yugoslavia, neither hawks nor doves in the United States or Europe were prepared for intervention in mid-1991, when Yugoslavia began to fall apart. Yet prevention isn't impossible. The cold war was won primarily by a preventive strategy— deterrence. In the Bosnian crisis most of the deterrence was self-deterrence by the West against its own actions. NATO's Kosovo operation, for all of its bumbling character, was an exercise in prevention. The problem was that NATO acted too late.

The most effective element of prevention is the credible threat of force. It's axiomatic that force should be called on only as a last resort—axiomatic, but often wrong. In Bosnia U.S.-led NATO air strikes against Bosnian Serb military installations early in the war would probably have deterred further aggression and produced a negotiated settlement. An aggressor doesn't have to take a stronger power seriously if that power visibly shrinks from the use of force. As soon as the Bosnian Serbs realized that they could no longer act with impunity, the picture changed dramatically. Milošević might have reached the same conclusion in Kosovo if NATO had struck sooner.

There's an important role for the United Nations in ethnic conflicts, but it's not the role the United Nations was asked to play in Bosnia. In Bosnia the United Nations was playing by the rules of peacekeeping before there was a peace to keep. By UN lore, peacekeepers are lightly armed and can use their weapons only as a last resort; they are neutral observers and interposers between the former belligerents; and they can operate only with the consent of those belligerents. In the hot war in Bosnia, these conditions made the United Nations a symbol of weakness and a candidate for blackmail. Whatever the abilities or biases of its commanders, the United Nations had a serious problem. The success of its primary humanitarian mission depended on Serbian acquiescence in granting access to relief convoys. Not even the most accomplished negotiator could expect to wheedle concessions out of the Serbs for the relief effort while simultaneously calling in air strikes against them.

In European situations where there is a clear need for force, NATO, not the United Nations, should be the favored instrument where it can be. Where it isn't possible or advisable for NATO to operate, the military capabilities of UN forces need to be built up, with more troops, better training, and tougher rules of engagement. The United Nations's weakness reinforces its retreat to the concept that it must act "neutrally," even though in a war of aggression neutrality inevitably favors the aggressor. If the United Nations had been better able to protect itself in Bosnia, it might not have shown such shameful solicitude toward the Serbian side.

For the United Nations to be effective in ethnic conflicts, it will need the military capabilities to enforce peace, not just to maintain peace once it's been achieved. There's much to be said for a UN ready reserve that can be called up quickly and dispatched to areas of potential conflict. Such a force might have prevented the massacres in Rwanda. The major reforms needed in the United Nations's ability to deal with ethnic conflicts require the full support of its leading members, especially the United States. Yet the U.S. Congress seems interested only in crippling the United Nations rather than reforming it. The predictable result of this dereliction will be greater pressure on the United States to take on problems that a reformed United Nations might have been able to handle.

Finally, much greater emphasis needs to be given to the Organization for Security and Cooperation in Europe (OSCE). This is an offshoot of the Helsinki process, which began in 1975 and played an important role in achieving human rights progress in the Soviet Union and Eastern Europe. The OSCE includes in its membership all the countries in Europe, plus the United States and Canada. It can thus enter complex ethnic situations with little negative baggage. Its greatest potential asset is an ability to mediate conflicts, to negotiate on behalf of minorities, to monitor elections and human rights observance, and to broker disarmament agreements. It played a useful role in organizing elections in Bosnia and monitoring violence in Kosovo.

For all these ethnic challenges, the role of the United States will be key. Our power remains unique and respected. Our involvement in other ethnic dilemmas need not be as deep as it has been in Bosnia and Kosovo. Europe should do much more where its own direct interests are affected. Yet Europe's failure in Bosnia was precisely the reason why America had to intervene. America also had to play the leading role in Kosovo. European countries were too divided, and some countries were not acceptable to all of the parties. Each crisis will require its own assessment of American interests and capabilities. What shouldn't be debatable is that the United States—in political support, in assistance to multilateral institutions and mechanisms, and, at times, in direct involvement—should be engaged.

Our own stature as a multiethnic society gives us a special responsibility. Of course we haven't always lived up to the standard set by Martin Luther King Jr. when he said, "I dream of a day when my four little children will not be judged by the color of their skin but by the content of their character." The spasmodic pressure against immigrants, legal and illegal; pseudoscientific efforts to prove genetically that blacks are intellectually inferior; conversely, the racist vilification of Jews by the African-American demagogue Louis Farrakhan; the insistence, in the name of multiculturalism, that group rights are more important than individual rights; the failure of our social policy to prevent the emergence of a black underclass—all these are challenges, if not already setbacks, to America's achievement of its own ideals.

Yet even our inadequate attempts to struggle with these intractable issues confirm our legitimacy in helping others to overcome their ethnic divisions. We have had the good fortune to see ourselves as an American nation in a nonethnic sense. The word "nation" appears five times among the 272 words of Lincoln's Gettysburg Address. Tragically, Yugoslavs never saw themselves as a nation.

Whatever our defects, America remains the most successful multiethnic experiment in existence. While the beleaguered Albanians appeal to our power and our support for freedom, the Bosnians see us also as a model of what a multinational society should look like. They will not be the last people to do so. We have the power and we still have the moral force. Most of all, we stand for the simple proposition that people of all ethnic strains can live together, not without tensions, but with tolerance, civility, and even mutual enrichment.

THE LAST CABLE

12 MAY 92
FM AMEMBASSY BELGRADE
TO SECSTATE WASHDC IMMEDIATE
FROM WARREN ZIMMERMANN
SUBJ.: WHO KILLED YUGOSLAVIA?

With U.S. recognition of Slovenia, Croatia, and Bosnia, and the proclamation of a new "Yugoslavia" by Serbia and Montenegro, the old Yugoslavia we knew is dead. Before we move into a world of five new Balkan states—communist and noncommunist, turbulent and calm, authoritarian and democratic, militant and moderate, viable and hopeless—it might be worth a final glance at what has been destroyed and why.

> "Who killed Cock Robin?"
> "I," said the sparrow,
> "With my bow and arrow.
> I killed Cock Robin."

It was nationalism that put an arrow in the heart of Yugoslavia. While the antecedents go back centuries, the nationalism that spawned the process of Yugoslavia's destruction began in 1987 in Kosovo, when Slobodan Milošević, the young leader of the League of Communists of Serbia, listened throughout one

long night to the stories Serbs told him of mistreatment by Albanians. That experience gave Milošević the issue that brought him
his power and charisma. Brandishing the issue of Serbian nationalism, he abolished the autonomy of Kosovo, then of Vojvodina,
purged all opposition in Serbia itself, and finally turned his nationalist aggressions on his neighbors.

Ironically, it was Slovenia, the only republic containing no Serbian minority, which Milošević first attacked. Serbia and Slovenia have always been natural allies, and Milošević's enmity
toward Slovenia was ideological rather than ethnic. What Slovenia, even back in the late 1980s, stood for was democracy, a decentralized Yugoslavia, and a freer market—just the kind of
Yugoslavia Milošević despised and feared. In December 1989
Milošević tried to displace the Slovenian government by a hostile
mass rally of Serbs in Ljubljana, then followed that failure by declaring an economic boycott against Slovenia. These were the
first shots in the nationalist war that led to the destruction of Yugoslavia. Croatia became Milošević's next target, a fat one.
Franjo Tudjman's victory in the May 1990 Croatian elections
brought to power a narrow-minded, crypto-racist regime hostile
to Serbia and to the Yugoslavia that it erroneously believed Serbia
controlled. Both Milošević and Tudjman had a strong interest in
Satanizing each other; given their characters, the job was not difficult. With the ancient enmities of Serbian and Croatian nationalism now pitted against each other, the odds of preserving and
developing a Yugoslavia along the progressive Hungarian or
Czechoslovak model plummeted. Violence became probable. As
Vladimir Šeks, a prominent militant in Tudjman's party, said of
one of the ethnically mixed areas of Croatia: "If we win, there
will be no more Serbs; if they win, no more Croatians." With people like that in charge, there could no longer be much hope for a
country whose very name—"Land of the South Slavs"—symbolized ethnic tolerance. As Milovan Djilas, the last great Yugoslav,

said to me the other day, Yugoslavia could not survive conflict between Serbs and Croats for they are its defining nations.

> "Who saw him die?"
> "I," said the fly,
> "With my little eye,
> I saw him die."

The death of Yugoslavia had many witnesses. The most prominent signatures on the coroner's report are those of the European
Community and the United States. Both Western Europe and
America were long-time friends of the deceased, midwifing its
birth in the aftermath of one war and helping it through another,
protecting it against its rapacious Soviet neighbor, paying the
bills for its profligacy, and encouraging it on the path to democracy. In Yugoslavia's terminal illness the Western countries did
what they could to nurse the patient back to health. The Europeans, in the person of Jacques Delors, offered an enormous economic carrot condition on the country's staying together, while
the Dutch, in the EC presidency, played the role of hectoring
father-confessor, urging the invalid to become a better European
in order to save its soul. The United States brought to bear the
weight of its traditionally good relations, its great power status,
and its moral authority to keep the country on the united and democratic path so hopefully begun by the Marković government in
1989. All in the end was to no avail; like everyone else, the Western countries were no more than witnesses at Yugoslavia's fu-
neral.

Could it have been different? Were there things the West could
have done to avoid the breakup and the bloodshed? Conversely,
should we have seen earlier that Yugoslavia was finished and
tried to provide a peaceful burial? Don't look for objectivity from
me on these questions. I was a part of our policy; I believed, and

still believe, that it was the right one. I leave it to the Ph.D. candidates to argue the details. In a general sense, I am convinced the failures do not lie with the Western witnesses to Yugoslavia's death. The failures lie within the corpse itself.

U.S. policy toward Yugoslavia was simple and consistent from the very beginning of the nationalist period heralded by Milošević's rise. We were for unity but not unity imposed by force. The Marković government represented the two interlocking qualities of unity and democracy. We were right to support it, weak as it was. The alternatives to Marković were Milošević's kind of unity, which meant dictatorship, or Tudjman's kind of separatism, which meant war. Nearly two years before the Croatian war began, this embassy stressed, and continued to stress, that the breakup of Yugoslavia could not be accomplished without massive violence. Much of the criticism of U.S. policy toward Yugoslavia is based on the assumption that we were blind to the pressures for independence and therefore failed to get on the bandwagon. We weren't blind; we just saw that the bandwagon was headed for Armageddon. Nationalism polarizes; in Yugoslavia, with the collapse of the Marković experiment, there was no middle ground between Tudjman and Milošević for the West to cultivate. Marković's Yugoslavia tended toward democracy, Milošević's Yugoslavia away from it. That's why the U.S. and the EC were simply present at the destruction instead of contributors to the creation.

> "Who'll dig the grave?"
> "I," said the owl,
> "With my little trowel,
> I'll dig the grave."

There were many gravediggers of Yugoslavia, including the unusual suspects Slovenia, Croatia, and Serbia. But there is one who stands out. Slobodan Milošević, one of the most duplicitous politicians the Balkans have ever produced, is duplicitous in this as well. Milošević poses as the protector and savior of Yugoslavia. Just two weeks ago he wrapped himself in the Yugoslav flag (with the red star cut out, of course) and renewed the Yugoslav national anthem. "Yugoslavia exists" has been his war cry ever since the secessionist rumblings began. It's all bunk. Milošević is not a Yugoslav; he is a Serbian imperialist. His maximum aim of three years ago was to dominate all of Yugoslavia; hence his effort to overthrow the democratic-leaning government of Slovenia and bring the Croats to heel. When that failed, he gave up on Slovenia and went to war to keep Croatia in Yugoslavia. Thwarted again, he tried to force Bosnia and Macedonia into a "Little Yugoslavia" controlled by Serbia. Finally he has fallen back on the "Federal Republic of Yugoslavia" which disclaims territorial pretensions but has a provision in its constitution for admitting parts of other states. He is currently pursuing actively a civil war in Bosnia designed to deliver two-thirds of its territory to the Serb minority there and is collaborating in the expulsion of non-Serbs in mixed areas of Croatia with the aim of making those areas ethnically clean.

Since his assumption of power, Milošević's crimes against Yugoslavia include the following:
- Violating the Yugoslav constitution by removing the autonomy of Kosovo and Vojvodina;
- Imposing trade boycotts on Slovenia and Croatia (an act akin to Massachusetts shutting off trade with Maine and Vermont);
- Stealing $1.8 billion from the National Bank of Yugoslavia before independence, and arrogating to Serbia all of Yugoslavia's hard currency reserves and other assets after independence;
- Trying to destroy the Yugoslav presidency, first by preventing the normal presidential rotation to Croatia in May 1991, and

then by trying to pull the Serbian members off the presidency altogether;

- Waging an unceasing battle against Marković and all he stood for: a Yugoslav-wide market economy, an overall standard of human rights, and an electoral mechanism that emphasized Yugoslav elements and downplayed national factions;
- Pursuing an aggressive war (together with the army) in Croatia across a republican boundary;
- And finally, expanding the war into Bosnia through his proxy Karadžić, with help from thugs like Arkan and the collusion of the JNA.

Milošević could never have succeeded in, or even attempted, his destruction of Yugoslavia without an essential accomplice— the JNA. The army's betrayal of Yugoslavia was nearly as egregious as Milošević's. Ostensibly the bulwark of "brotherhood and unity," the JNA allowed itself to be turned into a killing machine on behalf of one national group. It is true that the JNA was provoked in both Slovenia and Croatia, though it is also true that with Croatia the original provocations came from the JNA itself in its pre-war "anti-fascist" efforts to destabilize Tudjman. In any case, the bombardment of Dubrovnik and the destruction of Vukovar were criminal assaults against, in the one case, Yugoslavia's most famous town and, in the other, a peaceful ethnically mixed city. Moreover, the JNA's collusion in the Serbian takeover bid (in Bosnia) was prompted by no hostile actions at all from the plurality Muslim population. The JNA's proud Yugoslav partisan tradition is now buried forever in the rubble of Vukovar.

The bill of particulars against Milošević is not meant to imply that his enemies and rivals were pro-Yugoslav. On the contrary, Slovenia and Croatia seceded from Yugoslavia without even serious efforts to reconcile their differences with Belgrade. But even here Milošević was the prime catalyst for their disaffection.

Slovenia would almost certainly have tried to stay in Yugoslavia if Serbia had had a less aggressive leader; as recently as two years ago Milan Kučan won election as Slovene president on a pro-Yugoslav platform. Tudjman, anti-Yugoslav as he is, was floating proposals for a Yugoslav confederation even after the war broke out, and Milošević was torpedoing them one after another. As the EC stepped in, Milošević bobbed and weaved, blocking political agreements and bringing Montenegro to heel when [its president] Bulatović wavered. Innocent bystanders like Gligorov and Izetbegović, who sought doggedly to broker a Yugoslav settlement, never had a chance against Milošević's combination of aggressiveness and intransigence. Historians can argue about the role of the individual in history. I have no doubt that if Milošević's parents had committed suicide before his birth rather than after, I would not be writing a cable about the death of Yugoslavia. Milošević, more than anyone else, is its gravedigger.

> "Who'll be chief mourner?"
> "I," said the dove,
> "I'll mourn for my love,
> I'll be chief mourner."

Yugoslavia has few mourners today. It deserves more. Yugoslavs fought bravely by our side in World War II against our common enemy. Hitler's decision to destroy Belgrade in April 1941 caused him to delay his invasion of the Soviet Union and perhaps cost him Moscow. Tito later tied up German divisions that would otherwise have been available against the allies on the Western front. After the war Tito was the only Eastern European leader with the guts to stand up to Stalin, thus giving impetus to national communism and indirectly to the movements toward independence in Eastern Europe. He also created—or, more accurately, tolerated—a more open communist society than existed anywhere in the world. Economic management was decentralized and borders were open—a feature on which Khrushchev in his memoirs commented with envy. As one who has lived in all three countries, I can attest that the quality of life in Yugoslavia in the Tito period was a lot closer to Spain's than to the Soviet Union's. Tito left a country that was in fact ripe for economic and political reform, a country far ahead of the others in Eastern Europe. Unfortunately, Tito also left two poison gifts that were to destroy Yugoslavia—dictatorship and nationalism.

While Tito was no nationalist, his methods ironically made the rise of virulent nationalism inevitable. Both elements of Tito's "brotherhood and unity" were enforced with a police state apparatus. Nationalists routinely went to jail; Tudjman and Izetbegović, now the presidents of independent republics, both did time in Tito's prisons. In the decentralized and weak Yugoslavia bequeathed by Tito after his death, nationalism, suppressed since the war, awoke like a militant Rip Van Winkle. Unfortunately, it awoke in a Yugoslavia which had not had enough democracy to blunt nationalism's antidemocratic character. Moreover, the people who used nationalism most aggressively—Milošević and Tudjman—had both been schooled in Tito's communist authoritarianism. In distinction from the less militant nationalism of Izetbegović and Kučan, they took readily to all the techniques of communist control—mass parties, control of the press, centralization of the economy, and the like. In sum, Tito bears no less responsibility for the destruction of Yugoslavia than for its re-creation in the ashes of World War II.

There is a lesson here, not only for the Balkans but for all the ex-communist countries of Europe. The lesson is that there is more in common between communism and nationalism than might seem the case. Both dogmas are rigidly collectivist—the individual counts for nothing in comparison with the collective. And both are militantly exclusivist—whoever doesn't belong is an enemy to be exterminated. The battlefields of Bosnia, no less than those of Nagorno-Karabakh, are a warning to the world that if the rights of the individual are not given primacy, then they will surely be destroyed.

There have been two Yugoslavias so far—the pre-war Yugoslavia of the Karadjordjević's and the post-war Yugoslavia of Tito. Just created is a third Yugoslavia—Milošević's. As noted, it is no more than a disguised Serbia and a platform for Milošević's claims on other states containing Serbs. It is surrounded by unstable neighbors whose trust Milošević has lost, and it is eaten from within by minorities whose hatred Milošević has earned. Thanks to Milošević, Serbia—with a stronger democratic tradition than most other Balkan republics—is now consumed by nationalist frenzy; and the many decent, talented Serbs, appalled by the bloodletting, are marginalized. Instability has become a cliché and a permanent condition in and around Milošević's Yugoslavia. I fear that the crisis now visited upon the fragments of Yugoslavia may last a whole generation—a 20-years' crisis. Nationalism, the Balkan killer, will have to run its span. During this process, one can hope, people will begin to realize that their national passions haven't brought them welfare, or peace, or happiness. They may remember that they once lived together, and pretty well, and that their relations with each other were marked by civility and tolerance. They may also recall that the Yugoslavia they lived in, while not free, was certainly freer than the internecine jungle they inherited, and that it had a more civilized and broad-minded view of the world outside as well. One day they might talk about restoring economic ties and then gradually about creating a political framework. It will all make perfectly good sense since, after all, most of their mini-states are not really viable on their own, their ethnic groups are still inextricably mixed together, and they're condemned by geography to be neighbors forever. Somebody—it will take a great democratic leader, probably from

Bosnia—might suggest forming a state. It won't be called Yugoslavia, but it will have historical antecedents. As part of its inauguration ceremonies, I would like to imagine that somebody will leave a rose, just one, on the tomb of the Yugoslavia that has just perished.

> All the birds in the air
> Fell a-sighin' and a-sobbin'
> When they heard of the death
> Of poor Cock Robin,
> When they heard of the death
> Of poor Cock Robin.

ZIMMERMANN

ACKNOWLEDGMENTS

This memoir is based on my own memory of the events described, supplemented by the opportunity to draw from diplomatic cables from the years 1989 to 1992. I am grateful to the Department of State for its cooperation in a project that I hope will enlarge knowledge and understanding of a complex international crisis. The conversations described are reconstructions. No transcripts were made of the actual exchanges, but I am confident that I have reproduced not only their essential content but also their tone and spirit.

Parts of this book appeared in different form in *Foreign Affairs* and the *New York Review of Books*. I thank their extraordinary editors, James F. Hoge Jr. and Robert B. Silvers, for their encouragement and guidance.

Five surveys of the Yugoslav crisis have been particularly useful to me as an aid to recollection and a challenge to interpretation. *The Death of Yugoslavia* by Laura Silber and Allan Little (Penguin Books, 1995) is a fascinating and even exciting narrative about the period from the rise of Milošević to the Bosnian war. The five-part BBC television series (*The Death of Yugoslavia*) with which the book is linked is a remarkable piece of television journalism, adding much that is new to the historical record. *The Yugoslav Drama* by Mihailo Crnobrnja (I. B. Tauris, 1994) is a clear account by a Yugoslav insider, a liberal Serb who has moved to Canada. Susan L. Woodward's *Balkan Tragedy* (Brookings, 1995) illuminates such difficult issues as economic decline and self-determination; while she is less critical than I of Serbian actions, her book is unique in the depth of its probing of the central problems. *Broken Bonds: The Disintegration of Yugoslavia* by Lenard J. Cohen (Westview, 1993) was the first study, still a good one, of the Yugoslav disaster.

A number of friends took the time to read my entire manuscript and contributed extremely helpful suggestions for which I will be long in their debt: Avis Bohlen, Mihailo Crnobrnja, Max M. Kampelman, Slobodan Lekić, Herbert Okun, Dennison Rusinow, James Swigert, Edwin M. Yoder, Teeny Zimmermann, and several Yugoslavs whose assistance was enormous but who would prefer to remain unnamed. I also benefited greatly from the generously offered expertise of Michael Einik, David Gompert, Arnold Kanter, Henry Kelley, John O'Keefe, Ambassador Ernest Petrić, Robert Rackmales, Walter R. Roberts, Louis Sell, and Tim Zimmermann. None of the above should be held responsible for opinions expressed or errors committed.

Others who helped and encouraged me along the way were Jodie T. Allen, Joan Bingham, Owen Harries, and Margaret Jay. I thank Janet Birkler, Nebojša (Neša) Janković, Ana Logar, Rosa Pace, and Helena Santina for easing the technical requirements of getting a book out in a limited period of time. Luke Zahner took time off from his graduate studies to do a prodigious amount of research and fact-checking for the book; my gratitude to him is special.

James Thomson and David Gompert, president and vice president respectively of RAND, gave me the opportunity and the facilities, after my departure from government, to begin writing about my experiences in Yugoslavia. David P. Calleo, Dean Acheson Professor and Director of European Studies at the Paul H. Nitze School of Advanced International Studies (SAIS) at the Johns Hopkins University, invited me to teach a graduate course on Yugoslavia, which helped sharpen my own thinking on the subject. Paul Wolfowitz and Stephen F. Szabo, Dean and Associate Dean for Academic Affairs, respectively, of SAIS, were also generous in supporting the book project. Without Stanley Karnow's conviction that I should write a book about the Yugoslav crisis, I might never have started. I owe a singular debt of gratitude to all of them.

Peter Osnos, publisher of Times Books, and John Mahaney, executive editor, have given me all kinds of support during the writing process. Eleanor Wickland contributed industry and creativity to the project. All three helped turn a chore into a pleasure. Vicky Macintyre did a skillful and sensitive job of copyediting. Gail Ross introduced me with good humor into the mysteries of literary agency.

Finally, my wife Teeny shared with me a six-year adventure in Yugoslavia. She played an enormous role in the mission I had been assigned to carry out. Her cheerfulness, good sense, and manifest willingness to help people in trouble made her a lodestone for those in pain. The support she gave them, and me, is beyond description and is the reason for my dedication to her of a book that she had a large part in living as well as writing.

INDEX

for, 187, 232; Russian support for, 225; self-determination of, 77, 176; territory of, 191, 200, 231, 232; and U.S.-Serbian relations, 198; and Yugoslav unity, 162. *See also* Karadžić, Radovan

Bosnian-Croat Federation, 77, 231, 233, 235

"brotherhood and unity," 38–39

Brovet, Stane, 86

Bučar, France, 70–71

Bulatović, Momir, 68

Bulgaria, 15, 149–50

Bush, George, 46, 47–48, 122, 176–77

Bush (George) administration, 188–89, 215–16, 218, 223. *See also specific person*

Carrington, Peter, 159, 161–63, 164, 170, 171, 173, 177, 240

Central Intelligence Agency (CIA), 42, 84, 219–20

Cheney, Richard B., 46, 87, 219

China, 101, 102, 108

Christopher, Warren, 222, 223, 225, 226, 227–28, 231

Čičak, Zvonimir, 105

Clinton (Bill) administration, 216, 219, 221–26, 231–32

communists: and "brotherhood and unity," 38–39; characteristics of, 36–41; and demise of Yugoslavia, 211; and democracy, 38, 40–41; as dominant in republics, 18, 37; and elections, 66, 69; and JNA, 54, 86, 87, 89, 91; and nationalism, 36, 38, 39–40, 69, 117, 211; staying power of, 35; and Yugoslav presidency, 33; and Yugoslav unity, 38. *See also* League of Communists of Yugoslavia; *specific person or republic*

Congress, U.S.: and Croatia, 130–31, 139; and Kosovo issue, 8–9, 14, 16, 47, 126–29, 130; and Marković's Washington visit, 46–47; and U.N., 243; and U.S. intervention in Bosnia, 137, 225–26; and Yugoslav crisis, 126–27; and Yugoslav elections, 129–30; and Yugoslav unity, 130

constitution: of 1974, 13, 16–17, 39, 69–70; of republics, 70. *See also specific republic*

"contact group" plan, 231

Ćosić, Dobrica, 93–94, 201

Croatia, 9, 18, 218; and arms embargo, 155; arms supplies for, 181; army of, 94, 113, 120, 132, 151, 154; and Baker-Milošević meeting, 134; bombing of palace in, 155–56, 163; and Bosnia, 74, 77, 115–17, 122, 132, 136, 181, 194, 235; and Carrington plan, 161, 170; cease-fire in, 160, 164, 184; communists in, 55, 66, 71; and creation of Yugoslavia, 5–6; and demise of Yugoslavia, 212; democracy in, 75; economy of, 73; elections in, 66, 67, 71, 94–95; ethnicity in, 143–44, 184; and Europe, 158–59, 176–77; expansion of, 61; human rights in, 105, 106, 109, 132; independence of, 113, 122, 132, 134, 135, 138–43, 146, 148–49, 151–52, 164; and JNA, 84–85, 90–91, 94, 95–102, 111, 122, 126, 135, 137, 142, 143, 146, 150, 151, 153, 154, 156–60, 164, 184; and Marković, 49, 73, 112, 113; media in, 74, 75, 109, 117–18, 120, 121, 122; and Milošević, 25, 102, 125, 145, 146, 150, 157–58, 160–61; nationalism in, 53, 61, 67, 71, 76, 78, 91, 118, 186; peacekeeping forces in, 158–59, 160, 161, 172, 184; recognition of, 139, 173, 176–77, 191; refugees in, 224; and Serbia, 72, 73–74, 76, 77, 95, 111–12, 120, 121, 122, 126, 131–32; and Slovenian independence, 146; Tito's battle with, 6; Tudjman's goals for, 72–73; and U.N., 155, 160, 161, 172, 184; and U.S. Congress, 130–31, 139; U.S. relations with, 109, 110, 132, 154, 183, 196; and World War II, 6, 74, 75, 76; and Yugoslav unity, 35, 42, 61, 72, 73, 83, 94, 136–37, 154–55. *See also* Bosnian Croats; Bosnian-Croat Federation; Croatian Serbs; Krajina region; Tudjman, Franjo

Croatian Democratic Union, 61, 67, 71

Croatian Serbs, 84, 124, 130–31, 213; and cease-fire, 160; and JNA, 95–96, 153, 160–61, 163; and Milošević, 92, 120, 145, 160–61, 162, 234; and nationalism, 121, 235; oppression of, 74, 75–76, 95, 120, 132, 139, 152–53, 179, 231–32; population of, 92; and self-determination, 77, 92, 160; and

ABOUT THE AUTHOR

WARREN ZIMMERMANN first served in Yugoslavia in the late 1960s; he returned as the United States ambassador from 1989 to 1992. After thirty-three years in the U.S. Foreign Service, he left the government in 1994. He is the Kathryn and Shelby Cullom Davis Professor in the Practice of International Diplomacy at Columbia University and has also taught at the Paul H. Nitze School of Advanced International Studies at Johns Hopkins University. He is a senior consultant at RAND and a Distinguished Fellow at the New School for Social Research. He and his wife, Teeny, live in the Washington, D.C., area.